MELLOW MISTS AND WALNUT WINE

A RECIPE FOR LIFE IN THE FRENCH COUNTRYSIDE

LINDY VIANDIER

LIFE AT LES LIBELLULES (BOOK TWO)

And now here is my secret, a very simple secret: it is only with the heart that one can see right; what is essential is invisible to the eye.
Le Petit Prince (The Little Prince),
Antoine de Saint-Exupéry

CONTENTS

Foreword   1

Part I

THE BLACKBERRY SUMMER

Second Summer   5
Let the Games Begin   8
It's a Cat's Life   13
Going Dutch   17
Tian of Courgettes and Tomatoes   20
Men in Kilts   22
Sunflowers and Sangliers   27
Buried Treasure   32
We're All Made of Stars   38
The Shape of Things to Come   40
Don't Be an Ass   44
Cool As a Cucumber   49
Cucumber Salad   51
The Joys of Country Living   53
Mirabelle Jam   56
Follow the Leader   57
Be Careful What You Wish For   59

Part II

THE RELUCTANT AUTUMN

Topsy-Turvy   65
Birds of a Feather   68
Don't Judge a Cook by its Nationality   72
Poulet à l'Estragon   74
Computer Says Yes!   76
Roll Out the Red Carpet   79
Salad Dressing   83
Oaty Apple Crumble   85
Kindred Spirit   87
A Bridge in Time   89
The Magical Mystery Tour   93

The Past Revisited 97
Country Cousins 100
Golden Nuggets 104
Vin de Noix 106
Here's One I Made Earlier 108
Flowers of the Field 112
Sugar Plum Parcels 116
The Holly and the Ivy 118
'Tis the Season 121

Part III
THE CRYSTAL WINTER
The Spice of Life 125
Pain d'Epices 128
The Ghosts of Christmas Past 130
The Night Before Christmas 135
Strudel Tarte Soleil 138
A Rose for Winter 141
Spectacular, Spectacular! 144
Fairground Attraction 150
Oysters and Foie Gras 153
The Icing on the Ceiling 157
Sapin d'Hiver 160
Galette des Rois 162
Now is the Winter of Our Discontent 164

Part IV
THE SPRING OF CHANGE
Everybody Needs Good Neighbours 171
Season of Change 174
Garden of Morning Mist 177
Almost French 180
Huitres Chaudes 183
Down the Hatch 185
Coq au Vin 188
Everything's Coming Up Roses 191
Marie's Fondant au Chocolat 194
Shipshape and Bristol Fashion 196
Dancing in the Moonlight 200

Part V

THE PASTEL PALETTE OF PRINTEMPS

Spring Clean   207
Rillettes de Thon   210
Going Past the Apricots   211
A Rainy Night in Dijon   214
The Trail of the Owl   219
Gardening by Numbers   223
Ding Dong Bell   225
Easter Lamb   228
Spring Lamb   229
Not so Home Alone   232
Lime and Ginger Tart   235
Dining with the Viandiers   237
Soupe de Moules   239
Radio Ga Ga   242
A Day to Remember   246

Part VI

THE SEASON OF FRIENDS

June Is Busting Out All Over   255
Sowing the Seeds of Life   257
A Little Night Music   260
Melon, Yellow Pepper and Ginger Gazpacho   265
Top Gear   267
The Early Birds   271
The Good Life   276
Cucumber Soup with Fresh Mint   279
The Language of Friendship   280
Cat Chess   286
A Fête to Remember   288
Home Alone Two   292
Warm Courgette and Avocado Salad   296
Skies of Stars and Storms   298
Micro Break in Autun   301
There Is a Green Hill   305
Call the Midwife   308
Puy Lentil and Haloumi Salad   311
Heidi in the Hay Loft   313
All Dressed Up and Nowhere to Go   317

Lindy's Tabbouleh   323

Saturday Night Fever   325

The Sound of Silence   329

Glossary—Conversion from Metric to US Cups   331

Message from the Author   333

Book Club Questions   334

Acknowledgements   335

FOREWORD

*M*any of you came on a journey through the seasons in *Damson Skies and Dragonflies* with my husband, Mr (*monsieur*) V, and me during our first year at Les Libellules, our 300-year-old, fairy-tale cottage in the Burgundy countryside.

We are now twelve months into what we envisage as a ten-year restoration project and continue to live most of the time in Paris, while working on the house over occasional weekends and holidays—hence the slow progress.

As our second summer mellows into autumn and a new journey begins, I continue to delight in my new-found love of nature, even making peace with an old adversary.

So, find that cosy corner or shady spot and join me again in the magic of Les Libellules.

PART I
THE BLACKBERRY SUMMER

AUGUST AND SEPTEMBER 2018

You ate the first one and its flesh was sweet,
Like thickened wine: summer's blood was in it,
Leaving stains upon the tongue and lust for picking.
'Blackberry Picking', Seamus Heaney

SECOND SUMMER

I left you in the garden at midnight, so this is where you can find me at 8:30 in the morning on the 1st of August, the start of our second year at Les Libellules. For me this is merely the turn of a page on the calendar, but for you it may have been a year or more since we last met.

The air is refreshingly cool and the ground laden with dew. I'm pruning the masses of rosebushes surrounding the terrace before the sun rises any higher. This time last year I didn't know a thing about gardening, and if truth be known, my knowledge is still pretty primitive, but I'm learning from the garden itself. What was once a complete mystery is slowly revealing its secrets to me like rose petals opening one by one.

During the day, the air reverberates with the sounds of heat: the humming, buzzing and droning of insects, the dominant species being wasps, hornets and undernourished houseflies. The music of the night is hedgehogs snuffling in the bushes, crickets chirping in the grass, and owls whoo-whooing in the trees.

The hot, dry summer has prevented many plants from flourishing, notably the Virginia creeper that covered practically everything with its rampant foliage last year. The bonus of this stunted growth is that I can now see more clearly where parts of plants have died and weeds are choking others. I've discovered blackberry bushes that were completely obscured from view, though their berries are small and shrivelled, as now they are in direct sunlight. Every morning I take a walk before breakfast, inspecting the plants for signs of change; this way I'm getting to know them. I cut back anything that looks desiccated and diseased to a point where it is green and healthy. I deadhead roses to encourage a second batch of blooms and tame the wildflowers that have gone to seed to avoid them running riot next spring. And, naturally, I talk to them all.

Beneath a clump of these wildflowers, I've uncovered a group of snails sheltering from the heat. I can't leave them exposed, so I place them beneath a nearby rosebush. Again I marvel at the fact that I spend a good half an hour rehousing snails. How much I've changed. Not only am I enjoying working in the garden, I'm actually finding it addictive and get a great sense of satisfaction when I see things beginning to take shape.

I realise now that what I considered full summer before I lived here is really the beginning of autumn. The changes have appeared earlier than usual this year due to the lack of rain, but I think the signs were there last year; I just failed to see them.

This year is exceptional though. The temperature is constantly hovering around 36 degrees. The poplars and horse chestnut trees are already turning yellow, gold and brown, and their leaves are fluttering to the ground like tiny symbols, lining the lane with a deep, crisp frieze. The conkers are larger than golf balls and also look ready to fall. When I compare recent photographs with those I took twelve months ago, the difference in the colours of the landscape is remarkable. Last year's photos were vibrant and lush, and I wrote of the myriad shades of green. This year, all has a parched appearance, with a canvas of muted shades of yellow. The cattle in the fields are having to eat hay that normally would be saved for winter, so I don't know what farmers will feed them with when winter does arrive.

The heavy rain at the beginning of the year produced a bumper crop of apples, but the tree is also losing its leaves a good eight weeks earlier than last year, and our grapes that were sweet and succulent last August are clinging to the vine like shrivelled raisins. We're planning a trip to Dijon next week, so it will be interesting to see how the vineyards are faring. Hopefully these aren't the signs of things to come. Only time will tell.

What I've learnt today: A group of snails is called an escargatoire. I ask myself what other gems of knowledge I will uncover along with the snails as our second year at Les Libellules unfolds...

LET THE GAMES BEGIN

*W*e've hit the ground running. Our first major delivery of building supplies has just arrived on an enormous lorry that's somehow managed to squeeze itself between the house and the outbuildings. It's come to drop off a large quantity of sand and cement to lay the foundations for the new extension that will house the elephant-sized fuel tank. Marcel the builder is here to check that all is in order for him to start work on Saturday morning. At the same time, the men to clean and treat the roof tiles arrive also.

Our neighbour Fifi, who, along with Mr V, mowed down my precious wildflowers last May, sees their van parked outside as he's cycling past, makes an emergency stop and comes running into the house. '*Qu'est-ce que vous faites avec ces mecs? Ce sont des voleurs*' (What are you doing with these types? They're robbers), he asks, making it glaringly obvious that he doesn't trust these workers, though admittedly he's never seen them before in his life. It's enough for him that they're not local to arouse his mistrust. Add to this the fact they're maybe Moroccan or Algerian, with creased brown faces and accents that sound like they're clearing their throats as they speak, and he's doubly suspicious. Even someone from that grand metropolis, Dijon, would make him twitchy.

I discover that the men are Turkish, which in Fifi's opinion is worse than being Moroccan or Algerian, as 'at least *they* speak French'. One of them is already up on the roof, hurling down chunks of moss like a demented bird in the throes of nest making. Marcel, who is at the back of the house marking out the measurements for the foundations, is receiving a fair amount of this on his head. Luckily, he's wearing his hard hat. Without warning, the workman at the front of the house sets his jet-powered hose into action on the roof, adding a fountain of chemicals and dirty water to pour over the besieged Marcel, who's crouching with a tape measure on the other side.

An exuberant use of the P-word (equivalent to the English F-word) follows, and Fifi gives me a self-satisfied 'I told you so' look. To top it all, as I've not had the chance to close the shutters at the front of the house, the dirty water is cascading down all the windows and doors, plus one window in the utility room is open. The garden table is still on the terrace, and the once-cream parasol is now a moss-splattered mess. The Turks are on a mission it seems to finish as quickly as possible and get on to their next victims, so they carry on regardless while I dodge beneath their water cannon, trying to shut the window and gather up my potted geraniums to move them to a place of safety.

Job done, the roof looks amazing, and the men clean all the paths and patios after them. Mr V tells me to let the rain wash the windows, but as we haven't seen any real rain for over two months, I think it could be September before this happens.

* * *

The house is guiding Mr V as the garden is guiding me. His work here is dictated by priorities that change as quickly as bubbles at the top of a flute of champagne.

This afternoon it's the hot water bubble that has surfaced, or should I say, the lack of it. The creaky, old boiler is once again not working, and this time the heating engineer is 800 kilometres away on the Côte d'Azur.

We've discussed having a backup in the form of an electric hot water tank, as it isn't economical to fire up the London telephone box-sized boiler every time we want to shower or wash some pots and pans.

But to fit the water tank, we must first take off all the old *crépis* (a sort of rippled interior render pronounced crepee) in the little corridor between the dining room and the boiler room. Then we will need to patch up the wall, where half of it will inevitably come down along with the *crépis*, paint the walls and block off the door leading from the dining room. This is something that was scheduled for autumn, but I'm now wedged into a confined space in a temperature of 41 degrees in the shade with a paintbrush in my hand. Mr V, having done all the preliminaries, is on the other side of the door, building a frame to fit plasterboard into the alcove we've created in the dining room. I'm visualising it decked out with rustic shelves crammed with cookery books and hand-painted jugs brimming with meadow flowers. It's a good job I've got an imagination as this is far from the reality we're faced with.

The bad news is that the shop supplying water heaters is closed until the 21st of August, so we're boiling kettles to wash the dishes, and it's cold showers all round. This is fine as the weather is so hot, but I really don't like washing my hair in cold water. Just to add to the joy, the electric kettle has also given up the ghost, so we're boiling water in a whistling kettle that we picked up in a *vide grenier* (attic sale) in May. The sound of it tooting away on the hotplate conjures up nostalgic memories from when I was a young child and electric kettles hadn't reached the average kitchen, certainly not my mother's cramped kitchenette, which I don't believe even had an electric socket. How quickly times have changed.

* * *

Aid has come in the form of our neighbour Jacques, who is a fount of help and information. He is our *chevalier* (knight) in shining armour. He knows a retired plumber/heating engineer (of course he does) who he'll call to see if they can come out this evening to look at the boiler.

I'm doubtful as it's the second Saturday in August, and only mad fools like us renovating a ruin are not on holiday.

Eight o'clock on the dot, Jacques rings as arranged and tells us that he and his friend Pascal will be here in ten minutes.

I'm expecting Pascal to be a pot-bellied plumber, but up pops 'Sacha Distel'[1] in denim hotpants which are only marginally longer than those Fifi wears, but somehow not offensive in the least. He has an abundance of silver-fox hair, piercing blue, crinkly-edged eyes, and tanned, muscular legs and arms which are shown off to their best advantage by his white, sleeveless vest. His voice is deep and melodic, and his Sacha-worthy teeth are flashing me a smile. I half expect him to plant a kiss on the back of my hand when he takes it in his firm, reassuring grip. Add to all this the fact that with a few swirls of a spanner he gives me hot water, and he's elevated to the position of Poseidon in my opinion.

Jacques is beaming. He gains genuine pleasure from helping people. He truly is one of the most giving people I've ever met, and I thank fortuity for the day I casually invited him to join me for coffee on the terrace.

Mr V is an incy-wincy bit jealous and *bofs* to one side my outpourings of admiration for Pascal's plumbing skills. (*Bof* is a frequently used French expression that can mean yes, no, maybe, I don't know, I don't care or something else along those lines.) Between Pascal and Marcel, Mr V is stuck between a rock and a hard place. At this moment he's hacking away with a hammer and chisel at the *crépis* surrounding the boiler, in a peacock display of capable manhood. *Crépis* and plaster are tumbling to the floor, and mushroom clouds of dust are rising in the air. Mr V attended the same school of planning as the Turkish roof cleaners, and he's left curtains at the window; bathmats on the floor; towels hanging on rails; shampoos, soaps, toothbrushes and wash gloves all in the path of falling masonry, so I'm now dodging debris, scooping up what I can and moving it outside.

The boiler room is partitioned off from the bathroom, and we believe that this part of the house used to be the scullery. When we moved the large piece of marble from under the bathroom window, we discovered a stone slab like a shallow sink that sloped slightly towards a drain hole in the wall. Now, as the plaster comes down from above the boiler room window, an ancient wall has appeared with a large, wooden lintel supporting rough-hewn stones of various sizes; we think we've uncovered a former doorway. I get carried away, imagining all the people who've passed through this door and stood at that sink, and once again feel the presence of the past reasserting itself as we modernise certain aspects of the house. We're now going to leave these beautiful stones exposed when we finally create the new bathroom.

What I've learnt today: A partition is a faux ami *(false friend). In French it means a musical score. This caused a lot of confusion when I mentioned taking down* le partition*, and the plumber thought I was off to write some music.* Un cloison *or* une séparation *are the French terms.*

---

1. A French singer who was something of a heartthrob in the '70s.

IT'S A CAT'S LIFE

Flaubertine the farm cat and her brood are still installed in the garden. She may not have turned into an extraordinary mother overnight, but she *has* turned into an extraordinary hunter. Driven by the desire to be free from feeding the kitties, she's taken to the fields and regularly returns with a fat dormouse dangling from her jaws. Calling the kitties with a strangled cry, she deposits her prey for them to devour then slopes off, job done, to the den she shares with the other vagrants. I feel sorry for the dormice. They're really quite beautiful creatures—mottled grey and white with rosy-pink paws, but a not-so-pretty, long, broad, rat-like tail. Being naturally sleepy, they're easy pickings for Flaubertine. Today she's deposited her prey on our patio, and it's the first thing I see when I open the shutters, lying limp and forlorn with its throat ripped out in what I hope was a swift death. The sad thing is, the kitties are just playing with the little corpse, showing no interest at all in eating it. Maybe this is part of their training; nature can be cruel.

I for my part have developed a trick to help Penny, the runt of the litter, to get her fair share, not of mice, I must add. I've been giving the kitties a small serving of cat food twice a day to supplement the mice, but Penny, being weaker and less boisterous than the other two,

13

couldn't get a look-in. This was resulting in her becoming even more weak and listless, lying in the shade while Poly and Belle practised their hunting skills on flowers and stones, and each other. So I began sneaking a little plate of food under the hedge for her. She's cottoned on to this quickly. When I go outside and call the kitties in the morning and evening, Poly and Belle come bounding from their little lair and launch themselves onto the wall where I put the food bowl. Penny, however, has begun to hang back and waits until they're occupied eating, then she darts beneath the bushes and waits for her little, glass plate. The result is that she's now actively joining in with the fun and games, and in turn she's becoming more accepted by her siblings. Mr V, being a countryman at heart, tells me it's the 'law of nature' and the 'survival of the fittest', but I can't help playing Mother Theresa to the cats.

While we're on the subject, I'll take this opportunity to explain how we came to have our official cat, Pussy Willow, as that's a story in itself...

Six years ago, we were on holiday in the foothills of the Pyrenees mountains in Southwest France that form the border with Spain. Mr V is keen on mineralogy and had discovered there was a place in these mountains where you could find a particular kind of quartz. So off we went with a picnic for a day's prospecting. With only sketchy directions on a map that a man in the nearby market had drawn on a paper napkin, we were soon lost. Seeing a wide bend in the road with enough space to pull in and consult the Ordnance Survey map, we stopped the car and decided this was just as good a place as any to have lunch.

It was then that I heard what sounded like the cry of a baby coming from the forest behind us and went to investigate. I'd been walking for ten metres or so when the path I was following forked, one branch climbing into dense pine trees, the other descending into thicket. A pair of eagles were circling above the lower path, so I took this way to see what was attracting them. After another couple of metres, a tiny, undernourished, but strikingly beautiful kitten jumped out of the long grass at the edge of the path and began following me. I stopped and picked it up. It didn't resist, and I could feel its little ribs and shoulders sticking through its rough fur.

I took it back to the car and gave it some ham from our sandwiches, some yogurt, which it licked hungrily from my finger, and some water, which it also eagerly drank. Mr V told me to put it back, as someone else would find it. But I think you all know by now that was never going to happen.

We were staying at a *chambre d'hôte* (guesthouse) run by an Englishman, Chris, who I telephoned to ask if it was OK to bring the kitten back, to which he agreed, providing we kept it in the bathroom and didn't allow it in the bedroom as it would most certainly have fleas. We'd commented on the enormous size of the bathroom when we first arrived; now we knew why it was necessary.

Chris very amiably supplied a cage big enough for a bed, litter tray, bowls of cat food and water plus a giant climbing apparatus. We bought a travel box, a cushion, and a harness with a lead, and took the kitten, who we'd now named Pussy Willow, out in the car with us each day, taking her sightseeing on the lead. As she was so small, she inevitably ended up on Mr V's shoulder or being carried in his straw hat.

At the end of the holiday, we took her back home to Paris, where she grew and grew until she became the size of a small tiger, and I have to say, equally wild when she was young, but now she's my best friend and constant companion. She's at my feet at this very moment, a gentle breeze ruffling her gorgeous, titian-coloured coat, her jade-green eyes blinking at me contentedly.

What I've learnt today: Cats find you.

＊　＊　＊

Flaubertine has just trotted onto the terrace with another limp, grey body drooping like a fat moustache from her mouth at the most inopportune moment. We have our Dutch neighbours, Pieter and Eva, and their city-folk friends over for an apéritif. I hold my breath as

Flaubertine slinks beneath the table, hoping for her to emerge unnoticed at the other side, but the mouse brushes against the leg of one of the women, who, thinking it's just a cat, puts her hand down to caress it. On discovering that she's stroking a dead mouse, she lets out a huge scream, which in turn causes Flaubertine to drop the mouse and run for cover. Unfortunately, the poor creature is *not* quite dead and proceeds to drag itself across the terrace. I'm all for saving it but am outnumbered by hysterical women and practical men, so Mr V swiftly disposes of the mouse to put it out of its misery. The apero moment is somewhat spoilt, to say the least, and not even copious amounts of Pastis can rescue it. Our guests make a hasty departure, citing an early start in the morning as an excuse, leaving Mr V and me to finish our drinks with a disgraced Flaubertine and three disappointed kitties watching us from the terrace wall.

I think the kitties have begun to realise that Flaubertine is a rubbish mother, and that I'm a safer bet. They like to stay within sight of me while not showing the slightest concern where *she* wanders. Pussy Willow for her part is displaying maternal mannerisms towards Penny, rolling on her back in front of her, but the sight of Poly makes her hackles rise.

I must add that the mouse incident took place under the nose of Pussy Willow, who watched it all with the detached superiority of a cat who never has to hunt for food.

GOING DUTCH

*W*e're up early to go shopping in Saulieu before the sun comes into full force. The little town is already buzzing with tourists when we arrive, mainly German and Dutch. The Germans are tall and well-built and are mostly wearing shorts, revealing sturdy, tanned, hairy legs (both sexes). The Dutch are also tall, but slender and eclectically dressed in cheesecloth and Indian cotton, the women in earthy-coloured maxi dresses and the men wearing long, loose tunics over baggy pants as if they've stepped out of a Beatles LP cover from their Maharaja days. A distinct whiff of wacky baccy is floating around some of them, many of whom have dreadlocks. Most are carrying colourful woven baskets that are on sale in the market. I make a mental note to wear a maxi dress and bring enough cash to buy a basket myself next week.

The street cafés are jam-packed with people drinking coffee, cognac and wine. I can't get a seat at my usual haunt, Café Parisien, so I wander a little further away from the small town centre and discover a smart brasserie, and a pizzeria cooking pizzas in a wood-fired oven. Both look good places to go for a meal without the prospect of being presented with a calf's head in a pot or a snail pizza, which we've been faced with before, but both are also full, so I head back to the market to meet Mr V who has been to the 'no girls allowed' builder's merchants that I had the singular pleasure of experiencing last winter.

The market is even more of a hive of activity than usual. A Romany equestrian circus is in town, and they're putting on a publicity show next to the wine bar. Long-haired men in baggy-sleeved, white shirts, tight, black pants and knee boots are playing violins and an accordion while a lithe youth juggles large, wooden skittles, and a sultry young woman, looking like a wanton Disney Esmeralda, twists and twirls in a provocative dance. The wine bar is also packed to the hilt as the Romanies are attracting a fair crowd. All this is being frowned upon by some holy sisters who are selling religious statuettes and plaques made from plaster, but they're also attracting a reasonable amount of interest. Life here is so full of contrasts.

I fill my non-colourful wicker basket with carrots, radishes and long sticks of celery, all of which have an abundance of leaves and roots laden with earth still attached. I then buy a string of fat bulbs of smoky purple garlic, and two ripe, fragrant melons. Mr V is in an optimistic mood and purchases a new batch of twelve baby lettuces, stating it's too hot for the slugs and snails to leave the shelter of the grass to devour them as they did the previous batch. Therefore, there's no time for me to linger admiring the toned thighs of the Romany musicians, as he's eager to get home and plant the lettuces before they begin to wilt.

Back at Les Libellules, Mr V is busy planting the lettuces. The tomatoes have continued to flourish, and one plant has produced a huge, ridged, beefsteak variety that look like small, fiery-orange pumpkins, perfect for stuffing with minced beef, rice or couscous and baking in the oven. Jacques has been watering them while we weren't at the house. We didn't ask him to do this; he just noticed they were looking thirsty as he was cycling past, so he hopped over the fence, filled a watering can from the *mare* (pond) and gave them a much-needed drink.

As last year, courgettes[1] from kindly neighbours regularly arrive on the doorstep, so here's a traditional French way of using courgettes and tomatoes—in a tian, a colourful dish of finely sliced vegetables slow-baked in the oven.

---

1. Zucchini.

TIAN OF COURGETTES AND TOMATOES

Serves 4

Ingredients

1 medium/large shallot, finely chopped
1 large clove of garlic, crushed
A good glug of olive oil, plus extra
A knob of butter
4-6 large, ripe beef tomatoes
1 large aubergine[1]
2 large courgettes, roughly the same width as the tomatoes and aubergine. (I like to use one green and one yellow.)
1 tsp dried rosemary
1 tsp dried thyme
Salt and pepper to season

Method

Gently sauté the shallot in a little olive oil for 5 minutes to soften, taking care not to brown.

Add the garlic and continue to cook gently for a further minute.

Lightly butter the bottom of a round 20 cm (8 in) casserole dish and spread the shallot and garlic mixture on the bottom.

Slice the tomatoes, aubergine and courgettes into ½ cm (¼ in) rounds.

Arrange them in alternate slices in a circle around the outer edge of the dish, standing them on their sides like dominoes.

Continue towards the centre until the casserole dish is filled with a wheel of colour.

Drizzle with olive oil, sprinkle with the rosemary, thyme and seasoning, and bake in a preheated oven for around 2 hours at 180 C/gas mark 4 until the vegetables are soft and slightly golden.

I sometimes add some slices of mozzarella between the vegetables, and as I'm allergic to aubergine, I substitute that with fine potato slices, which also work well.

This dish is delicious served warm with grilled chicken, pork steaks, salmon, or haloumi as a veggie option, or served cold as a starter drizzled with a little balsamic vinegar.

It's guaranteed to raise an 'aaahhh' at the dinner table, and the smell when cooking is divine.

---

1. Eggplant.

MEN IN KILTS

*L*ars, my Dutch neighbour Pieter's Rastafarian cousin, has arrived again in his psychedelic Bob Marley-graffiti transit van. Three camper vans are now parked outside our neighbour's house with an odd assortment of occupants, including: A pale, bearded man who looks like the 17th-century Flemish artist Van Dyck. A robust, middle-aged lady with short, bright-vermillion hair who always seems to be pushing an empty pram and carrying a baby. A youngish, ginger-bearded male who resembles Shaggy Rogers in *Scooby-Doo*, and a thin American woman with a severe, snatched-back bun. Add to that a young female artist from Amsterdam, and it's an eclectic mix.

This time, much to my disappointment, Lars doesn't appear to have brought his accordion as he did last year. Instead I'm woken to the sounds of 'Wonderwall' being strummed on a guitar and hummed along to with the odd snatch of lyrics here and there. Due to the intense heat, Lars has piled his dreadlocks on top of his head in what looks like a bizarre parody of Marge Simpson. On his feet are a pair of black Dr. Martens boots. He's also wearing a skirt, a wrap-around style in the same earthy-coloured cotton that I saw people wearing in the market, teamed with a black vest top that reveals his tanned, sinewy arms. The effect is surprisingly manly, and I don't know why more men don't wear skirts. Lars looks infinitely more attractive than the ageing Fifi in his denim hotpants. I compliment him on it, and he says it's cooler and healthier than shorts in this heat, the only problem being mosquitoes getting to places you'd rather they didn't. I wonder if he's gone commando under this flimsy garment, which doesn't have the weight of a Scotsman's kilt to hold it down should a sudden gust of wind arrive. But as the morning is still, without a breath of air, I guess we can all relax.

He's the only one awake, so I invite him over to share our French version of an English breakfast with wafer-thin rounds of French bacon, fried tomatoes fresh from the garden and a huge bowl of scrambled eggs made from a cocktail of hen, duck and goose eggs that Noëlle, the wife of the deputy mayor I've christened Pappy Cardigan, brought for me. Lars has been travelling and makes me envious with tales of adventures in Corfu, Albania, Armenia and Azerbaijan. It seems this is what he does—what a wonderful, nomadic existence.

The other residents are still in bed, as according to Lars, they keep late hours, talking and drinking. They *do* seem to have some odd nocturnal practices. Every evening after dark, when I'm on the terrace typing up notes, I see them file past Les Libellules. They appear wearing sundresses, shorts, T-shirts and sandals, even flip-flops—hardly kitted out for a hike in the hills. They march past in earnest, calling *'bonsoir'* and *''ello'*, then disappear; as to where, I have no idea, as I never see them return. Maybe one evening I'll ask if I can tag along.

⁂

Marcel has also just arrived *de bonne heure* (early), bearing gifts in the form of a box of a dozen eggs still warm from his hens. I pick more tomatoes and rustle up more scrambled eggs, and he enjoys breakfast on the terrace with Lars, Mr V and me while the morning is still cool.

We're joined by Flaubertine, Poly, Penny and Belle, then Fifi and Jacques, who must have the same homing instinct as the cats at meal times. I give the cats a bowl of scrambled eggs and the 'boys' coffee and croissants.

Marcel and Mr V disappear to start work. Mr V advised me to make a large percolator of coffee to last all morning, but evidently things are done differently here in the country than in Paris. Marcel prefers a beer. It's still only 9:30, and he's on his third (granted small) bottle. I'm not sure about the wisdom of this as he's wielding a seriously big pickaxe, but he's a seriously big boy, so I guess he can handle it. Mr V, on the other hand, is positively lightweight, both physically and metaphysically. One beer he is fine; two he sings; three he sleeps. As I'm relying on him to drive me to the supermarket this morning, I'm hoping he limits himself to one and doesn't get caught up in macho bravado.

The cats, now satiated, have also disappeared to escape the mounting heat. All except Penny, who sits a safe distance from me, watching as I write. I get up and approach her slowly in a meandering manner, until I'm about two metres away, then stoop down to her level. She then does the most curious thing. She begins to zigzag across my path from right to left, getting a little closer each time. I think I've seen lions or tigers do this on wildlife programmes when they are stalking their prey. To see this behaviour in a tiny kitten with a cry so high-pitched and feeble that it's barely audible is incredible. She comes to a halt just beyond stroking distance and sits looking at me with an expression that says, 'I want to come closer, but I'm too timid.'

* * *

Marcel is an artisan, it appears. He's mesmerising to watch when he begins spreading the final layer of concrete on the foundations that are strong enough to support the Titanic, let alone the fuel tank. He smooths and observes, smooths and observes, and from time to time takes a giant spirit level to verify that his eye is good and all is even—which of course it is.

What I've learnt today: A man in a skirt is extremely manly indeed
—providing he has the legs for one.

⁂ ⁂ ⁂

I don't want to be writing this, and I've held off for 48 hours in the hope that I may be wrong, but I haven't seen Belle for two days, and I'm once again heartbroken. I had hoped that one of the Dutch visitors had taken her as she is so pretty, but after making enquiries, sadly this is not the case. I'd said to Mr V just two days ago that I had concerns for her. I don't know why I felt like this as she was the one closest to her mother, plus she was lively and playful and held her own in the food chain. I once witnessed her dragging a mouse carcass across the garden like a lion with a wildebeest, but she tended to be accident-prone. It was Belle who we had to rescue from a drain last month, and I had to free her from a can that she'd stuck on her head. She also tended to go inside the house and hide out of sight, so you wouldn't know she was there unless you'd seen her enter. (I found her cowering behind my washing machine on a couple of occasions, and I always did a 'Belle check' every evening.) It's this tendency that I fear may have been her downfall. It distresses me no end to think of her alone and afraid, having sneaked into somewhere and being unable to get out and starving to death.

Flaubertine feels her loss also, and she's gone into a decline, even turning her back on food, and more worryingly as she's still feeding the other two kitties, not drinking. I've been giving her bowls of half milk, half water, as she refuses water point blank. I stand watch over her as thankfully she drinks, but I'm afraid that when we wake tomorrow, she may no longer be with us.

I somehow have to harden myself to this aspect of life here, but it's an unexpected obstacle to overcome. My Dutch neighbour Eva, also a cat lover, has told me that she went through the same emotions regarding these semi-feral felines when she first arrived from Amsterdam seventeen years ago, but you have to get used to it. I'm far from getting used to it, but deep down know that I must.

* * *

I'm happy to report that Flaubertine has not only survived the night, but she's begun to drink and eat a little with encouragement.

SUNFLOWERS AND SANGLIERS

a mystery is about to be solved. I was on the terrace writing after dinner, and the dwindling Dutch walking group approached, shouting their usual *'bonsoir'*. The professional route-marchers appear to have left the party, leaving an amiable, relaxed quartet. They called me to join them, so I'm changing out of my flip-flops to catch up with them at the crossroads.

As I leave the garden, I hear the first rumbles of distant thunder and question my sanity in continuing into the dusky evening. But curiosity gets the better of me, and I sprint to meet them. Rather than head towards one of the two closest villages, we turn onto the main road and hug the grass verge for about 30 metres, then cross the road and take a lane I'd never noticed before, as we usually pass this way by car. There, laid out like a mantel before me, is everyone's vision of life in rural France: fields of heavy-headed sunflowers as far as the eye can see, and I had no idea that they were virtually on my doorstep. Their petals fold in upon themselves, and their vibrant colours appear more silvery cream than yellow in the fading light. Then the sky lights up with a sudden flash of lightning, and they are illuminated like a photographic negative against the now purple/black background. All five of us stand enthralled as fork lightning pierces the clouds to the west. The air has freshened a little, and I can smell rain. We hesitate whether to continue or turn around, but there's really no contest. We quicken our pace and continue through the countryside that's now being lit by strobe-effect lightning.

It is both dazzling and exhilarating. The hairs on my arms bristle with the electricity in the air and the thrill of this spectacle of nature. It is also a bit scary, as we are out in the open as flashes of light appear to strike the ground around us. Mr V thinks I'm still on the terrace writing; he would think I'm mad if he knew I was out here. I've never been this way before, so I'm not sure how far we are from home. My heart is pounding, and it's not just due to the speed with which we're walking. The distant rumblings of thunder are getting nearer, with shorter pauses between each clap. I'm beginning to agree with Mr V. I must be mad.

Finally I see a sign for the hamlet, and we enter by another path, past the cottages, shutters drawn against the oncoming storm. Then it happens. We are outrun. Soft summer rain begins to fall in warm, heavy drops. It feels so good against my hot, sticky skin. I throw back my head and let the rain run down my face and neck. This is what we so desperately need.

Once again the rain is short-lived and has hardly penetrated the sun-baked soil, but there's a damp, earthy smell in the garden this morning, and I take this brief respite to type a little before breakfast, and the threatened 41 degrees heat hits us. This, we are promised, is the last day of the heatwave, and temperatures are going to drop by a massive 12 to 14 degrees tomorrow to a more bearable 27 to 29.

Immediately after breakfast, Mr V and I are on the road to do some business at the bank and post office. Something slow-moving up ahead is causing the traffic to roll at a snail's pace. One by one cars tentatively pull out and overtake what surely must be a tractor. But as we get closer, I can make out the keyhole shape of the back of a Romany caravan; three Romany caravans in fact, each being pulled by two clopping Shire horses. It's the troupe from the market, moving on to another town. The caravans are painted in bright blue, green and red, and the middle one is in fact not a caravan at all but a yellow, covered wagon, exactly like those seen in Wild West movies. Behind the wagon a man in a red bandana is riding a horse, leading two others by long reins. This is what's causing the holdup, as drivers are having to pass the convoy of caravans and horses and must wait for a long, straight stretch of road in which to do so.

Nine horses plodding along in the heat are leaving behind a fair trail of pungent manure, which Mr V thinks is *dommage* (a shame) to leave on the road as it would be good for the garden.

As we pass, I hear the tinkling of tiny bells fastened to the horses' broad leather collars. There are also bells and small, coloured lanterns around the curtained doors. The Romanies smile and wave at everyone who passes, putting me in mind of a line from Dylan Thomas's 'Under Milk Wood':

> *There's the clip clop of horses on the sun-honeyed*
> *cobbles of the humming streets.*

Business done, we're back on the road to get home before the sun comes into full, blistering force. We pass another field of sunflowers I hadn't noticed before (maybe there is crop rotation, and they were not here last year). Mr V slows down for me to take photos from the car. The sunflowers merge into fields of corn 'as high as an elephant's eye'. The now crisp, brown husks are peeled back, revealing rows of yellow, beaded maize. Suddenly a spikey, whiskered, black head with a large, black nose and small, beady, black eyes thrusts out from the bamboo-like stalks. It's a *sanglier*—a wild boar. I've never seen one so up close and personal, and it is enormous, and not in the least cute and cuddly.

I let out a squeal of both shock and delight, which causes Mr V to come to an abrupt halt in a little clearing at the side of the road. He warns me not to get out of the car in case the animal charges. The last time someone said this to me, I was in a safari park. This boar looks like a mean beast, and I have *no* intention of getting out of the car to risk being gored by its trophy-worthy tusks. The corn is swaying as if being blown by a sudden breeze, then six or seven other animals in varying sizes emerge; a couple are small and downy, the others as big and bristly as the first. They forage around at the base of the plants, looking for fallen husks, ramming their ample rumps into the stalks to encourage more to tumble. Mr V says it's unusual to see them in broad daylight, but it can be dangerous if you come across one with your car at night, as being all black, they're virtually impossible to see; only their eyes, like shiny beads of jet, are visible glinting out of the darkness.

It's these beasts that the hunters will be chasing across people's land once the season starts in autumn. Given the choice, I don't know who I'd prefer to meet: a drunken hunter with a loaded shotgun or a raging wild boar.

We drive back through the now shimmering heat to calmer climes: the gently mooing cows in the field opposite the house and languid cats stretched across the terrace.

It's now 8 p.m., and we're going blackberry picking. The full moon is the colour of champagne, hanging low in the strawberry-ripple ice-cream sky. The berries aren't as big and juicy as last year. But along the hedgerows, there are still rewards to be had for those brave enough to stand astride the dried-up brook and stretch across the brambles to reach the abundance of plump prizes on the other side. This is the first evening that it's been cool enough to walk out, and it's invigorating. The air smells of cows and corn, and feels fresh against my bare shoulders and arms.

My arms and legs are scratched by the thorns on the brambles that reach out like witches' fingers and hook into my skin. They wrap themselves around my wrists and ankles in a menacing manner, warding me off stealing their fruit. I'm put in mind of Rapunzel, and the prince falling from her tower into the thorns that scratch out his eyes and blind him, his sight finally being restored by Rapunzel's tears. Needless to say, I'm careful to avoid branches springing back and catching me in the eye.

We each fill a basket full of berries and head back through the hamlet as the sun is disappearing behind the poplars. Hands and arms stretch through windows, slamming shutters in a procession before us, obscuring the golden glow that had spilled onto the pavement from inside. Here and there one stays open, giving a glimpse of a family or group of friends gathered around a table lit by candles and lamps as they share a meal, too engrossed in conversation to notice our shadowy figures passing by.

A small boy and girl race up and down in the darkness on their scooters, as it's been too hot for them to play outside during the day. The boy, aged around four, has a life-size toy rifle made from wood slung across his back. Mr V tells me that the boy's grandfather is a hunter. The children both stop and wave and shout '*bonsoir*' as we pass. Their grandmother keeps a watchful eye from behind lace curtains and waves also. Back inside Les Libellules, we too close our shutters; all but one, so I can watch the Harvest Moon as she saunters across the sky.

What I've learnt today: Don't pick blackberries from the lower part of the brambles, as foxes urinate there, and their pee is poisonous.

BURIED TREASURE

J've just returned from a trip to Wales to celebrate my mother's 90th birthday, and although still a respectable 27 degrees, the intense heat that I left behind five days ago has departed. Its departure has heralded the return of the intense light, and once again I am dazzled by the piercing blue of the sky. Miraculously, patches of green have also begun to sprout amongst the stones and barren earth. Although we've still not had any real rain, the morning dew is heavy and refreshing now that the nights are cooler.

It's 8 a.m., and I'm walking in the garden, inspecting the plants. The miniature roses have responded well to my inexpert pruning, and there's an abundance of tiny, deep-pink flowers adorning their spidery stems. My sandalled feet are cool and wet as I walk through the newly appeared grass to the tomatoes. Six or seven fat, ripe fruits are begging to be picked. Once again, my nose is prickled by their sharp, tangy scent which stays on my hands even after washing.

The cooler air has also seen a return of the tiny, cornflower-blue butterflies plus slightly larger white ones and a handful of sun-faded orange moths. Yellowy-green salamanders are motionless on the wall of the *pigeonnier* (where families once kept pigeons in a circular loft), unruffled by the gentle breeze that sways the tree I call the feather tree. All is calm, and I feel myself slip back into the rhythm of life here, at one with nature.

⁎ ⁎ ⁎

Renovation work has continued in my absence. The *mare* that had such an abundance of life last year has been dredged, revealing retaining stone walls. This is not the higgledy-piggledy pond we thought it was; each stone has been meticulously cut to size and placed in position. I imagine the craftsmen who constructed these walls, as this is a work of art and beautiful to behold. The *mare* is also much deeper than we imagined. I'm amazed at its depth at the far end which is over three metres. Mr V estimates that the total capacity of water when full is about 60 cubic metres. I'm even more amazed that so much water has dried up during this drought. The bottom now resembles a muddy river bed after the tide has gone out.

A friend of Jacques has removed mountains of earth and sludge with a mechanical digger. But he stopped working when he unexpectedly struck stone on the bottom for fear of damaging both his equipment and what lies beneath, so it was safer all round to remove the last layer manually. Jacques is helping clear the mud from the shallower end that has thoroughly dried out. He is breaking it up with a pickaxe, and Mr V is shovelling it into a wheelbarrow. The old Chinese proverb 'many hands make light work' is proving to be true, as they are picking and shovelling away like two of the seven dwarves, Jacques being Doc and Mr V alternating between Happy and Grumpy, depending on how things are going. Mr V is pushing the wheelbarrow up a precariously placed plank and dumping the contents on the bank, where I would like to plant a woodland garden. All the dead branches from the trees damaged in the spring storms have also been deposited here, and the ground, crisscrossed with tractor tracks, more resembles a landfill site than the enchanting arbour I envisaged.

A quarter of the way in, where the *mare* becomes considerably deeper, they hit a problem, literally. In addition to large cobbles that we can now see lining the bottom, they uncover two huge stone slabs. Jacques becomes highly animated and says the *mare* is obviously much older than the present house. The Knights Templar were in this area during the 12th century and were known to have created *mares* in order to bury their gold in large chests. Slabs such as these were placed over them to protect their buried treasure. The possibility that the Templars could have constructed our *mare* blows my mind, as more layers of history are added to the weight we already carry.

We've just discovered three stone steps leading down to the deepest part of the *mare* where past occupants would have collected water for their vegetables. How I wish I could make a tear in the fabric of time and take a tiny peek into the past to observe them for five minutes.

The more of the *mare* that's revealed, the more we see the outstanding craftsmanship of these men an astonishing 800 years ago. We have now exposed part of the original boundary at the shallow end. A cylindrical stone some twenty centimetres in diameter, stretching from the woodland bank to beneath the part of the house that will be my utility room, indicates that the *mare* was once much bigger than it is today.

This boundary stone would have been essential to prevent the cattle who drank from here advancing and soiling the water. We've also uncovered some seriously strong foundations supporting the utility room building, which has been added at a much later date to the rest of the house. Jacques thinks there was probably a cow shed here originally for the cattle that would have been kept when the property was a farm. He also says that he thinks the *pigeonnier* and the part of the house attached to it are the oldest section, as according to the '*cadastre napoléonien*'[1] this is the only part that resembles the current building.

The presence of the *pigeonnier* indicates, as it's the only one in the hamlet, that this was the home of the local nobility. Jacques tells us that nobles who had a *pigeonnier* were disliked by the peasants who worked the land, as their pigeons ate the grain; the nobles ate the pigeons, and the peasants often went hungry. The more pigeons they had, the more grain the birds ate; whoever lived here kept a substantial number. I, having a pigeon phobia, can only think of the noise and the smell. Not such a romantic image as the Lady of Shallot figure I'd dreamt up, sitting in her ivory tower regarding the world through the reflection in her mirror.

> Four grey walls, and four grey towers,
> Overlook a space of flowers,
> And the silent isle imbowers
> The Lady of Shallot.
> *'The Lady of Shallot', Alfred Lord Tennyson*

* * *

Now that the *mare* is almost entirely dry apart from the deepest part next to the steps, we've been able to reach the big, juicy blackberries overhanging it that aren't scorched and shrivelled by the sun like those on the path. Jacques is in his long shorts and a pair of Mr V's wellingtons, almost knee deep in water with a bucket to collect the berries. Mr V tells me to come see *le petit canard* (the little duck). He's in his element, splashing around like an overgrown four-year-old in a puddle. It's a joy to watch him taking pleasure in the simple things. Many people could learn a thing or two about the true meaning of life from this gentle soul. He's no simpleton though; he is a brilliant mathematician and an inventor. Maybe he's worked out the mathematical formula for happiness...

Jacques has become even more excited than usual. He's seen something glinting in the mud beneath the water. Perhaps he has indeed found the Templars' treasure. He's scratching away with his bare hands.

'Maybe it's a Napoléon,' he says, 'a gold coin.'

He can make out the outline of a head encircled by a laurel crown, and where there's one, there could be many. Alas, the treasure turns out to be the gold foil wrapper from a piece of chocolate money, so we won't be giving up our day jobs just yet.

I wonder how the chocolate money got into the *mare*. Maybe a child threw it in with the chocolate still inside, like throwing a coin into a fountain to make a wish. I hope that it came true.

＊　＊　＊

We've just unearthed some treasure. Well, not exactly treasure, but a couple of interesting items. One is a large horseshoe that's been well worn by what must have been an enormous Shire horse. It still has some of the original nails intact, and Jacques says that looking at the way it has worn down, it came from a front left foot. I'm going to clean it and hang it on the exterior door of the *pigeonnier*.

Jacques has found an interesting spoon that appears to be made of copper, with engravings on both sides of the handle, and Mr V has dug up an eating utensil. It is something between a spoon, a fork and a knife and probably used for scooping up, stabbing and cutting food. It's quite primitive-looking and could have been buried here a long time.

We've also found half of a beautiful blue and white floral plate with a seal on the back similar to those found on silver and gold; there's a number painted in green and the word 'Germany'. This dates it after 1871 when Germany became a country; maybe someone visited there and brought it back as a souvenir, or perhaps it has a connection with the occupation. I know that German officers were billeted in this area, so I'm presuming they were in this house. Once again, I feel history close in like a concertina, bringing the past into touching distance.

What I've learnt today: There are two schools of thought on which is the correct way to hang a horseshoe. Ancient folklore suggests that the position should follow the lunar cycle, hanging it pointing downwards during the waxing cycle from the new moon to full moon to fill it with luck, and pointing upwards during the waning cycle from the full moon to new moon to keep the luck.

---

1. A nationwide land registry ordered by Napoleon Bonaparte in 1808.

WE'RE ALL MADE OF STARS

I'm outside taking advantage of the cool evening air. Mr V has rigged up an electrical socket to enable me to charge my laptop and continue to work outdoors. I'm listening to an old CD. It's Wishbone Ash's *Argus*, and it is still one of my favourite albums of all time. The track is 'Leaf and Stream', and it fits perfectly with my mood this evening. The words speak of thoughts being carried into dreams like a fallen leaf in a stream. How beautiful is that?

Earlier this evening the newly independent Poly and Penny entertained us after dinner by playing 'leapcat', hopping like furry frogs into the pots of geraniums along the terrace wall. This began with Poly sitting in one of them and flattening the plants while he surveyed us with his overlarge, green eyes. He plucked up courage to leap to the next then proceeded from pot to pot, jumping down from the last one and running back to the first to begin the process again. I must add that these geraniums have been a gross disappointment, and no amount of watering and cajoling has encouraged them to produce more than a few straggly stalks with a smattering of sparse flowers drooping from them, so I'm happy for Poly to give them their just deserts.

Penny then surprised us by also managing to leap onto the wall and proceeded to play a delightful game of 'follow the leader' with her brother, jumping in unison one pot behind. The game ended abruptly when Poly smashed a pot, and although Mr V and I simply laughed, Poly promptly hightailed it to hide beneath the feather tree, maybe due to fright, or maybe his male pussy pride had been compromised.

Pussy Willow has joined me in the tranquillity now that all the invaders have left. She rolls onto her back at my feet in pussy bliss, purring and rubbing her damp nose on my bare toes.

The stars begin to come out one by one as if someone is flicking a celestial switch. Venus is the first to appear, rising in the east and drifting across the ink-black sky like an amber diamond; others swiftly follow until the sky is studded with countless constellations. Once more I'm in awe of how much closer they seem to be here; it's as if heaven and earth could stretch out their hands and brush fingertips, as in Michelangelo's masterpiece in the Sistine Chapel. The stars appear as specks to me; in reality it is I who am the speck. But we're made of the same matter, the stars and I. I am made of stardust, and so are you.

THE SHAPE OF THINGS TO COME

*M*r V has removed all the tiles from the utility room roof and insulated above the rafters. This room will have a lot of water pipes running through it, and we don't want them to freeze. It's as hard to imagine it freezing as it was to imagine it stopping raining last winter. The seasons are so extreme here.

The nights are beginning to draw in, and the sun has disappeared behind the poplars by 8:45, taking the heat of the day along with it. This is a blessing, as I'm sitting at the table writing with the sound of crickets and Neil Young. Les Libellules seems to have rekindled a love of '70s music in me. Flaubertine is chilling with Neil on the terrace wall, and Pussy Willow is playing at hunting—stalking real or imaginary prey amongst the molehills.

I've acquired a little secretary—Poly is sitting behind my laptop, and from time to time he pops his head and paw around the screen and taps on my keyboard adding multiple pppppps and lllllls to my story. I've just told Flaubertine that she's now immortalised in two of my books, but she looks unimpressed. She would prefer that I was Peter Mayle or Gerald Durrell, but I'm just Lindy Viandier, feeling at this moment that I'm mad to be slaving away at a hot keypad when I could be inside with a glass of wine, watching something inane on French TV.

This coming weekend, serious work is about to commence, as the new extension to house the elephant-sized fuel tank begins. The preliminaries for moving the tank have already taken place. The foundations that Marcel made are now thoroughly dry and can support an empty tank, though it will take another couple of weeks before we can fill it. All we need to do now is drain the 100 litres or so that remain at the bottom.

Pascal the plumber has dropped off an empty 100-litre oil drum for us to syphon the fuel into, and Mr V gets to work with a pump and a hose. Then we hit a problem. The seemingly almost-empty tank has more than the estimated 100 litres left inside, the problem being we have nothing to drain the contents into.

I run from house to house, asking if anyone has a spare drum; Fifi, Jacques and Pieter can't help, but Patrice from the farm behind has three 60-litre barrels, which he drops off. We fill all three, and there's still fuel in the tank. Mr V now begins syphoning it into five-litre, plastic containers, but after he's filled six of these and there remains a residue in the bottom of the tank, we're at a loss. It feels as if it's never going to stop. It's like an enchanted fuel tank; the more we drain, the more it fills.

Then Fifi arrives with his trailer. He's been ringing around, and a farmer in a village fifteen minutes away has two brand-new, 100-litre drums that he'll give us for free as they're taking up space in his barn.

Fifi has been drinking, and I query the wisdom of Mr V getting into a car with him, but he assures me they're only going on country roads, plus our trailer is already loaded with rubble from the *mare*.

They return safely 40 minutes later and proceed to drain the remainder of the tank, tipping it at an angle to reach the last drops. Mr V is up a ladder to do this as the tank is as tall as he is. Fifi is feeding the hose into an empty drum, getting fuel all over his hands. When the first drum is full, he steps outside and lights a cigarette despite his fuel-soaked fingers; he's also using one of the filled, 60-litre barrels as a table on which he's placed an empty plant pot as an ashtray. I envisage him and half of the house going up in a flash. Mr V says it's only oil, not petrol, so not flammable, but I lure Fifi to the actual table, now on the patio at the other side of the garden, and give him some kitchen paper to wipe his hands.

With the last drum almost full, we've drained exactly 500 litres from the 'empty' tank.

Time to offer Fifi a small beer then Mr V will drive him the 500 metres up the road home.

* * *

Pascal is coming this morning to power-wash the inside of the tank, but first it must be moved out of the utility room and into the garden. Before this can happen, the now full drums and barrels must be moved from the terrace, where they've spent the night, into one of the outbuildings. Three of these contain 100 litres of fuel, so it's no mean task. Plus, the tank itself is over 70 centimetres wide, and the doorway only measures 78 centimetres, so there's not a lot of room to manoeuvre.

Jacques is first on the scene with a *diable*, which literally means 'devil' but is a tall frame on two wheels that tips back and makes it easier to transport heavy loads. I have no idea what this is called in English, but they have them in warehouses and DIY stores. Even so, Jacques and Mr V must get the drums onto the devil in the first place. I ask how they're going to do this, and Jacques simply flexes his muscles. Sure enough, half an hour later, all the drums are in the 'hangar' as Mr V calls the outbuilding.

He and Jacques now turn their attention to the tank. Incredibly, between the two of them, they get it out of the room without taking the doorframe with it as I envisaged. And with the aid of various planks of wood, they have it at an angle, bottom up and ready to clean.

The effect of this is immediate. The scale of the room can now be appreciated, and I get to work with a tape measure and graph paper, planning where all the appliances will eventually go, plus marking out where I would like Mr V to put electrical power points. I allocate places for storing the garden furniture and also the ironing board, clothes airer, hoover, mops and brushes. After I've brushed and steam-cleaned the floor, and opened the door and windows, there's barely a trace of the overpowering smell of fuel that pervaded the room and seeped into the rest of the house. I now have a pleasant place next to the window where I can put the garden table in winter and write, looking out onto the terrace.

Fifi and Pascal are amazed when they arrive to see that most of the heavy graft has been done. We just need Pascal to power-wash the interior of the tank and leave it to dry before moving it to its new home at the back of the house.

Moving the tank into position is a lot trickier, as it must be carried across the garden, out of the narrow gate, around the side of the house and along the entire length of the back, as the *mare* blocks the shorter route. It's all hands on deck with the four men each taking a corner and me guiding them to avoid obstacles such as molehills, holes in the ground, rocks, paving slabs and cats and kittens lying in their path. Eventually it's positioned on its platform to make sure it fits.

All that's left is for Pascal to drill through to the utility room to rig up a temporary fuel supply from one of the 100-litre drums to the boiler while the extension is being built.

This is one of those moments when you realise nothing is simple in a house as old as this. I'm waiting expectantly on the other side of the wall to see the corkscrew end of the drill emerge. When it does, it's a good metre lower than expected, smack bang in the middle of where I was going to put a wall cupboard. So, back to the drawing board for me, but the loss of a cupboard is a small price to pay for the gain of a room.

DON'T BE AN ASS

*W*e've come to visit Pappy Cardigan and Noëlle, who have a menagerie of chickens, ducks, geese, cats, rabbits and a donkey. Apart from having a penchant for real animals, Noëlle also has an impressive collection of animal statues dotted about her garden and balancing on walls and window ledges. The gates to her house are guarded by two alabaster eagles with wings poised to take flight, plus there are stone squirrels, frogs, hedgehogs, rabbits and ducks wherever you look. The most impressive, until now, was a large, life-like owl whose eyes followed you everywhere and who, Noëlle said, kept the foxes at bay from the rabbits and chickens. But nothing could have prepared us for the sight that greets us on coming up her drive. There, smack bang in the centre of the lawn, is a life-size horse. This is no majestic stone statue. It is made from a sort of resin, therefore in full glorious colour, and looks like something that has come from the forecourt of an American thrift store selling cowboy boots and belts with silver-dollar buckles. I am, to say the least, taken aback and, unusually for me, lost for words. As with the owl, the horse's eyes follow you, but unlike the owl, the horse is baring its teeth.

'Oooh that is...big,' I manage to get out under the watchful eye of

Pappy Cardigan who is flashing me a warning look not to say what's really going through my mind.

Mr V follows my lead with a hesitant, '*Ouiaaa, impressionant.*'

'Isn't it just impressive?' replies Pappy Cardigan with more than a hint of irony.

Noëlle obviously loves it, and that's the most important thing.

She asks us if we'd like to go to feed her real donkey. Now, if you know me, you know that I love donkeys, and my daughter Kate once created a photo file of me entitled 'the woman who strokes donkeys'. I even received a donkey sponsorship as a birthday present, and each time I visited the UK, I went to The Donkey Sanctuary, standing in the mud and rain waiting for Billy O to show himself. But Billy O was no fool and had no intention of leaving his cosy stable for a mad woman with a bag of carrots.

Noëlle's donkey, however, is not the type you would want to plonk your child on the back of for a saunter over the sand. He is demanding, has some decidedly uncouth habits and…he bites.

He's called Pilot, and he is eyeing us menacingly as we approach his field. Noëlle calls his name, which unfortunately comes out as Pee-y-lot, sounding very much like 'pee a lot' to me, to which I reply with words to the effect of, 'I bet he does,' eliciting strange looks from both Pappy Cardigan and Noëlle. Mr V, who speaks excellent English, knows exactly what I mean and gives me a half-stern, half-amused look.

Pee a lot lives up to his name and treats us to the sight of his impressive little-boy donkey part which gushes out pee with such force that both Mr V and I get our legs splashed. I know Cleopatra was said to have bathed in asses' milk, but I'm not sure if urine has the same properties. Then he swiftly goes into his next party piece, simultaneously braying from one end and breaking wind from the other; he does this when he gets excited apparently. Well, he must be thrilled to see me, that's all I can say.

In all honesty, this is the first donkey I have ever disliked, and one I will definitely not be stroking.

After we leave Pee a lot to snortle his way through his dinner, we go to feed the geese. Noëlle must specialise in aggressive farm animals, because she warns us to approach with caution as they act like guard dogs. The guard geese see us coming and waddle forwards at an impressive speed. I'm hoping they're just running towards Noëlle as she has a bag of grain, but they leap (geese leap?) onto the stone wall surrounding their enclosure and begin flapping their wings and honking in an alarming manner.

'They do this at the postmistress,' says Noëlle, 'but they never actually attack.'

I'm digging my nails into Mr V's arm, thinking the postmistress must be made of stronger stuff than I. Noëlle goes on ahead, scattering grain on the ground, and thankfully they all jump down and start pecking.

Next it's the chickens' turn. After the donkey and the geese, a cackle of hens pecking perilously close to my feet is my least traumatic encounter this morning.

Feeding time ends with the rabbits, who again are not the cuddly bunny variety I'm used to; these are russet-coated, feet-thumping creatures the size of dachshunds. They're eyeing me with the same menacing glint as Pee a lot and beating the ground so loudly that they sound like galloping horses.

This was not at all what I imagined. I had visions of distributing food to a Beatrix Potter-like menagerie of tame animals. I must remember next time we pay Noëlle and Pappy Cardigan a casual visit not to come at feeding time.

What I've learnt today: Not all donkeys are docile.

Back at Les Libellules, our menagerie has developed some unsavoury habits of its own. A fast-food restaurant has opened on the terrace— Chez Flaubertine. Dish of the day is mouse: field mouse, dormouse and vole depending on how hungry you are. Flaubertine is so grateful for the food that I'm giving her and the kitties, she has decided to show her gratitude by bringing me mice, dropping them at my feet with an immense sense of pride, and not at all expecting the shriek that I let out each time I'm presented with another 'gift'. One is under my chair now as I write. If it continues at this rate, mice in the area run the risk of becoming an endangered species. I take back all that I said about Flaubertine's mothering skills. She gives the kitties at least three mice each per day, then lets them suckle from her to drink. She herself is looking much better. She no longer has a runny nose and eyes, has put on a little weight and is looking more like her former, pretty self.

Penny is also a little prettier than she was. Mr V said she could hardly get any uglier, which I think is a mean thing to say. She and Poly are so close, it's really sweet to see, washing each other and sleeping curled one around the other like ferns in a forest. They're extremely eclectic in their diet. Last night they shared our chilli with kidney beans, and this evening's calamari and hummus went down a storm. They've also polished off a plate of paella and a tuna pasta bake in the past. They're particularly fond of cheese, and mustard-flavoured crisps as, I must admit, am I.

✳   ✳   ✳

Flaubertine and Pussy Willow have never got on and growl and tail-thrash at each other whenever they come face to face, so I was astonished to see Flaubertine rush to defend Willow yesterday afternoon when a large, mean-looking tomcat attacked her. Between the two of them, they saw him off, giving a whole new meaning to the slogan 'Girl Power'. What's even more astonishing is that I've seen Flaubertine cower in the presence of this beast on other occasions. I've a nasty feeling that this is the father of the kitties, and he was after Willow as his latest conquest. I showed my gratitude to Flaubertine with a large bowl of milk. She in turn continued to show her gratitude to me by leaving a little vole on each of our four doorsteps this morning.

This time last year, I was afraid of standing on giant snails; this year, it's poor little sacrificial rodents.

What I've learnt today: There is nothing like a common enemy to bring two warring factions together.

COOL AS A CUCUMBER

There's been a sudden drop in temperature, and a fine drizzle hangs over the garden like a cloak of cobweb. This has invigorated the kitties who are leaping and tumbling in the cool, damp air which in turn has invigorated the apple tree, and its abundant fruits have developed a delicate rose blush on their white/green skins.

Mr V was right in his assumption that it was too hot for the slugs and snails to venture out to eat our salad plants, as they too have blossomed overnight, and we have twelve crisp, curly lettuces of a presentable size. So we're about to have our first lettuce-cutting ceremony. I've never grown lettuces before and am really amazed that these have flourished. Choosing the 'winner' is a serious business. There are four nominees out of the twelve. Mr V has opted for the biggest of the bunch. I dither between the two curliest.

Jacques has arrived and tells us to cut the one that's most open, as the others will still be good next weekend. So, head wins over heart, and I produce a knife, a salad spinner, and my camera to record the momentous event. Mr V has never dug up a lettuce either, so Jacques demonstrates where to make the fatal cut, and Mr V holds up his trophy like the head of Marie Antoinette as I take 'one for the album'.

What I've learnt today: The name La Petite Bergère *(The Little Shepherdess) was attributed to Marie Antoinette, who liked to dress up and play at being a shepherdess or milkmaid when she was in her garden at Versailles.*

* * *

One salad variety that we didn't plant this year, but must do next, is cucumber. Fortunately they've been arriving on the doorstep with regularity from neighbours who have a glut of them. Dark-green, thick-skinned, odd-shaped fruits, not at all like the vibrant, thin-skinned batons that you find sweating in plastic on supermarket shelves, they're crisper and less watery and perfect in a Greek salad or tzatziki, both of which I've been making a lot of in the recent temperatures. But you don't want to be reading a Greek recipe in a book about life in France, do you? So here's another staple favourite of mine during the summer months.

I first ate this simple salad as a starter in a restaurant in the medieval city of Provins, southeast of Paris, and have continued to make it ever since as either a starter or to accompany fish.

CUCUMBER SALAD

Serves 2 to 4

Ingredients

1 medium cucumber
2 tbsp of light olive oil. (If you can't find light olive oil, use sunflower oil.)
1 tbsp tarragon vinegar
1 tbsp lemon juice
2 tbsp light crème fraîche
1 tbsp fresh mint leaves, finely chopped
1 tsp fresh tarragon, finely chopped

Method

Wash and finely slice the cucumber. (I leave the skin on for added texture, plus it's much easier to slice.)

Mix together the oil, vinegar and lemon juice with a hand whisk.

Add the crème fraîche a little at a time, continuing to whisk gently.

Add the cucumber to the crème fraîche dressing, cover and put in the fridge for around 30 minutes to allow the cucumber to soak up some of the dressing.

Sprinkle with the fresh mint and tarragon immediately before serving.

This is delicious and refreshing served as an entrée with a little warm, crusty baguette to mop up any dressing that remains on the plate.

THE JOYS OF COUNTRY LIVING

$\mathcal{W}$e're on our way to a *vide grenier*, probably the last of the year. We are early for once; only around twenty or so other vehicles are lining the lane leading into the village. In an hour this will be more like 200. It's the village we visited last year with the restaurant that serves *tête de veau* (calf's head), so we won't be having lunch there.

There's the usual array of rusty, old farm implements and enormous pots for making jam, and presumably cooking cows' heads, but also something that took me by surprise. A large selection of hunting rifles is there for the buying, with people picking them up and expertly looking down their barrels. Some serious-looking knives are also on display. Life here in the country is totally different from in Paris where security is extremely tight, and you even have your bag searched to go into Marks & Spencer. I express my surprise to Mr V which is met by his stock response of '*bof!*'

I fall lucky at the first stall and buy a beautiful oval mirror in an antique gilt frame surrounded by rose motifs for the rose bedroom. It's in immaculate condition and a steal at €15. Mr V then barters down from €70 to €50 a Louis-Phillipe fireside set of a heavy brass shovel, brush and tongs balancing on a classic stand, also in near-perfect condition. We'd seen a similar set in Paris, in not such good condition, also for €70 so are delighted with this find. Then I lower the tone by buying a brightly painted, wooden-duck wall plaque to hang tea towels and aprons on, but the €1 price tag softens the blow. I also pick up four much-needed egg cups for 50 centimes each, two of which are fine bone china and either Chinese or Japanese. We of course buy an obligatory oil lamp (goodness knows how many we have now). This one reminds me of the emperor dragonflies that gave the house her name—Les Libellules (The Dragonflies). The base is made from orange onyx with an Art Deco-style brass stand and a turquoise-blue glass bowl.

An unusual number of enormous dogs are being dragged around, or rather dragged away from each other. I think their owners must be holidaymakers, as these mutts are too well-bred to be farm animals. There are also stalls laden with fresh produce: huge, succulent melons and punnets of dusky-purple plums that the sellers are offering you to taste before you buy. The two village *boulangeries* (bakeries) are selling tempting, freshly baked, flaky croissants and rich, aromatic coffee from tables on the pavement, and both are offering samples of their delicious varieties of bread. Needless to say the queues are growing longer and longer outside their shops. I sample the melon and buy a coffee and a large, toasted almond croissant and am glad I only ate blackberries and yogurt for breakfast.

As we're leaving, I see a lady selling mirabelles by the kilogramme from the boot of her car. They're a bit bruised and battered and wouldn't look pretty in a tart but are perfect to make jam. Mirabelles are tiny, oval, amber-coloured plums that grow on the tree between our garden and the one behind. They are mainly found in the Lorraine region in the extreme east of France, but I've been surprised and delighted to see an abundance of them being sold in markets and at the roadside here in the Côte-d'Or. There are two varieties: larger, sweeter fruits that are best eaten fresh, and smaller, firmer ones that make excellent tarts, jam and even brandy.

I'd like to preserve some next year as we did with Jacques' cherries last year, but this time I'm just making jam, which is simple to do.

As the fruit is only grown in certain regions and its season is short, *confiture de mirabelles*, as it's called here, is quite expensive and much sought-after in the more upmarket supermarkets, hence, even at around €7 a jar, it doesn't stay on the shelves for long. I, however, have managed to make six jars from a €1.99 kilo of mirabelles and a €1.79 bag of sugar. The joys of country living.

MIRABELLE JAM

Makes 6 x 340 g (12 oz) jars

Ingredients

1 kg (2¼ lb) freshly picked mirabelle plums (best picked first thing in
the morning when they're plump with dew, not in the heat of the day
after the sun has dried their skins)
800 g (1¾ lb) of sugar
The juice of one lemon

Method

Wash the mirabelles, put in a large, heavy-bottomed pan with the
sugar and stir constantly while bringing to the boil.

Reduce the heat and add 2 tbsp of fresh lemon juice and simmer for
around 20 minutes until the mixture begins to cling to a wooden
spoon as it is lifted from the pan.

Sterilise 6 jam jars in boiling water and fill with the jam while it is still
hot, then seal the lids tightly and put the jars in a cool place to store
(the 'buttons' on the top of the lids should invert, indicating the jars
are airtight).

This will keep for around a year if unopened, but it lasts around a
month in my house.

FOLLOW THE LEADER

I've just taken some empty cartons and bottles to the recycle bins at the crossroads. Mr V was in the garden raking up all the long grass and straw that he'd cut from the molehill-infested land in front of the terrace. The kitties were having a whale of a time jumping in the miniature haystacks that he'd made; that is until Penny saw me passing, leaving the fold. A look of sheer alarm crossed her face, and she ran towards the fence, found a little gap to squeeze herself through and began chasing after me. Poly was quick to follow his sister's lead, and I found myself being trailed by two kittens while their mother lounged on the terrace wall either unawares or unconcerned.

They came almost to the crossroads before stopping, further than Flaubertine had ever been with me, and much further than Pussy Willow would come. I hurried to the bins and back, and on seeing their little, shadowy forms waiting for me in the middle of the road, I whistled and called to them. Immediately they sprang forwards and began running towards me. At the same time, the sheep in Monsieur Mouton's field also began hurtling towards me at a speed that I didn't know sheep could reach, especially these dull, languid creatures. Not only were the sheep running, they were baaing—loudly— terrifying the kitties who had never seen a sheep and only heard far-off baas, not this hullabaloo, which I have to admit alarmed me too. Waving my arms and telling them to 'shoo' and 'shut up' was having no effect at all.

The kitties have now hidden themselves underneath our neighbour Marie-Claire's car. Here I am on my hands and knees trying to coax them out, as this is also the home of César, a belligerent little terrier. Right on cue, Monsieur Mouton has arrived to herd up his flock for the night, something that I've already unwittingly done. He stops his car and asks me if I've lost something, and also if I know why his sheep are making such a racket. I tell him that I'm trying to coax two kittens from under the car, and he, with his still dodgy hip replacement, gets down on all fours beside me to help persuade them to come out. This of course has the opposite effect, as the sight of a large, almost toothless man thrusting his huge, hairy hand in their direction makes the kitties shrink back even further, and I have to say that I'd do the same.

The sheep, however, seeing their food supply so near and yet so far, reach a crescendo, in response to which Monsieur Mouton apologises for deserting me in my quest, but he must feed his sheep before the entire hamlet comes out to investigate the noise. Seizing the opportunity, I run towards Les Libellules with two little furbies scampering at my heels. I'm touched by how trusting they are of me, Poly particularly; his saucer-like eyes follow me everywhere. When we return to the terrace, I offer him my hand, expecting my customary scratch, but instead I am licked tenderly. Penny, however, still prefers to show her affection by digging her needle-like claws into my thigh.

What I've learnt today: Don't whistle near sheep, or you could cause a stampede.

BE CAREFUL WHAT YOU
WISH FOR

*A*fter a week away, Mr V and I are driving back down to Les Libellules on a glorious, late-summer evening with the low sun filling the car with coppery light. The telephone wires we pass on the way are like airport departure lounges, crammed wing to wing with birds waiting to take off for their winter residences. I muse over conversations they could be having.

'What did you do all summer then?'

'Oh, I just chilled by a swimming pool. And you?'

'I went up to the mountains; it was too hot to hang around here.'

'Doris on the wire behind said she went to the coast to escape the heat, but it was crowded, hardly a branch to be had.'

I'm always a little sad to see the birds leave as it signals the end of summer. This is our last visit in September. The next time we're here, we shall be well into autumn, and our focus will shift more and more indoors as the days get shorter, and no doubt wetter.

September has proved cooler and kinder than July and August, but there's still been no rain to speak of. The heavier dewfall, however, has revived parts of the garden, and I'm surprised to see six blood-red velvety roses on the once spindly now ornamental, rose bush in the centre of the garden. The valerian has also sprung back to life with a second flurry of deep-pink flowers, but alas no little Belle to play with them.

It's strange. Poly and Penny are not here to greet us either, despite Flaubertine being under my feet as I'm getting out of the car. I call, 'Kitties,' but they don't come, so I call them by name and bang the side of a tin of cat food with a fork, but there's no sign of them bounding towards me as usual. I ask Flaubertine where they are and tell her to go and find them. She gives me a prolonged response, which I understand to be that she doesn't know where they are either. I can't believe this is happening again and feel an element of guilt that I've somehow wished this upon them.

I couldn't bear the thought of Poly suffering, watching him grow thin and scraggy and losing his swagger, and had been trying to find a home for him and Penny once they were able to leave their mother. The fact that both kitties have disappeared in such a short time gives me hope that they've found another safe haven as we weren't here, or someone has taken them in, but given their wild nature, and me being the only human that they would let near them, this seems unlikely. I console myself with the fact that if they have died, then they knew only love and happiness in their short summer lives, and the hardship of winter never touched them. But *they* have touched me. I see their ghosts everywhere. Like a transfer that a child rubs from a paper onto its arm, traces of the kitties are rubbed from my memory all over the garden. Jules Verne wrote: 'I believe cats to be spirits come to earth.' I can believe that also.

I'm in the shower at this moment. My thigh still bears the marks of Penny's sharp, little claws that she hadn't yet mastered the art of retracting when she tried to climb upon my knee. I miss them. Flaubertine cuts a sad and lonely figure, calling the kitties to come to eat a mouse she's caught or drink the milk that she's still producing. She cleaves to me as she has never done before. I realise that I, poor as I may be, am her only friend.

What I've learnt today: French swallows travel a staggering 10,000 kilometres to winter in Sub-Saharan Africa in a crossing that takes between five and seven weeks, sometimes flying for 60 hours non-stop, living off their fat reserves.

⁂

We need to go shopping, but the road is blocked for repairs, so we take a different route, driving through a sunshine-infused corridor of yellow-headed sunflowers and golden maize. Ahead is a low hillock crested with the lollipop forms of trees like a scene from a calendar. The sunlight is swallowed by the shade of an arcade of tall trees with huge baubles of mistletoe dangling from their almost bare branches like sinister, giant hanging baskets. We emerge onto a flat plain where white Charolais cows are honey blonde in the soft morning light. The sky is milky blue with smudges of high cloud, and little troops of birds are amassing in the hedges then take off in a chattering frenzy as the car passes.

We won't be back in time to see the bread lady, so I've left a hessian bag with the money for two loaves hanging on the doorknob. The idea of doing this in Paris and expecting your bread and change to be there when you return is unthinkable.

⁂

We've just arrived back, and the hessian bag is where I left it, but now two floury, rustic loaves called *pains de campagne* are poking their pointy heads out of the top, and my twenty-centimes change is in a little money bag in the bottom. The postmistress has also left something for us, a note to say that I received a parcel last Tuesday, but rather than leave it in the postbox outside, she will keep it in her van until we're here. I really am living 'The Life Less Ordinary'.

Back in 2005 I received an 'inspirational diary' for Christmas. I was recently divorced, and a new, uncertain future was stretched out before me. On the first page of this diary, I wrote the following words:

'My promise to myself for 2006 is to live a more adventurous life.'

That April, I met Mr V, and the rest is history…

PART II
THE RELUCTANT AUTUMN

OCTOBER AND NOVEMBER 2018

L'automne est un deuxième ressort où chaque feuille est une fleur.
(Autumn is a second spring when every leaf is a flower.)
Albert Camus

TOPSY-TURVY

*O*ctober has arrived as radiant, warm and dry as July. The only tell-tale signs that the year is in its tenth month are the sun hovering low in the west at seven in the evening, and the fields shorn of corn basking in its softly fading light. We pass little troops of deer foraging amongst the remaining stubby stalks as we drive back to Les Libellules, and I'm reminded that we'll soon be in the hunting season. We've already discovered cartridges in the woods behind the house, though we haven't seen or heard any activity this close up to now.

Les Libellules is an array of colour with the roses and valerian enjoying a second spring before they go to sleep for winter. Dainty white butterflies and more dragonflies than I've seen all summer are flitting amongst the flowers. The sky is an unbroken arc of blue, and the trees, having begun to change colour in August, seem to have regained some of their greenery. The ground is strewn with dandelions, which I'm sure shouldn't be around at this time of year. The seasons have gone topsy-turvy.

I'm strangely catless in the garden. It feels odd and empty, as if we've forgotten something. Pussy Willow is flat-sitting in Paris as we're only here for two nights. We haven't seen Flaubertine since we arrived, and I've given up any hope of ever seeing the kitties again. I must admit to feeling a little lost, but on the plus side, the sun is no longer punishing and the temperature a pleasant 26 degrees. It's such a treat to be able to eat outside in the sunshine still, and having enjoyed what seems like an eternal summer, I'm dreading the winter, which must inevitably arrive.

* * *

I have a glimmer of hope. Pieter has just told me that a couple at the far end of the hamlet have adopted three kittens. Deep down I know that the kitties would never have gone that far on their own, as they stopped at half this distance when they followed me just days before their mysterious disappearance. But still I'm hurrying down the lane, my heart pounding expectantly.

I arrive at the house. All is quiet. There are cars in the drive, but no one appears to be home. I call out 'Penny', 'Poly', 'Kitties', all to no avail. I crunch up the gravel path on the far side of the house that leads to the back door, and there, perched on a window ledge, are indeed three kittens, but alas, not Poly, Penny and Belle. They are a mishmash of grey and white fur and sharing a large bowl of milk. They pause and look at me. These are the fortunate ones who have found a home. I'm naturally disappointed but also heartened by the fact that someone has taken these three in, so maybe someone has taken ours.

Back at Les Libellules, Flaubertine makes her appearance. She looks well, too well. Her stomach is bulging a little at the sides, and when I put my hand underneath, I can feel her nipples. It has been two weeks since we last saw Poly and Penny, so surely the teats would have shrunk back by now if she was no longer feeding them? I hope the poor little mite is not expecting another litter.

* * *

It's now evening, and I'm on the terrace, reading. Flaubertine has reappeared and joined me. I sense she wants to do something she never does—sit on my knee. I fetch a blanket from indoors, spread it across my thighs and pat it, but instead of jumping up, she goes to sit on the wall at the other side of the table. Still, she looks pleadingly at me. I tell her to come, and she tentatively crosses the table, which is usually forbidden, and slinks down onto my knee. She begins purring loudly and padding like a kitten, with needle-like claws. I'm glad I had the foresight to cover my knees.

We stay there together until past midnight. When I go in for the night, I leave the blanket on the chair for her.

BIRDS OF A FEATHER

Flaubertine is not the only one who has reappeared. The crows that so hastily departed in the storms last June have returned, settling back into their former nests where they can and building new ones where they can't. This time I feel none of my previous animosity towards them. I've been observing them for a while now. Their resilience astounds me, not only their resilience, their sense of community. I can see birds that have nests helping others who have not to reconstruct their colony in the treetops. Their cawing isn't just a senseless racket as I first thought but appears to be a sophisticated system of communication, issuing a mild warning cry to be on guard if a stranger approaches, and a much more forceful call for a mass evacuation if a predator is near. Mating pairs also converse with each other, and the colony as a group signals to guide and direct the young birds who are now making mass fly trials.

It's the fly trials that first sparked my interest in these animals who have been so much maligned by history and legend. Initially the flights were just a couple of hundred metres in a large, sweeping circle with adult birds leading and bringing up the rear, and a handful of scouts on the outside to prevent any of the fledglings straying from the group. They leave around the same time every evening, just before

8, but return later and later, flying further and further as their wings become stronger.

Tonight is the first time that the young birds have been out alone. Two adults went a couple of hundred metres towards the southwest with them, then returned. The youngsters were obviously ecstatic to be independent at last, cawing exuberantly as they passed overhead and disappeared across the fields into the amber dusk. The adults, however, have been unnaturally quiet for a good hour, as if all ears are straining to catch any sound from their precious offspring. Finally I see a black mass on the horizon—they are returning. The adults refind their voices and begin calling excitedly. As they approach the trees, individual fledglings peel themselves away from the group and return to the nest where proud parents are waiting to make a big fuss of them. They're just like human mums and dads greeting their children at the gate after their first day at school, excited to hear what their son or daughter has to say about their adventure.

I never thought I would ever hear myself say this, but I admire these birds so much. They are clean, well-organised, look after each other and have a real community spirit. *Liberté, Egalité, Fraternité*[1] indeed. If humans conducted themselves like crows, the world would be a safer and happier place.

Prompted by my new-found admiration and respect, I've done some research and discovered that my opinion of crows falls short of the facts. They're not only the most intelligent *birds* on the planet, they are one of the most intelligent *animals*. With a brain size to body ratio on par with humans, they've been described as 'feathered apes', their intelligence being compared to chimps, elephants and dolphins.

Humans, apes, elephants and crows are the only species known to make tools, but humans and crows are the only ones believed to make tools in order to make another tool. This has been observed in studies carried out in the French department of New Caledonia in the South Pacific. A crow is filmed using a stick to retrieve another longer one from a box in order to use it to reach a piece of food in a second box.

Crows can live up to twenty years and, following a prolonged courtship, mate for life. The young stay with their parents longer than any other bird, on average five years. They live in family units with relatives supporting each other. Older siblings share responsibility for younger ones, helping to provide food, very much like human civilisation.

So, no more playing the scarecrow for me. From now on we live in harmony.

*　*　*

A little additional crow tale. If you're reading this book, then you are already familiar with Mel Beswick's wonderful illustrations that have so perfectly captured the essence of my original photographs. Mel and I were taking some time out from designing book covers to visit one of my favourite places in Paris, the Montparnasse Cemetery.

We were discussing crows and how they'd been portrayed throughout history and recent popular culture, particularly in the film *The Birds*. The cemetery seemed to have more than its fair share of them perched on the headstones in a menacingly Hitchcockian manner. One particular bird that was pecking around on the ground not too far away seemed to be observing us and listening to what we were saying. I said if we left the cemetery and returned wearing Halloween masks, then we would get a completely different reaction, as crows can recognise faces and judge whether a person is perceived a threat based purely on appearance, something we humans all do instinctively.

As I spoke, a couple emerged from another path, both aged around their mid-thirties. The man was small and extremely thin with long, dark hair tied back into a ponytail. He was dressed all in black—trainers, jeans, jacket, baseball cap—and had an unkempt-looking beard. I didn't like the look of him, and although he may have been a perfectly decent guy, I wouldn't have wanted to come across him alone in a lonely place. The crows, however, were positively spooked by the sight of him. They began hopping about on their gravestones, flapping their wings in an alarming manner and letting out warning cries. Our little friend on the ground hastily ran from where he was pecking to position himself on the other side of us so that we were in between him and what he evidently saw as a threat.

After the couple moved off in another direction, all was calm once more. We clearly looked like the good guys.

What I've learnt today: While researching crows, I discovered that their collective noun can either be 'a murder' or 'a wake', while ravens, who are part of the crow family, have the collective nouns of 'an unkindness' or 'a storytelling'. I think A Storytelling of Ravens would make a good title for a book, don't you?

---

1. Liberty, Equality, Fraternity is the national motto of France.

DON'T JUDGE A COOK BY ITS NATIONALITY

I've discovered that it's not only crows who have a false reputation. I am British, and in the eyes of some French people, that means I can't cook. If you've been following me so far, you'll know that I love to cook, and I'm not half bad at it. Still, this wasn't enough to convince Vincent (the partner of my Parisian friend Marie) when I invited them for dinner.

Half an hour before they were due to leave, Marie caught Vincent in the kitchen eating a baguette stuffed with ham, cheese and salad.

'What are you doing?' she asked. 'We're going out for dinner soon.'

'Ah yes, but Lindy is English. This means there will be nothing that we can eat,' Vincent responded.

It was no use Marie trying to convince him otherwise; stereotypes are notoriously difficult to shake off, so she left him to it.

When they arrived, we welcomed them, as customary, with a flute of champagne and an array of nibbles for the apéritif. I had pushed the boat out, as Marie is an excellent cook, and I wanted to impress.

I'd prepared rillettes *de thon,* a sort of tuna pâté, to serve with small rye-bread toasts; little glasses called *verrines* layered with foie gras and fig chutney; goat's cheese with sundried-tomato tapenade, and smoked salmon with cream cheese and cucumber purée. For a starter

I'd made a *soupe de moules* (mussel soup) with homemade garlic and parsley croutons.

Vincent was by now beginning to get the picture that this was *not* going to be the dinner of beans on toast followed by jelly that he'd anticipated.

The main course was *poulet à l'estragon*—chicken in a tarragon and white wine sauce—served with timbales of rice cooked in coconut milk. Next came the cheese board. I'd prepared a platter of four cheeses: a French Brie, Roquefort and Comté plus an English Wensleydale with apricots for them to try. It was now that a red-faced Vincent had to confess, admitting that if he took cheese, he would not have room for the dessert, which he imagined would be excellent after the rest of the meal. He was glad he passed on the cheese when presented with my homemade lime crème brûlée. I told him he could have beans on toast and jelly next time.

Here is the recipe for *poulet à l'estragon*. If you want the recipes for rillettes *de thon, soupe de moules* or another lime dessert, you'll have to wait until spring or cheat and look ahead…

POULET À L'ESTRAGON

Serves 4

Ingredients

1 tbsp butter
4 free-range chicken breasts, each cut into 3 pieces
1 medium shallot, finely chopped
1 clove of garlic, finely minced
1 tbsp tarragon vinegar
100 ml (4 fl oz) white wine (I prefer a slightly sweet wine with this dish)
1 tbsp cornflour[1]
4 tbsp crème fraîche
200 ml (8 fl oz) clear chicken or vegetable stock
Freshly ground salt and pepper to season
4 stems of fresh French tarragon

Method

Heat the butter in an ovenproof casserole until melted but not brown and gently sauté the chicken portions until just sealed and lightly golden.

Remove from the pan, reduce the heat a little and add the shallot and garlic and sauté until soft, taking care not to brown.

Add the vinegar and white wine and deglaze the pan.

In a mixer, mix the cornflour, crème fraîche and stock into a smooth paste.

Return the chicken to the pan and season with salt and pepper.

Pour the crème fraîche and stock mixture over the chicken.

Add the stems of tarragon and cook covered in a preheated oven at 200 C/gas mark 6 for 30 minutes until the chicken is tender and the sauce has thickened.

Serve with rice or pasta and a crisp, dry Chablis to counterbalance the sweetness of the dish.

The smell when this is cooking is divine.

What I've learnt today: Check that you are using French tarragon, as the Russian variety is much milder, so you'll have to use a larger quantity.

---

1. Cornstarch.

COMPUTER SAYS YES!

J can't write a book about living in France in 2018 without the B-word rearing its ugly head, though I've deftly avoided it up until now. I am of course talking about Brexit. My intention is not to take a political stance, but this has undoubtedly had an effect on my life. The first of these effects came weeks after the referendum when I attempted to open an account with the French post office bank, *La Banque Postale*, and was refused as the computer said 'no' to my British passport as a form of ID. Arguing that the UK was still in fact part of the EU and that Article 50 had not yet been triggered was futile. The bureaucrat behind the counter was having none of it as he foresaw 'problems', even though I said that the account would be used to receive my French salary, and solely for use in France. We did, however, manage to wangle my name onto Mr V's account and convert it into a joint one, but they still wouldn't grant me a *carte bleue* (a French debit card).

So, when we were faced with a most amiable gentleman on a recent trip to the local post office near Les Libellules, Mr V casually slipped into the chit-chat about the heat and house renovations that although we had a joint account, it would be more practical if his *petite femme*[1] had one of her own. Cue for small, blonde English wife to put her *petit accent anglais* (little English accent) to good effect and flash her most alluring smile. He said that he personally couldn't see a problem with my having a British passport, but it was not his domain, and that he would make an appointment for us with Mr Renaud Flambeau, their financial advisor in Pouilly-en-Auxois. So off we go, ready to do battle with bureaucracy once more...

I smell success as soon as I clap eyes on Renaud. He bears none of the traits of the smug Parisian. He is wet behind the ears and desperately trying to appear not to be, and what's more, he has a trainee in tow. I'm glad I opted for smart, rather than casual, dress and persuaded Mr V to do the same; it makes us more of a force to be reckoned with. Now, this could go either way. Renaud could demonstrate his power by refusing me on the grounds that I have a British passport, as they did in Paris. Or he could demonstrate even more power by granting me what French red tape seemed so determined to deny me.

The charm offensive begins. Mr V is magnificent, blinding them with science, talking about the technicalities of his job, and I'm gushing about how we prefer the country to the town, and how we cannot wait to retire and move here permanently. I throw in the fact that I'm a writer, and if my book is a big success, I'll have my royalties paid into the post office.

Then the form-filling begins. The amount of paperwork is only slightly less than when we bought the house, and actually more than when we got married. Renaud is on a roll, asking me for proof of income, utility bills, *livret de famille* (French marriage certificate in the form of a book where marriages, divorces and children are documented), details of our joint account and so on. I'm whipping documents out of my bag like a magician pulling rabbits out of a hat.

Even Mr V is astonished, repeatedly saying, '*Oh là là*, you have that!'

'Yes,' I reply. 'I'm practically French. I've even brought *une prise de sang* (a blood sample).' At which Renaud falls about laughing and gives me a free pen that I'm soon to be in need of. After pushing aside the little niggle of the system once again not recognising my passport,

Renaud, in a flurry of authority, announces that it's of no consequence; it's only to prove that I am who I say I am. He can see from all my other documents that are now stacked between us in an impressive pile on his desk, and from my beautiful passport photograph, that I am indeed Madame Lindy Viandier. To verify this fact, I get to sign my name and initials on countless sheets of paper that I feel Renaud should at least explain, even if I don't read them before signing. But I don't want to give him time to change his mind and side with the computer. Steam is coming off the free pen as my signature gets more and more erratic. I hope it doesn't run out of ink.

Fifty euros is transferred from the joint account into my new bona fide French bank account, and I'll receive my *carte bleue* in the post in the next five days. Hands are shaken firmly (I actually want to kiss Renaud, but refrain), and we leave triumphant.

We wait until we're around the corner before pumping the air and saying, 'YES!'

What I've learnt today: The only thing that French civil servants like more than making rules is bending them.

---

1. *Petite femme* literally translates as 'little woman', and is a term of endearment in France for a wife; not so in British culture.

ROLL OUT THE RED CARPET

*W*e're now in the second week of October, and there's still no sign of rain. The conifers that we pass en route to Les Libellules are drooping like Christmas trees on the 6th of January, and the hedges are dry and dusty, with none of their usual lustre. The ground, however, is a glorious ochre, like a straw mat has been strewn across the land, bringing a beautiful harmony against the dense blue sky. Summer, it seems, is as egotistical as winter, keeping a tight grip on her domain. As winter kept spring at bay, she keeps autumn waiting in the wings, giving her no stage on which to perform her profusion of colour.

However, little hints that autumn is approaching *have* appeared in the Virginia creeper around the gate, which is now the colour of rosy apples with tiny touches of green and yellow. It trails across the ground in a thick red carpet of leaves. The actual apples are still disappointingly mostly green, and I wouldn't like to chance eating one. I'd make a *tarte tatin*, a sort of sticky, upside-down apple pie, but the weather is too hot for heavy desserts, and we're still eating tomato and mozzarella salads on the terrace at lunchtime.

Flaubertine is waiting on the wall when we arrive; she must have a sixth sense. She has a kitten with her. It's obviously not hers, but it's behaving as if it is, arching its back and rubbing itself against her affectionately, and she is happier to share her food with it than she was with Poly, Penny and Belle. It is jet black and around three or four months old with short, stubby legs and a rotund, little body, like a furry, black ball. I've not seen it before. I have no idea who its mother is, or was, as Flaubertine seems to have adopted it. I'm happy for her to have found some comfort, but I'm not giving Sooty a name...

One not so welcome habit that has resumed with Flaubertine's new-found surrogacy is the trotting across the terrace with dead rodents almost constantly. She's just passed under the table with a huge dormouse dangling limply from her jaws. I freeze, hoping she doesn't leave it as a present for me; thankfully she continues out of the garden and calls to Sooty or the kitties, but no one answers, and my heart breaks for her. She eats the mouse herself and comes crying to me. I put a chair next to mine and invite her to jump up beside me while I write. She's here now, purring and cooing, content that I'm near.

Flaubertine wasn't the only one waiting by the wall. Jacques was there also, balancing on his bicycle, waiting to tell us he has VIP tickets to the Bonsai San exhibition that's taking place in Saulieu over the weekend. I was underwhelmed by this news until I heard how internationally popular this event is. I had noticed an extraordinary number of tourists in the town as we drove through—people with suitcases going into the handful of hotels, and almost all the tables taken in restaurants that usually only have half a dozen diners. The tickets are normally €20 per person, and the acclaimed bonsai change hands for hundreds of euros.

Mr V adores plants, trees in particular, so I think there's a good chance we'll be going.

* * *

We've arrived at the venue for the international Bonsai San exhibition. Here too there's a red carpet, but it's the official variety. I wasn't expecting such a lavish function; the car park is two-thirds full at 10:15 in the morning. There are a number of camper vans and caravans, and looking at the registration plates, people have come from far and wide. Apart from French and Dutch, there are British, German, Belgian, Spanish and Portuguese. The exhibition hall itself is impressive—a large, modern building with a high, vaulted wood and glass ceiling that Mr V and I had no idea was here. Inside, rows and rows of prize-winning bonsai are displayed on black plinths set against a black backdrop. The effect is stunning, with the exhibits cleverly illuminated to show off their intricate branches and foliage. Some of them are what I imagined a bonsai tree to be; others are much bigger, reaching up to a metre high and wide, but still miniature in comparison to their full-size counterparts.

The international theme continues with, not surprisingly, stalls from Japan, but also China, South Korea and Mexico. A lot of broken English is being spoken around the room as experts and enthusiasts discuss together. Large sums of money are changing hands also; people are definitely not just here to window-shop.

I feel as if we've stumbled upon an alternative universe of bonsai lovers; they all seem laid-back, friendly people. I'm sure it has a lot to do with constantly touching trees. Touching though is one thing that you're not allowed to do in the exhibition, but people are genuinely pleased when you stop to photograph their displays, particularly the South Koreans, who insist on being in the picture. Some expert cropping will be required later, as I was angling for arty and ornamental, and I'm ending up like the local rag photographer at a village fête. I think the fact that I have a real camera, while most others are using their phones, is tricking the Koreans into thinking I'm official.

I'm in my element being amongst trees and taking photographs. Mr V has more serious interests, watching demonstrations and looking at the various tools required for cultivation, but we're not buying as we have neither the time nor place to spare, and nor, it seems, the money. Trees are changing hands for anything from €150 for a tiny specimen to over €5,000 for a grander/rarer one. I'm particularly attracted to a dense, little, mushroom-shaped conifer which is €3,500. Mr V said that would buy us a new boiler; this is how we think now before we buy.

In the end I buy a book; it's an illustrated version of *The Hidden Life of Trees*. Its magnificent, inspiring, full-page colour photographs made me feel calm and relaxed when I looked at them, so it could come in handy over the stressful months ahead at Les Libellules.

On the house renovation front, Mr V has now turned his hand to tiling the roof of the new extension to house the fuel tank. Marcel has sourced some original terracotta tiles from another dilapidated ruin, and Mr V is now seamlessly tying them in with the utility room roof so that it looks as if it's always been there. I am, as you can see, writing. But unlike way back in August 2017 when Mr V asked me if I had nothing to do when he caught me furtively scribbling beneath the curtains I was supposed to be sewing, he's just asked if it would disturb me working if he used the drill. Maybe it's my promise to buy him a Mercedes if I become rich and famous that has brought about this change of opinion. We can but dream.

SALAD DRESSING

*I*t's the 19th of October, and we've left Paris straight after lunch. I'm dressed as if it's July, as the temperature remains in the high 20s with no sign of rain. The trees are still green with hints of yellow here and there, but the ochre fields of two weeks ago are now chequered with chestnut-brown, freshly turned soil. I'm surprised to see so many calves born in our brief absence. I can't remember noticing so much new life this time last year. Speaking of new life, it takes Flaubertine about two minutes to materialise after we arrive. She looks extremely well and is pleased to see me, far and beyond wanting food.

We stopped at the supermarket at Saulieu on the way down. I'm putting groceries into the fridge, and something that looks like a small tadpole is on the bottom shelf. At first I think it's a piece of lettuce, but I pick it up carefully in case it's a caterpillar and that by some miracle it is still alive as it must have been in there for at least five days. Imagine my surprise to find that I'm holding a minute lizard no more than one and a half centimetres from nose to tail, and apparently dead. I put the poor little creature in the palm of my hand to take it to show Mr V, and an extraordinary thing happens. The heat of my hand brings this miniature miracle back to life, and it begins scurrying up my wrist, where I intercept it with my forefinger and pass it from hand to hand. It's as agile as an ant and perfect in every way. I take it outside and place it in some foliage growing close to a south-facing wall, where hopefully it will find a little crevice to hide itself away from the prying eyes of predators.

Not only am I happy to have discovered this little lizard but also not to have eaten it, as it must have come into the fridge along with a lettuce from the garden, which I did wash, but obviously not sufficiently.

I can now hear you all making mental notes not to eat salad *chez moi*.

What I did make sure was well and truly washed were the windfall apples that we found lying in the damp grass when we arrived. Their milky-green skins have now turned a soft lemony colour; Mr V tested one and declared it delicious. I'm not a big fan of apples, unless they're in a salad. I'm not a big fan of them cooked either, but as they're so abundant, it would be wasteful, and against all we're about here at Les Libellules, not to use them, so here is my surprisingly good variation of apple crumble using a flapjack topping.

OATY APPLE CRUMBLE

Serves 4 to 6

Ingredients for the compote filling

4 large apples, peeled, cored and finely sliced
A handful of raisins
8 cardamom pods
2 x 8 g (⅓ oz) sachets vanilla sugar (or 1 tbsp Demerara sugar)
2 tbsp fresh orange juice

Ingredients for the topping

100 g (4 oz) porridge oats
1 tsp ground cinnamon
30 g (1 oz) butter
1 tbsp runny honey or maple syrup

Method

Put the apples, raisins and cardamom pods in a saucepan and sprinkle
with the sugar.

Add the orange juice and simmer gently for around 15 minutes until
the sugar dissolves and the apples and raisins are soft.

Mix the oats and cinnamon together.

Melt the butter and honey or syrup together in a non-stick saucepan.

Remove from the heat and add the oat mixture.

Remove the cardamom pods from the apples and raisins and put the apple mixture into a baking dish.

Sprinkle the oat mixture over the apples and raisins and cover loosely with foil.

Bake in a preheated oven at 180 degrees/gas mark 4 for 30 minutes until the oats are cooked and the apples bubbling.

Remove the foil and bake for a further 5–10 minutes until the top is crisp and golden.

Serve with custard, crème fraîche or vanilla ice cream.

I made extra apple compote and custard and mixed the two together to make an apple fool which was delicious served cold the next day.

KINDRED SPIRIT

*W*e've just been to Dijon to get more building supplies. On the way back, we take a different direction to avoid the autoroute as the trailer is dangerously loaded with loot from Brico Dépôt and Castorama. We pass through honey-stoned villages that, if you removed the shutters from the windows, could be in the heart of the English Cotswolds.

We climb so high that my ears pop as I look down on the dense treetops of the forest below before descending into the gloom of the canopy. Ribbons of sunlight break through the branches, illuminating small patches of the road which is little more than a lane. As we emerge from the forest, the view below us becomes a sea of golden vineyards with bronze-skinned hired hands nimbly picking grapes and tossing them into baskets strapped to their backs. We're on the *Routes des Vins* (Wine Route), passing through villages with familiar names: Nuits-Saint-Georges, Vosne-Romanée, Vougeot, Gevrey-Chambertin. Mr V 'ooohs' and 'aaahs' at the memories that they're conjuring up for him. I would really like to stop and create a few memories myself, but the trailer is swaying in an alarming manner on the tight hairpin bends that rise and fall like a roller coaster. I'm on wing-mirror duty, watching to see if anything falls off, but am constantly distracted by the sights beyond.

Many of the vineyards we pass are called *clos de* something or other. Mr V explains that a *clos* was traditionally a walled vineyard (*clos* is the French for enclosure). Originally these were part of Cistercian monasteries; later they were built to protect the grapes from theft and to create a microclimate. The word is often used in the name of wines even when the wall no longer exists. The prefix *domain* is also associated with wines from Burgundy, while *château* is associated with wines from Bordeaux.

Eventually the hills are behind us, and we come to a flat stretch of road. Mr V stops the car to check all is OK in the trailer, and I get out to stretch my legs. I wander a couple of hundred metres, pausing at the pillared gateway of an elegant château. It's the Château Lamartine, the former residence of the politician and founder of the Second Republic, Alphonse de Lamartine. It thrills me to have stumbled upon the home of such a political giant tucked away in a quiet, little backwater, overgrown and seemingly abandoned. There's no splendour to honour his greatness, just a small, simple plaque on the wall, half hidden by ivy. I feel a connection with this man who two centuries ago was also a writer and poet, who loved nature, spirituality, history and theatre; all the things that I love. I could write pages of his quotes, as they are so insightful and mirror many of my own sentiments, but you can have the thrill of looking them up for yourself.

Here's one that I *will* share with you though, as I hope in some small way that I move you, and you are affected by *my* words.

The people only understand what they can feel; the only orators that can affect them are those who move them.
Alphonse de Lamartine, 1790–1869

A BRIDGE IN TIME

*I*t's only five days since we were last at Les Libellules; how quickly things change. The temperatures are still unseasonably warm for the latter part of October, with 26 degrees forecast for tomorrow, but the trees have turned from green to russet, and the late-evening light is painting them fox-fur red. We're cruising along nicely when out of the bushes on the right dart nine or ten *sangliers*. Mr V brakes and swerves to avoid hitting them, as they're like skittles scattering all over the road. They are young, no bigger than a medium-sized dog, but less furry and with horns, and quite... cute? I've told you that we've been warned about the dangers of encountering these beasties on the road at night, and I now see why. If I'd been behind the wheel, there would have been blood and guts everywhere; ours, and the *sangliers'*. Luckily Mr V is a more skilful driver.

The trees have now taken on the hue of smouldering embers in the rose-gold glow of the dying sun. The rays catch Mr V's face, transforming him into King Midas; he really is quite handsome in a certain light.

Speaking of embers, this evening we have lit our first fire this autumn, and I have to say, as much as I love sitting outside watching the sunset, I equally love sitting inside watching the logs come alive with flames. Of course, this is a play fire, just to take the chill off the room; it's a different story when an icy blast is passing beneath the door and biting at my toes.

*　*　*

I've been woken by Mr V trying to saw wood quietly in the loft. Looking at my watch, I see it's 7:20 in the morning, and it sounds as if there's a steam train chugging through the room. I know time is limited, and he has to work, so I drag myself bleary-eyed from the cosy, comfy bed and go downstairs to make him a plate of eggs and me a pot of coffee.

The smell of the freshly brewed coffee attracts Jacques, who has been busying himself in the *mare* while we were away, and he's now found a large, conical, wooden implement with an iron handle. We're not sure what this could have been used for, but we're thinking it's some sort of bung, maybe to cap off a drain. He's also found another large horseshoe, but still no treasure.

There have been noticeably fewer frequent callers and fewer donations of fruit and vegetables this year, as we're no longer the 'new kids on the block' and therefore less of a curiosity. I like this; it means that not only are we calmer but also shows that we're more integrated into the community. We're now part of the fabric of the place like everybody else, which gives me a sense of belonging.

Jacques, however, is still an almost permanent fixture and now like part of the family.

*　*　*

Another visitor I'm always happy to see is Noëlle. She's here now with Jacqueline, the elderly lady who lived at Les Libellules with her parents and brothers, Maurice and Guy, when she was growing up. It was Guy who was married to Léa who lived here before us. Jacqueline asks me if the *pigeonnier* is still the same. As she can't manage the stairs, I show her photos of it, telling her that I'd cleaned all the little chambers myself. She's happy about this, as she has a small *pigeonnier* in her present house, but the previous occupant sold all the clay interiors to a man who made them into lamps and jars for storing kitchen utensils. I tell her of Mr V's plans for a library, but that we're going to leave all the original structure intact behind the panels so that it could be uncovered again at any time in the future. She has given me the idea to leave a section exposed behind a glass panel when the room is finished, which will further preserve the history of the house.

Jacqueline is impressed with the *mare* and had no idea it was so ancient. She tells me that in all her years, she has never seen it dry up and blames global warming. She also talks of her father, Fernand Lefebvre, the gentleman Jacques told me about on our first meeting last year, who collected postcards from around the world.

Monsieur Lefebvre sounds like a fascinating character. Jacqueline tells me that he was tall and slim with a mass of blonde hair and startling blue eyes. I think I'm falling in love. He was an artist, a musician and had a fine singing voice. My hit list before I met Mr V, who has none of these attributes, was a blonde-haired, blue-eyed man who could sing and play an instrument—and cook. I don't know if Fernand could cook, but as I was born around 70 years too late, it's irrelevant. Jacqueline points to the large central beam in the living room.

'This was the dining room when I was a child,' she says. 'My father had a rack for wine glasses attached to that beam.'

Apparently he'd cut off the feet from the glasses with a sabre, which was traditionally used for opening champagne. When someone visited the house, he would take down a glass (he must have been really tall), fill it with wine and hand it to them. They then had to drink it all before putting the glass down as there was no way of standing it up.

Now when I'm in the living room, each time I look up at that beam I will see a row of sparkling wine glasses waiting to be filled—and emptied.

I learn that it was Fernand who first ran the garage, and that his office was in the garden room, where I would like to have mine. Now, after hearing about its previous occupant, I can see why it has such a congenial ambience and attraction for me. It was also him who built the extension (where the giant fuel tank was) as a kitchen in 1926. He later added the terrace where we are sitting now, talking and drinking tea, with me scribbling notes on scraps of paper.

Not all the stories Jacqueline tells me are as pleasant as this one. We've already touched on the Resistance activity in this area. I'm now hearing that there was a German lookout tower on the hill behind the hamlet and a mini fort on the one facing. This fort was manned by two genial Germans, who were well accepted by the local community and often seen riding their bicycles to the *boulangerie* in the village. The local Resistance group *le Maquis Bayard* captured these two hapless invaders on one such trip to buy bread. The occupying forces weren't happy and threatened to set fire to thirteen villages in the area, including the one where Les Libellules is situated, if the prisoners were not released. The thought of Les Libellules being destroyed by fire makes me shudder. The occupants of the said villages pleaded with the *maquisards* to release the Germans, which they did, saving all the villages but one, which was tragically burnt to the ground. The mother of our neighbour Patrice was a little girl in that village and hid in bushes with her mother and siblings as they watched their house and all their belongings burn. But they were the lucky ones, as in other villages in the Morvan the residents were rounded up into the church and burnt alive along with the houses.

All this brings history out of the storybooks and into the real world. So many layers of it are buried here. I hope that I, in my small way, am keeping them alive.

What I've learnt today: The former lady of the house was Léa, not Leah as I previously thought.

THE MAGICAL MYSTERY TOUR

*M*r V is a man of mystery. He likes to play his cards close to his chest. Extracting information from him is like trying to prise open an oyster with a nail file. This morning he's acting more cagey than usual. Jacques is arriving at 8:30 to take us somewhere which is also a mystery to me. I've been told to wear my wellington boots, an old pair of jeans and to bring my camera, so I've packed a bag with 'emergency' coffee and chocolate just in case this is going to be a long-drawn-out affair.

Jacques arrives on the dot as usual, and we set off through the morning mist in a direction we've never taken before. Villages suddenly appear without warning, and the ruins of a 12th-century château emerge like a ghost ship from the fog. The mist floats above the fields like a silk scarf carried on the breeze. We rise above it, driving through hazy sunshine, then make a sharp descent as the road plunges into a valley obscured from sight. The sun comes up, but the haze lingers on the landscape, throwing the distance into soft focus. The foreground is all muted shades of clay, mustard powder, lichen and silver-green sage.

We stop at a roadside that appears to be in the middle of nowhere. In front of us is a large field with a small herd of Charolais cows grazing aimlessly. Jacques has the key to a high five-bar gate which is entwined with garlands of barbed wire. He demonstrates the peculiar wrist action required to manoeuvre the key into position to open the gate then relocks it, handing the key to Mr V to try. It swings open, and we enter a field dappled with cow pats, bordered by a fringe of gold- and copper-leafed oak trees. The oaks are part of a small wood nestling between two others. The wood is co-owned by Jacques and his siblings, some of whom want to sell. We're to become landowners it seems...

A point that I've not mentioned so far is that Jacques is carrying a rough horse blanket. I asked him why, and he mumbled something in French that I didn't catch. The reason now becomes apparent. There's a stile, a good metre off the ground without the usual foothold, and again encased in barbed wire. The blanket is to cover the wire while you cross the stile. Both being over six feet tall, Mr V and Jacques can accomplish this with ease. As I'm only five foot two and a half, it's a lot more challenging for me, and I concede that I must stay this side of the fence. Jacques, however, makes a gallant gesture and cups his hand for me to put my muddy boot into and propels me onto the stile as if I'm astride a horse; all that remains is for Mr V to catch me on the other side.

The other side is like entering another world. Tunnels of light entice me deeper into the wood. I weave between saplings and young trees. Clusters of golden acorns surrounding older oaks crunch like gravel beneath my feet. Shafts of muted sunbeams don't reach the ground but hover above my head like halos. I am entranced. Mr V appears to be also. His initial interest was to have a supply of firewood, but now I see that he too is under the spell of this enchanted place. He is mentally plotting out sites for his own saplings and inspecting trees that have been neglected and unloved for so long, seen only as a source of fuel, and not a source of beauty. He wraps his arms around an ancient oak to measure its girth; it appears to me that he's hugging it, and I want to do the same.

I see the completion date for the house renovations drifting further into the distance as he contemplates having his own forest, and I have to admit the idea thrills me too. I feel so at peace here. The silence is palpable, broken only by the gentle rustle of our footsteps as we walk through a carpet of fallen leaves. I could never have imagined having such a place where only we can go; our own totally wild, secret garden, made even more secret by its sheer inaccessibility.

I've done a foolish thing and lagged behind, taking the inevitable photos. Although out of the trees, I'm not, figuratively speaking, out of the woods. We'd stopped by a *mare* owned by a nearby commune, and I was attracted by a copse of elegant young trees closely grouped together, their slender trunks twisting and intertwining like maidens dancing in a circle. They made me think of the story of *The Twelve Dancing Princesses*, though there were more than twelve. I was clicking away at various angles when I noticed the sound of sporadic gunshots that had been in the distance were no longer sporadic *or* in the distance, but nearby and in earnest. There are hunters afoot.

Jacques and Mr V are a good 100 metres ahead of me, crossing a wide-open field, while I'm concealed in the shrubbery. I'm wearing a cream-coloured jacket and have blonde hair, so out in the open I would be easy to distinguish from a wild boar. I need to be visible as quickly as possible.

I have a dilemma, however. There is movement of an animal nature coming from the other side of the trees. A memory suddenly springs to mind of Jacques telling us not to stray into the adjoining field as there's a bull. I don't entirely trust cows, so I don't relish the prospect of coming face to face with a bull. I want to get out in the open as soon as possible but am afraid of attracting the attention of a raging animal. My heart is thumping, and I'm staring at Mr V's back, willing him to turn around and wait for me, but he goes marching on. So, torn between both wanting to draw attention to myself and not wanting to draw attention to myself, I dig my nails into my palms and screw up my eyes (goodness knows how this will help me in either event). I walk forward as quickly and quietly as I can, given the rough terrain. I finally catch up with Mr V who takes my hand and, sensing my disquiet, gives it a comforting squeeze. The Charolais cows continue to chew their cud, regarding us from a comfortable distance as we make our way back to the car. And I breathe a heavy sigh of relief.

THE PAST REVISITED

*J*acqueline is here again. She has brought a wonderful sepia photograph of Les Libellules. On the back, in flourishing handwriting, are the words 'Résidence Dard 1910'. The photo shows the house as it is now minus the kitchen extension. In its place there's another part of the house leading back from the *pigeonnier* forming an L shape. Jacqueline says this part was destroyed in a fire before her family bought Les Libellules. It's difficult to tell from the photo, but it appears to be made of wood. There's also a large tree where the small terrace is now. But apart from that and the lack of shutters, everything is exactly the same.

I get tingles in my hands and a peculiar sensation in the pit of my stomach looking at this scene that I know so well and have photographed so many times myself.

Once more Les Libellules reminds me how enduring she is and how transient we are.

There are four people in the picture: One barely visible without the aid of a magnifying glass, looking out from the present kitchen window. Another a stout lady in a black dress standing in front of the garden room. And two children, a girl aged around six or seven with a large, white bow in the side of her hair, and a boy a couple of years older dressed like Christopher Robin in a smock dress, standing near the tree. We shall have to wait until we are back in Paris to do some research into the family Dard to see if we can identify anyone in the photo.

⁂

Mr V has been scouring the net, and we've found our family. Louis Dard is the likely owner. He was born in 1876 and was a vet; his wife, Marie, was born in 1879. Only one child of the right age is listed in the archives—Emma, born in 1903—so this is our little seven-year-old girl with the ribbon in her hair, but the boy must be a friend, neighbour or relative. Louis and Marie had a younger child, a son, Jean, born in 1910, so the stout lady in the garden could be Marie Dard, heavily pregnant.

⁂

Jacques has confirmed that the little girl in the picture is indeed Emma Dard and that she lived here in the hamlet with her husband. She too was an *institutrice* (schoolmistress) in the local primary school, as was Léa, the previous occupant. So, as I taught medical English in Parisian teaching hospitals for nine years, it seems that I'm continuing the line of female educators; the only difference is that I have two daughters, who also work in education, and Emma and Léa were both childless. Emma must have lived to a ripe old age, as Jacques said it wasn't too long ago that she died and that she was an incredibly fat, old lady. He's not sure if she's buried in the local cemetery. I still haven't found the time to go and investigate as we've had a busy weekend, but this has been earmarked for our next visit when it will once again be *la Toussaint* (Halloween). This time though, unlike last year's fiasco, I'm well prepared with bags of sweets for the little trick or treaters.

⁂

The birds know something we don't. They sense autumn approaching. They gather together and take flight in unison like vast shoals of fish, swirling in formation in the ocean of deep-blue sky. They chatter incessantly, and the air is charged with their song and anticipation.

We, down on the ground, however, are lulled into what is no doubt a false sense of eternal summer. The garden continues to bear fruits of lettuces and tomatoes, and even the blackberry bushes are still producing fat, juicy berries, albeit they are now raspberry red not black. The only signs that autumn is around the corner are the slight nip in the air at the start and end of the day, and the morning mist that hovers above the fields is no longer the golden haze of summer, but silver grey. The colours of the land are also hinting at a seasonal change. The chequered landscape has given way to vast stretches of tilled earth the colour of cinnamon, which in turn give way to fields of deep rich green planted with neat rows of cabbage, kale and spinach.

Mr V and I eat what is maybe, if the birds are correct, the last al fresco lunch of the season and discuss our plans for the woodland. He wants to make space for the young saplings to receive enough light to flourish, and to begin his plantation. I would like to make a small clearing to serve as a picnic area with a rustic table and benches, and also build a little wooden playhouse hidden just out of sight from the picnic area with a swing hanging from the bough of an oak tree. I, as you can see, have fallen through time into a future full of grandchildren, who, like Christopher Robin, are safe to explore, play and learn about nature in their own secret woods. I'll make trails for them to follow, at the end of which they will find some delightful little curio such as a giant toadstool or woodland animals. I'm imagining Easter egg hunts and birthday parties, and I'm getting totally carried away.

Now it's time to pack up my fantasies along with everything else and head back to the reality of Paris.

What I've learnt today: The young saplings will need to be protected by wire cages, or they will be eaten by deer roaming the woods.

COUNTRY COUSINS

*A*fter ten days in Paris, we're once again en route for Les Libellules. The birds were right it seems. Summer has disappeared in a puff of smoke and left in its place a dreary, wintery day. Not a hint of crisp autumn sunshine as we head down the ironically called *Route du Soleil* (Route of the Sun)[1], just bleak clouds and persistent rain; even the hill of happiness, the boundary between our city and country lives, looks miserable. Pussy Willow, however, is a little ray of sunshine, sitting patiently between my feet as we proceed along practically deserted roads. Mr V finished work at lunchtime (not before eating lunch—perish the thought), and we're approaching the hamlet at 5 p.m. The bonus hour when the clocks go back has been and gone, so dusk is almost upon us this early in the evening. Vestiges of a previous snowfall cling to the sides of the road, and an oversized Hunter's Moon hangs low in the sky like a large, bronze milk bottle top circled by a ring of silver, indicating frost is in the air.

It's Halloween. The 'empty chairs and empty tables café' that we drive past on the way to the hamlet has pumpkins on the tables—but still no one sitting at them. The pumpkins make it look even more forlorn than usual, and I once again feel sad for the owner, but presumably he does have customers inside otherwise he would have closed long ago.

When we reach the hamlet, the trick or treaters are out in force, and as last year, all together in one troop so as not to continually disturb people; also as last year, accompanied by two adults making sure they are all polite. Mr V comments that they are more numerous this time, and he is right; there's the addition of two little Count Draculas and a Snow White wearing a token witch's hat, all of whom appear to be aged around three. I act suitably alarmed by the little vampires, and suitably impressed by the pretty witch costumes of the girls, particularly Snow White's. I distribute the obligatory rubbishy sweets into their eagerly outstretched bags, and off they go.

Flaubertine also comes looking for treats. I feel deeply sorry for her, as the long, hot summer is seemingly over, and she now has to face another cruel winter. I would like to let her into the house, but Pussy Willow is having none of it, growling and snarling, and hissing and spitting like a banshee. I feed Flaubertine and give her lots of fuss. After eating, instead of disappearing back to the den she shares with all the other nameless cats, she sits in the little shelter Mr V built in the corner beneath the feather tree, where Penny also used to take refuge. The shelter has had an upgrade. Mr V has since made a tiled roof to protect it from the rain, with thick polystyrene underneath the tiles as well as on the floor and sides to give some insulation, but it's still open to the elements. I can't understand why Flaubertine doesn't snuggle up in one of the boxes of pinecones on a shelf in the garage as Poly did. There she would be safe, warm and dry; but I guess she's claimed her territory, and she doesn't want to lose it.

What I've learnt today: The Hunter's Moon is the name for the full moon in October, while the Harvest Moon is in September. Every four years, the Harvest Moon occurs in October, and the Hunter's Moon is moved to November.

✳ ✴ ✳

Pussy Willow has crossed the line from town to country cat. She's caught her first mouse. I saw her busy in the bushes early this morning and was horrified to see her emerge with a tiny field mouse clasped in her jaws. Thankfully it was dead when she proceeded to play with it, tossing it in the air as I'd seen the kitties do. I'm a little saddened by this, but Mr V is at the window with his camera, displaying all the pride of a father on sports day when his child wins their first race.

Flaubertine is also watching the spectacle with feline fascination from the kitchen step. To her, mice are food, not playthings, plus Flaubertine has no capacity for play. She does, however, have a capacity for stealth, so while Willow was preoccupied, she took the opportunity to sneak into the kitchen and polish off what was left in her bowl.

Pussy Willow now has a dilemma. She wants to come inside, but Flaubertine has installed herself on the kitchen step, so Willow goes to the garden room and sits looking up expectantly at the door. Her problem is she still has the mouse in her mouth, and in order to meow for me to open the door, she must let it drop and risk Flaubertine snatching it from under her nose. They sit there frozen into stalemate for a good ten minutes until Pussy Willow decides on another tactic. She approaches the living room door and proceeds to jump up at the window like a Jack-in-the-box—now you see her; now you don't— with her trophy still clasped between her teeth.

This is where Mr V's parenting duties come to an end. When I ask what I am to do, he tells me it is my cat and walks off to drill some holes. Finally Pussy Willow gets the point of the hunting game and devours the poor little mite on the step, leaving not a scrap for Flaubertine.

This exercise has, however, created an unprecedented respect between the two. It's as if Pussy Willow has passed a country-cat initiation test, and in turn, she has understood that this is what Flaubertine must do to survive. Flaubertine is now content to remain in the little shelter beneath the feather tree and not approach either me or the house while Willow is in the garden. Willow for her part is ignoring Flaubertine, so a truce of sorts.

Spurred on by her success, Pussy Willow is stalking through the long grass in front of the terrace. It's now my turn to watch anxiously from the window, as two fat robins are merrily pecking for worms beneath the hedge. While I can just about tolerate her catching a field mouse, I shudder at the thought that she could kill one of these beautiful, sociable creatures, so I tie a fat ball to the tree to encourage them out of the immediate reach of preying paws.

---

1. The A6 motorway linking Paris to Lyon which becomes the A7 from Lyon to Marseilles.

GOLDEN NUGGETS

*M*r V and I are off foraging while the early morning mist still clings to the earth and the dawn sky is streaked with pink. We drive a short distance through the sleeping village to a nearby hill, parking the car at the bottom. I take a large, wicker basket from the boot[1] and climb the hill. Overnight rain has dampened the grass, and it seeps through the toes of my suede boots, soaking my feet. At the top of the hill stands a solitary walnut tree, its trunk twisted and bent by the wind into a corkscrew and the ground beneath its branches strewn with plentiful autumn gifts—parcels of walnuts, wrapped in their skull-hard shells.

We gather them as eagerly as squirrels until the basket is brimming and too heavy for me to carry alone, then slip and slide back down the hill with our loot, like two pirates with golden nuggets.

As we drive home, the village is beginning to come to life. People fling open shutters, and tractors trundle before us while our walnuts rattle down the bumpy lane.

This for me is one of the unexpected joys of country living—gathering nuts in the countryside. My walnuts always used to come minus their shells, often halved, in plastic, supermarket packets. Now I have baskets of them stored to last me through the year. I use them as snacks for an aperitif, to make winter salads with apple and Roquefort cheese, to garnish other soft cheeses and to put into fruitcakes and tarts. But Mr V likes to make *vin de noix* (walnut wine). *Vin de noix* is very popular as an aperitif in France and is also delicious to accompany cheese, to add flavour to a fruitcake, or even added to chocolate mousse. Each region has its own particular recipe, most commonly using green nuts gathered in June around the time of *la Fête de la Saint-Jean*. But if, like Mr V, you make it from the dryer autumn nuts, the wine is less bitter though will take much longer before it is drinkable (at least twelve months as opposed to three if you use green nuts), so patience is required.

The longer you leave it the better, as it improves over time. Sediment may develop on the bottom, which is normal. Just avoid disturbing it by not shaking the bottle before serving. Here's Mr V's recipe, passed down from his grandmother in Normandy.

---

1. Trunk.

VIN DE NOIX

Makes 6 x 75 cl (1 ⅓ pt) bottles

Ingredients

40–50 dry walnuts, roughly crushed in their shells (some recipes use
only the kernels)
3.5 ltr (6 pt) red wine
1 ltr (1 ¾ pt) brandy
350 g (12 oz) raw cane sugar
1 tsp ground nutmeg
1 tsp ground cinnamon
A 4.5 ltr (8 pt) glass demijohn

Method

Mix all ingredients together in a large pan (a pan for jam making is
ideal) until the sugar is completely dissolved.

Pour into the demijohn.

Keep in a cool, dark place and stir the mixture daily for two weeks.

Continue to store in a cool, dark place for twelve months.

Pass the wine through a sieve to separate the nuts, then use a funnel covered by a piece of muslin (or a clean pair of tights) to sieve the wine into the bottles.

Seal the bottles with airtight stoppers so the alcohol doesn't evaporate, and store in a cool, dark place as before.

Serve in port or sherry, not wine, glasses, as *vin de noix* is quite strong.

The wine has a slight syrupy consistency and is also delicious drizzled over ice cream.

HERE'S ONE I MADE EARLIER

J've made it to the Christmas decoration workshop as the meetings have changed from Wednesday evenings to Saturday afternoons. We're all assembled in the former schoolhouse halfway up the hill in the village. It's just one large, high-ceilinged classroom with a blackboard running along one wall and a single, long, narrow window two metres or so from the floor giving a tantalising view of the sky and hillside. Two double desks from a bygone era with attached benches and inkwells sit beneath the window. There are no indoor toilets; these are outside in the little playground and are built for smaller bottoms than ours. Jacques shows me where his desk used to be. I'm fascinated that he went to school here. Then I learn that almost everyone in the room did. Léa was the schoolmistress to many of them, and the school only closed a couple of years ago due to lack of pupils, which is a shame, as judging by the growing numbers of trick or treaters, they'll soon be able to fill a class.

As the meeting is taking place between 2:30 and 5, and this being France, everyone except me has brought something for *le goûter*, the traditional sweet snack at four o'clock when children come home from school, but everyone I know continues with this tradition into adulthood. Solène, who I met last year at the Advent get-together held in her barn, produces a large, loaf-shaped apple cake from her bag. Fabienne and Celine, two neighbours that I remember from last year's *Fête des Voisins* (an annual tradition that takes place all over France where *voisins* (neighbours) get together for a sort of street party), have also brought homemade offerings, Fabienne presenting something that resembles an extremely long, thin jam roly-poly filled with her plum compote, and Celine a brioche sprinkled with crystallised sugar. Valerie from the farm behind Les Libellules has made delicate, chewy tuile biscuits sprinkled with flaked almonds. There are plates stacked with madeleines and various other miniature cakes, bottles of orange squash for the children, and two coffee percolators, one for making coffee and another heating water to make tea. I am conscious of my lack of contribution to this impressive spread, and although there's more than enough to go around, I feel that this isn't just about putting food on the table, so a yogurt cake will be arriving with me next time.

Not only have I not brought a cake, I've also not brought any art and craft materials or examples of my handicrafts to show off either. Everyone else has bags bursting with paints, pinecones, rolls of ribbon, tubes of glue and tubs of glitter. A trestle table at the back of the room displays their creations: tin-can lanterns with holes drilled in them to allow a tea light to shine through; garlands of miniature pinecones sprayed green and decorated with tiny, red bows; empty, gold-coloured picture frames with baubles hanging where a picture would usually be. In addition to this, there are two giant snowmen, each made from three tree stumps turned on their sides, bolted together and painted white. A couple of ladies whose names I don't know are in the process of knitting gaily coloured striped scarves for the snowmen's necks and making equally brightly coloured pompoms as buttons for their chests. Fifi is trying out various hats to fix onto their heads; Solène tells me that it's he who has made them. A little group of men is helping him decide on the hat; this is serious business if we want to make it onto French television again as we did last year.

Another man has sliced slim branches, stripped of their bark, on an angle and drilled a hole at the top so they can have Santa and reindeer faces painted on them then be hung on the Christmas tree. I'm helping a woman called Aimée, who tells me she's a garage mechanic and not at all artistic, to paint a base coat on them: brown for the reindeer and a flesh colour for the Santas. A dispute has broken out about the shade of brown we're using. It looks fine to me, but Celine, who I discover is a perfectionist bordering on being a control freak, insists it's too pale and we should mix it with black, but this just turns it into a sludge-grey colour. From deep within my memory comes an image of mixing green and red watercolour paints to make brown in an art class at school. I proceed to mix away on the plastic plate serving as a palette and create a nutty, non-sludgy brown. Celine declares that I've found the perfect shade for a reindeer, and I'm promoted to group paint mixer, making the perfect pink for Santa's face and the perfect green for the Christmas trees being painted on another table.

While the paint is drying, I go and see what Jacques is up to on the tin-can lantern table. His designs are a little abstract, to say the least, and in my opinion, he's not using the cans to their full potential (Celine's tendencies are rubbing off on me). I set about making a template of a star with rays of starlight radiating from it that can be used on both the front and back of a can. Jacques is impressed, especially when I tape my design in place so he can drill through the points I've marked. He asks me can I do the same for a Christmas tree. My artistic juices begin to flow, and I'm producing templates for holly leaves, candles and bells. A small audience has gathered behind me, and I admittedly begin showing off; I have to regain my respect after arriving empty-handed. I'm now producing angels with halos, and wise men bearing gifts. People are photographing my designs on their phones to make their own tin-can lanterns at home. I feel as if I'm Valerie Singleton[1] (a veteran *Blue Peter* presenter for you babies out there).

I'm on a roll now and think why stop at paint for the tree branch decorations, so I cover Santa's hat with glue and sprinkle sparkly, red glitter over it. More 'ooohs' and 'aaahs' follow, and I proceed to give him a glittery, white beard. Next I cover the star and angel in golden glitter, and the Christmas trees in green and red. This is when I get the idea for my pièce de résistance—a coat-hanger Advent crown mobile as seen on *Blue Peter* during the '60s and '70s. I have the coat hangers; now I need to find some cheap baubles and tinsel. But for those of you who haven't got a clue what I'm talking about, YouTube has tons of videos showing you how you can do this at home.

Have fun...

---

1. A British children's television programme, now the longest-running children's TV show in the world.

FLOWERS OF THE FIELD

$\mathcal{T}$oday is Mr V's birthday, and we're driving down to Les Libellules to spend the first of what I hope will be many birthdays there. The sandstone-hued fields are screened by poplars the colour of English mustard, and the roadside bushes have turned a deep shade of burgundy red. Autumn has at last decided to show up at the ball, and like Cinderella, she's wearing her splendid ballgown, but alas, also like Cinderella, her time to dance will be brief before the clock strikes winter and her adornments tumble to the ground.

The hill of happiness rises before us in the distance, looking like a bronzed iced bun, with the copse of pine trees perched like a cherry on the top, the sharp contrast against the deep-blue sky behind the hill making it stand out like a cardboard cut-out. We cross the mythical border into our magical kingdom; we're almost home.

I've got a cool bag full of 'cheats' from the freezer shop Picard, as I don't want to spend the little time left in the day cooking. We're going to be feasting on an *entrée* (starter) of lobster and scallops in a cream sauce flavoured with white wine and thickened with egg yolk, followed by sole meunière, a selection of cheese, and Mr V's all-time favourite dessert—rum baba. A bottle of white Mouton Cadet is already chilling in the fridge.

Flaubertine is at my heels as soon as I set foot out of the car, raising herself on hind legs like a circus bear for me to stroke her head. As this is a short visit, Pussy Willow has stayed in Paris, so Flaubertine can come in and have a warm by the fire without skin and fur flying. A letter is waiting for us in the mailbox. It's an invitation from the mayor to a ceremony at 10:45 on Sunday morning to mark 100 years since the end of the Great War. I find it particularly poignant that the centenary actually falls on a Sunday; we will truly mark the 11th hour of the 11th day on the 11th month 100 years on.

It's not only autumn that is like Cinderella, as I'm discovering why she always has a broom in her hand and soot on her face. The open fire is a filthy beast, and the floor is constantly strewn with bits of bark and leaves, so I have to sweep up a small pyramid of debris at least three times a day. When I see television programmes set in the past where people are gathered around a log fire in a gleaming, clean room, I have a strong urge to contact the director and give them a reality check. But, filthy as it is, I love it, and playing at being Cinderella is a small price to pay. Still, it will feel good to dress up a bit to enjoy the celebratory meal this evening.

*　＊　＊

It's Armistice Day. The sun is shining; the sky is clear and blue, and a soft, warm breeze is ruffling the washing on the line. We set off for the assembly in front of the small *mairie* (town hall) in the village. When we arrive a crowd is already gathered outside, weaving between each other like ants, pausing to plant a kiss on both cheeks of their friends and neighbours. Mr V and I approach the throng, and I'm targeted for much more cheek kissing than he is. All my new-found friends from the Christmas craft workshop are waving and shouting 'Bonjour, Leendee' and coming forward to not only kiss but hug me also. Mr V is a little taken aback but pleased at the same time saying, 'You're very popular,' with a certain amount of pride. We're all presented with a *bleuet* (cornflower) to wear in support of injured servicemen in the same manner as a poppy is worn in the UK.

Monsieur le mayor arrives looking, in my opinion, decidedly un-mayor-like in jeans and a checked shirt with one of the buttons undone. The only thing that gives the game away as to who he is is the enormous blue, white and red sash around his open quilted jacket. He asks us all to follow the young people of the commune down to the memorial. The older ones are bearing flags and large baskets of chrysanthemums decorated with blue, white and red ribbon; the younger ones, bouquets tied with yellow and white bows. We form a crocodile like school children on an excursion, and I link arms with Marie-Claude, an elderly neighbour, to steady her, as the path is steep and strewn with damp leaves. This raises a few eyebrows, as Marie-Claude is fiercely independent, but she pats my hand affectionately, giving me her full seal of approval.

We arrive in front of the memorial just outside the archway entrance to the church and graveyard. Large candles in storm lanterns have been burning around its base since yesterday evening, adding to the poignancy of the occasion. The flags are ceremoniously positioned at the four corners, and the mayor reads an address to the nation from the president. A basket of flowers is placed for each of the hamlets and villages that form the commune, then the youngest children place their bouquets in remembrance of all the children killed in both World Wars.

Noëlle is given the honour of reading the name and age of every young man lost from the commune during the 1914–1918 conflict. After each name is read, the crowd responds by solemnly saying 'mort pour la France' (died for France). At this moment, a sudden wind comes from nowhere, snatching the golden leaves from nearby trees and scattering them like poppy petals around the memorial. Then a flock of pigeons roosting in the tower above the archway takes flight, making a large circle in the sky before returning to their perches just as the last name is read. The whole experience is extremely moving, and I'm not the only one dabbing my eyes as the ages 18, 19 and 20 follow each name—young men cut down in their prime as flowers of the field.

Next comes the singing of the Marseillaise, the French national anthem. I only know the *'marchons, marchons'* part so stand in embarrassed silence. Mr V is tone deaf, so he stands in silence also, but everyone else gives a rousing rendition. When I apologise for not knowing the words, Marie-Claude tells me that she could not sing 'God Save the Queen', but she isn't living in the UK, and I *am* living in France. I give myself a 'could do better' note and vow to learn at least the first verse before next year.

The ceremony over, we head back up the hill to the town hall for *un pot,* the familiar term for taking a drink together. Glasses of champagne and plates of canapés are passed around to celebrate the peace that France has enjoyed since 1945. The mayor comes to talk to me, which is a bit of an honour, asking me how we're getting on in the house. Mr V looks on nervously in case I admit to anything that could result in the mayor wanting more tax from us. But I stick to telling him how much I love living in his commune, which seems to go down well. He tops up my glass and moves on to talk to Monsieur Mouton, who once again has scrubbed up well, though not as spectacularly well as he had at last year's Advent get-together in his leather jacket and winklepickers.

Celine from the decoration workshop has just offered me some plums, the last of the decent ones from her garden, which I accept with gratitude. Mr V and I have decided to stay at Les Libellules until tomorrow so we can relax and enjoy the occasion, and as I have nothing for dessert this evening, I can bake the plums with vanilla sugar and butter. This is a watered-down version of a dessert that I make regularly during the plum season, so I'm going to treat you not to what I'm making today, but my original recipe, as it's much more scrumptious.

SUGAR PLUM PARCELS

Makes 6 individual servings

Ingredients

30 g (1 oz) ground almonds
1½ tbsp caster sugar (I use Madagascan vanilla sugar for extra flavour)
6 medium/large, firm plums of any colour or variety
A knob of butter per plum
375 g (13 oz) pack of ready-made puff pastry, cut into squares large
enough to wrap each plum
Beaten egg yolk
Icing sugar for dusting

Method

Mix the ground almonds and sugar.

Scoop out the stones from the plums and fill each cavity with the
almond/sugar mixture.

Top with a knob of butter.

Place in the centre of a pastry square and fold opposite corners,
squeezing them together with the tips of your fingers to make a
parcel.

Brush with beaten egg yolk and bake in a preheated oven at 180 degrees/gas mark 4 for around 25 minutes until the pastry is golden and the plum juice bubbling.

Sprinkle with a fairy dusting of icing sugar when cooled a little.

Serve warm or cold with a little dollop of crème fraîche or drizzled with single cream.

THE HOLLY AND THE IVY

I'm at the second Christmas decoration workshop. Everyone is gathered in a circle, weaving wreaths from willow branches under the instruction of Christophe (the husband of Mireille, the former psychiatric nurse I met at last year's *Fête des Voisins*). He resembles a jolly Christmas elf in a green apron and red woolly hat that's miles too big for his head. It's clear that my *Blue Peter* tinsel and wire coat-hanger creation is not going to cut the mustard. I hastily hide my bag beneath one of the school desks, salvaging some scraps of ribbon and pinecones before I do. Christophe is a calm and patient teacher, and despite never having tackled anything like this before in my life, I manage to make two more or less circular wreaths, and, imagining that this was the hard part, feel quite pleased with my results.

The next step is to cover the willow wreaths with pine branches, which is easier said than done as they're extremely springy, and the florist's wire that we're using to attach them has been rationed to five insufficiently long pieces per wreath. The others are old hands at this and are expertly swirling the wire around their branches, leaving enough of them loose to give a natural, rustic effect. Mine, however, just looks like a disorganised mess; I'm clearly not hitting the heights of the previous workshop. I come up with the idea of taming some of the more wayward escapees with the salvaged ribbon, which works a treat, and a couple of the other ladies follow suit, though simply for effect, not out of necessity.

Now comes the decoration of our creations. This is under the watchful eye of perfectionist Celine, who has now adopted the role of an overbearing schoolmistress and is telling everyone what to do. In my case this involves her taking over entirely, spoiling for me the spirit of the workshop and the pleasure of making my wreath, even if I was making a pig's ear of it.

I'm feeling rebellious and can't see the point in taking something home to hang on the door that someone else has made, so I begin to take apart what she has done. This is evidently not a wise decision, and Fabienne is looking on nervously. Celine, for her part, looks furious at my insurrection. This is supposed to be a pleasure, for goodness' sake, a little departure from the dust and dirt at Les Libellules, but instead I'm sweating beneath the heat of Celine's glare. I feel like a naughty schoolgirl, but it's too late to turn back now, and soon all is stripped back to a bare circle of willow.

I'm not the only one who's not exactly relishing the experience. Across the table from me are three little girls and their mother of mature years, who I already made an enemy of at the last meeting as I presumed she was their grandmother. The middle child, aged around eight, proudly shows her mother her efforts. I was about to coo how creative it was to try to bury the hatchet, but she shoots the child down in flames and proceeds to criticise and change what she has made. I know these wreaths are to decorate the hamlet, but they're for Christmas, the season of goodwill and all that, not for a national art and craft competition. The poor little mite looks totally deflated, and I have to bite my tongue not to jump in and defend her.

Spurred on, I'm now determined to make a better job of mine. I begin taming the unruly pine branches, trapping the tips of one with the stem of the next and using pliers to twist the paltry piece of wire in place. I then secure it with a crisscross of narrow red and green ribbon.

Next, I use the places where the ribbons overlap to weave strands of ivy in and out around the wreath. This is beginning to look pretty darn good, even if I do say it myself. Fabienne obviously thinks so too, as she nudges me from behind and sneaks into my hand three miniature cow bells that have been sprayed gold and fastened with a tartan bow. I select some sprigs of holly that have plenty of berries and strip back the leaves at the bottom so that I have a good stalk to thread beneath the ribbon also. Then I secure this with small bows tied from what is left of the red ribbon, finishing the whole thing off with Fabienne's cow bells. Celine is now looking over with a face that would turn milk sour as Christophe and Jacques both congratulate me on my efforts, with Jacques adding, 'If this is your first attempt, imagine what you can do next year.'

Next year I'll be fully armed with ribbons and bows, and yards of florist's wire, and will have been practising since January.

'TIS THE SEASON

The feeling of rebellion is apparently in the air. The president, Emmanuel Macron, has just hiked up the fuel tax, and it's the last straw for a population already taxed to the hilt. A movement has begun, *les Gilet jaunes*, named after the yellow waistcoats that are compulsory for French drivers to have in their car in case of an accident. They're mounting roadblocks and protesting in Paris. Some of the protests have become ugly and violent, and access to many petrol stations has been obstructed, so Mr V and I are not entirely sure that we'll be able to get back there.

We set off early and are fortunate enough in our little backwater to find a petrol station not barricaded. Then we hit the A6 autoroute. It's like a ghost road; there's even less traffic than when we drove back while France was playing in the World Cup final. We have our *gilet jaune* on the dashboard to show our solidarity and pass through the first roadblock we encounter without any problem. The second, closer to Paris, is a little more militant, and three lanes of traffic are channelled into one, but again no aggression. The blockade is made up of young and old alike, and they're representing the poorer classes who are struggling to make ends meet, particularly in the rural areas where people have no choice but to use their cars, as public transport is practically non-existent. A lady in our hamlet has four children, and as the local school has closed due to dwindling numbers, she now must pay for a bus to get them to the one in a nearby town. If the fares go up, she'll find this extremely difficult. Likewise, the local *boulanger*, who delivers bread three times a week, said it would no longer be cost-effective unless she put up her prices, again hitting poor country folk in their pockets. Everyone understands the need for change to help reduce emissions, but foreign lorries are hurtling up and down country roads, and if governments really wanted to change things, then freight could be returned to the railways or canals.

We're now safely back in Paris without serious delay or incident, but *les Gilets jaunes* demonstrations on the Champs Elysées have hit the news for all the wrong reasons. It seems the season of goodwill is turning into the season of unrest...

PART III
THE CRYSTAL WINTER

DECEMBER 2018 AND JANUARY 2019

The air is blue and keen and cold;
With snow the roads and fields are white
But here the forest's clothed with light
And in a shining sheaf enrolled.
Each branch, each twig, each blade of grass,
Seems clad miraculously with glass:
Above the ice-bound streamlet bends
Each frozen fern with crystal ends
'A Crystal Forest', William Sharp

THE SPICE OF LIFE

*T*his time last year, we drove down from Paris through a winter wonderland; today we're driving through lashing rain and dangerously high winds. The hill of happiness looks forlorn drenched in grey, but the sight of it still makes my heart leap as we draw nearer to Les Libellules.

As we enter the hamlet, the fruits of the decoration workshops are on display. There's a group of Christmas trees made from old wooden pallets that have been painted green and white and adorned with silver and gold baubles. In the centre of the group is a much larger pallet tree painted red and with little bells that tinkle in the wind. There are also some snowmen made from pallets and one that Fifi made from three tree stumps. This jolly fellow, complete with pipe, is pointing the way into the hamlet. Les Libellules hasn't been forgotten, and she has three tree-trunk Santas standing like sentries in front of her.

The rain must have been falling heavily in our absence, as the *mare* is almost full. I thought it would take all winter to amass 60 cubic litres of water, but apparently two or three weeks in November is all it needed. I'm hoping this deluge ceases tomorrow as we're expecting Marcel to arrive with our *sapin de Noël* (Christmas tree) that he's bringing from the forest near his home. Mr V had grand designs on a two-and-a-half-metre monster, but I said I preferred a more modest, one-and-a-half-metre one while the room is serving as lounge, dining room and tool shed.

This will be our first Christmas at Les Libellules, and although I'm a little sad not to be spending Christmas Day with my family as we have done for the last nine years, I have to admit that I'm rather excited also. I've asked Marcel to find a small, bushy tree, so I'm eager to see what he comes up with tomorrow.

It's the day of the first Advent get-together which is taking place in Solène's barn as last year. Jacques is at our door even before Flaubertine. He comes to tell us that the *vin chaud* (mulled wine) is about to be served. But first I have to unpack the freezer bag full of goodies we've brought for Christmas. The disruption caused by *les Gilets jaunes* has begun to bite, and empty shelves have started to appear, so I've brought some beef for New Year and various things for an apéritif, just in case the situation worsens.

By the time we arrive at the barn, only dregs of the *vin chaud* remain, and it now resembles a lukewarm, wine-drenched fruit compote and doesn't look at all appetising. I've thrown caution to the wind and made a speciality of the region—a moist, spiced ginger loaf known as *pain d'épices*—which I place on the table, fully aware that it will be up for intense scrutiny. Solène is the first to come forward, and all eyes are on her as she savours the first bite as if she's a judge on *Le Meilleur Pâtissier*, France's answer to *The Great British Bake Off*.

I hold my breath. She smiles and says it is superb, moist and light and not too sweet, with just the right balance of spices. I'm now floating as lightly as my cake, and once more Mr V has reason to be proud of me and comes to give me an affectionate kiss on the top of my head. Solène is followed by Fabienne and Celine from the workshops. Celine has taken off her bossy schoolmistress hat, and now all three are voicing their approval and asking me for the recipe.

The men swiftly demolish the rest of the cake, and all agree it's worthy of a place in a Dijon cake shop. I'm sure you would all like the recipe too, but you'll have to wait until the end of the chapter.

Fifi is in an unusually sober and subdued mood, probably because Madame Fifi is in tow. She stays close to his side, keeping his trips to the wine vat in check. Monsieur Mouton is absent, as are quite a few others. I put this down to the driving wind and rain. The weather does not, however, deter Jacques from insisting that Mr V and I go out with him to light this evening's Advent candle. The candles, as last year, are in the jam jars we decorated in the workshops and are placed on shelves in the little wooden chalet. There, to my surprise and delight, hanging either side of the candles, are the decorations I made from the slices of tree branches covered with glitter. I can see Mr V is impressed with my artistic flair. There are two Christmas trees this year: one with white lights and silver baubles, the other much larger and decorated entirely in red, which truly is magnificent. The model of Mr Mouton's farm from last year is there also. It *had* been suggested that we make a model of Les Libellules this year as she was voted the prettiest house in the hamlet, but I think it was deemed too difficult.

When we return, the party is breaking up, and the kissing and handshaking begin once more. A couple of the men are forgetting their manners and instead of planting a kiss on each cheek, they land the second on my lips. Mr V says it's because they want another taste of my *pain d'épices*, but I'm not so sure...

Here, as promised, is the recipe. See if you get the same response.

PAIN D'EPICES

Makes a 900 g (2 lb) loaf (roughly 12 slices)

Ingredients

200 g (8 oz) plain flour plus extra to line the tin
100 g (4 oz) Demerara sugar
8 g (⅓ oz) sachet vanilla sugar
8 g (⅓ oz) sachet dried yeast
1 tsp ground nutmeg
1 tsp ground cinnamon
1 tsp ground ginger
½ tsp ground mixed spice
Pinch of salt
200 ml (7 fl oz) milk
100 g (4 oz) butter plus extra for greasing the tin
150 g (6 oz) runny honey
1 large free-range egg

Method

Mix together the flour, sugar, vanilla sugar, dried yeast, spices and salt in a large bowl.

Gently warm the milk, add the butter and honey, and then let them melt slowly.

Beat the egg with a hand whisk.

Alternate between adding the milk mixture and the beaten egg to the dry ingredients a little at a time, mixing well.

Grease the loaf tin with butter and sprinkle with flour, knocking off the excess.

Pour in the mixture.

Bake for 30 minutes in a preheated oven at 180 degrees/gas mark 4 with the top loosely covered with foil.

Remove the foil and cook for a further 5-10 minutes (checking to see that the top does not get too brown).

Use a skewer to test that the inside is cooked (if it comes out clean then the cake is cooked; if not, then turn off the heat and leave the cake in the cooling oven to dry out, testing again after 10 minutes).

I had some candied Sicilian orange and lemon peel left over from when I made my Christmas cake, which I sprinkled on top when I removed the foil, giving the loaf a festive flavour.

THE GHOSTS OF CHRISTMAS PAST

*I*t's Saturday morning and still bucketing down with rain. Marcel has rung to say he'll bring the *sapin* this evening as it's soaking wet and drying out in his garage before he puts it in his van.

I've spent the morning writing while Mr V has begun to block off the gaps in the roof of the *pigeonnier*. He plans to insulate it in the same way that he has the *grenier* but leave the large lower beams exposed. I've got my own grand designs for the panels that will form the conical ceiling. I'd like to paint them midnight blue with a pattern of gold stars or fleur-de-lys like Sainte-Chapelle in Paris. Either that or sky blue with clouds like the Sistine Chapel; you can't get much grander than that.

* * *

The rain has eased a little, so we've decided to call past Jacqueline's house on our way shopping as we have to return her photo of Les Libellules that was taken in 1910. From the outside, her house appears to be a small cottage wedged between two identical neighbours. Jacqueline seems to be expecting us, though we didn't say we were coming, as she opens the door before we knock and welcomes us into her cosy kitchen. A fire is burning in a cast-iron stove on which a kettle is steaming at the point of whistling. A teapot is at the ready, and a homemade fruitcake is in a tin on the table. Jacqueline offers us tea, but Mr V refuses, saying he doesn't want to disturb her, and we'd only come to return her photograph of Les Libellules. I can see that Jacqueline wants more than anything to be disturbed, so I say I would love a cup of tea. She bustles about getting an assortment of mismatched cups and saucers, then she pushes the teapot in my direction, asking me to pour, and the cake in Mr V's direction, asking him to slice.

'I always have a cake ready in case someone should call,' she says.

I get the impression that callers have become fewer and fewer. I compliment her on the cake, and also on how welcoming and snug her kitchen is. She asks us if we'd like to see the rest of the house. Again Mr V politely refuses, but I'm dying to see the other rooms. Jacqueline says we're lucky and that today the guided tour is free, so I proceed to follow her, with Mr V in tow. Guided tours of other people's homes are a pet British pastime. The French rarely invite neighbours into their home, and if they do, you are usually confined to one room, whereas in the UK, people proudly present their bathrooms and kitchens and the interiors to their fitted wardrobes to all and sundry.

The house is like the TARDIS and is in fact three houses in one with a labyrinth of corridors and adjoining rooms. The first room we go into leads directly off the kitchen and is what would be a spacious living room if it wasn't jam-packed with furniture. It's a treasure trove of Victorian, Edwardian and Art Deco splendour. Against one wall there's a beautiful, rose marble fireplace, above which is a large mirror in an intricately carved wooden frame. Against another is an enormous, ornate buffet with bow-shaped drawers and a marble top in a darker shade of rose than that of the fireplace. Everywhere I look there are elegant Art Deco lamps and ornaments, and a crystal chandelier that wouldn't look out of place in a château hangs from the deceptively high ceiling. Despite the grandiose furniture, the room retains a homely air, with a large, red, velour sofa strewn with tapestry cushions, and a highly polished coffee table partially obscured beneath a jumble of cookery and cross-stitch magazines. Even on such a dull day, light floods in from French doors that reach from floor to ceiling, stretching across an entire wall and looking out over a surprisingly large courtyard garden and the steep rise of the hillside behind.

Room after room follows, with me losing count after eight, each crammed with gorgeous furniture from four-poster beds to leather-clad writing bureaux; everything is in immaculate condition.

I ask Jacqueline if she keeps house herself, to which she replies, 'Yes, with a little help to spring clean two or three times a year.'

Given that she's getting on for 90 years of age and the house is so large, she puts me to shame.

Back in the kitchen, more tea is served, more cake forced upon us, and more stories about the former occupants of Les Libellules emerge. Jacqueline tells us that Louis, the father of Emma Dard, the little girl in the photo, died from injuries he received in the Great War and that his name is on the war memorial where we attended the service commemorating 100 years since the Armistice. I find this strange as, being born in 1876, this would make him thirty-eight when war broke out, and all of the names we'd heard read out belonged to young men of eighteen, nineteen and twenty. We take our leave of Jacqueline with the remains of the cake wrapped in foil, and promise to return, but instead of going shopping, we head off in the rain to the memorial on the windswept hill. I scour the names engraved on the stone column, but there's no sign of a Louis Dard. One side of the memorial isn't visible as a screen of holly trees grows right up to the surrounding railings. So I climb over them and go around to the back, and there is a single name—Louis Dard, 1876-1919. He was forty-three years of age. Emma would have been a young girl of sixteen, and her brother Jean a child of nine when their father died.

I wonder what happened to them and their mother after that. I know Fernand Lefebvre built the extension in 1926, so sometime during those seven years the family Dard must have moved out. A man of that age when the war ended was too old to fight, but as we know that Louis was a vet, I surmise that he must have been looking after the war horses. Life has been hard, it seems, for the former occupants of Les Libellules; this makes me feel even more privileged to be part of her history.

* * *

Marcel has arrived with the *sapin*. It's everything I asked for: almost as wide as it's tall, with an abundance of tightly packed branches, and a single stem standing proudly to attention, waiting to be graced by my golden-robed, porcelain angel. I put Michael Bublé on the CD player and begin to decorate the tree. Christmas has arrived.

I begin with the lights—traditional red, blue, green and amber. No one- or two-colour designer tree for me; this beauty is going to look like an explosion in a sweet shop. Next I attach some large, golden pinecones and some even larger golden baubles with mock red ribbons around their middles that we found in a dusty box on the shelves in the garden room. They look as if they've come from the 1950s or maybe earlier. I wonder if they were already in the house when Léa arrived, and how many past Christmases they've seen. Smaller pinecones and a selection of little, faux presents wrapped in red and green shiny paper are next to be hung, followed by an eclectic mix of wooden and pottery decorations that either I or my daughter Kate have bought in various parts of the world. This year a beautiful, carved wooden nativity scene that she purchased in Bethlehem takes pride of place in the centre. The rest of the branches are filled with sparkly red, blue, green and gold baubles and finally some delicate, gilt-filigree, giant snowflakes. *Et voilà!* There it is!

It seems I'm not the only one who's been adding festive touches to Les Libellules. Noëlle has just rung, inviting us to go and see her decorations, and she commented on our illuminations that she saw as she was driving past. Now, to my knowledge, we don't have any illuminations, but I also know that Mr V has a penchant for lasers and suchlike. So I've ventured outside in the freezing cold to see what she's talking about—and lo and behold, the utility room is hosting a disco. A light show of pink, mauve, purple and green is coming from the windows; it is borderline festive, with Les Libellules looking more like a nightclub on the Côte d'Azur than an ancient house on the Côte-d'Or. Apparently, unknown to me, this extravaganza has been switched on automatically between five o'clock and midnight every evening since we arrived. I suppose I should be thankful this is Mr V's only festive touch, as a couple of weeks ago, I had to drag him away from buying a projector that would have covered the walls with huge green stars and snowflakes. Alas, I don't think I will manage to contain him next year.

THE NIGHT BEFORE CHRISTMAS

*I*t's Christmas Eve, and the hamlet has once again attracted the attention of the media, though not TF1 (France's equivalent to BBC1) as last year, but a regional newspaper is coming to see our latest display. All the participants from the decoration workshops are gathered outside Solène's barn along with some other residents, and as this evening is the 24th of December, the last and largest Advent candle is to be lit at dusk.

The journalist arrives, and we all walk down to have our photographs taken amongst the wooden Christmas tree, reindeer and snowmen ensemble. It's bitterly cold, so we don't hang around too long but head back to the barn where a vat of hot cider is waiting. As it's only 4:30 in the afternoon, it's more the hour of *le goûter* than the apéritif, so everyone has brought a sweet rather than savoury dish.

I've made a strudel *tarte soleil* (sun tart) filled with mincemeat pie filling,[1] apple from our tree and the last of the candied orange and lemon peel left over from making the Christmas cake. It's visually impressive and tastes delicious, but it's outshone by Marie-Claude's simple offering of figs, dates and walnuts stuffed with marzipan, the figs and dates being stuffed with pink, and the walnuts green, a Middle Eastern dish festively arranged in a mosaic pattern on a large platter decorated with sprigs of holly. A feast for the eyes as well as the tongue.

I detect the faint jingle of bells above the chatter inside the barn. The children, already buzzing with excitement and bonbons, begin fizzing fit to burst.

'He's coming; he's coming!' shouts little Jojo, rushing in from where he has been waiting in anticipation outside. The other children dart out, and we all follow to see what the attraction is. I must admit, I'm buzzing a bit myself. At the end of the road, a small pony and trap is approaching. The pony is wearing felt reindeer ears and has tiny bells and coloured fairy lights on a large leather collar. A girl dressed as an elf is at the reins, and sitting beside her with a sack full of presents is Santa Claus. There are sweets for the children in cones of red, shiny paper tied with a green bow, and chocolates for the adults in smaller cones of gold, shiny paper tied with a red bow. After the presents have been distributed, the children take turns to ride in the trap. The pony proudly canters up and down the lane with its excited little passengers, such simplicity bringing so much joy to young and old alike, and once again I feel blessed to have been given the opportunity to be part of this community.

※　＋　※

Santa has left; the hot cider is cold, and night begins to envelop the hamlet. Time for us all to form a procession to the little chalet to light the final candle. This honour is bestowed on Jacques, as he's the one who has come out every evening in all weathers to light the 23 others. Fabienne links arms with me as we walk and calls me 'My Lydie'. Lydie is now my new name as no one seems to remember Lindy. As we progress down the road, some of the men peel away from the group and go to knock on the doors of elderly residents to bring them out to witness this important event that signals the start of the *Réveillon de Noël* (Christmas Eve).

Mr V and I return to Les Libellules to spend our first Christmas Eve here together. We're having a Franco/Anglais evening, with a buffet replacing the traditional roast meat and chestnuts of a French meal. The buffet consists of tiny vol-au-vents filled with snails in parsley butter, blinis with smoked salmon and crushed baies roses,[2] a cheese board, oysters, a selection of mini quiches and of course foie gras on fig toast. All washed down with champagne, what else? We also open our presents this evening. I have received, amongst other things, a box of my favourite Mon Chéri chocolates and some stylish thermal gloves from Mr V, which are very handy (no pun intended), as I've lost the pair I brought with me on Friday. Mr V has received the film *Elf* from my daughter Natasia, so we settle to watch this with a Mon Chéri and a glass of port as a digestif in front of a crackling fire. Apart from my family, what more could I want?

---

1. A thick compote of brown sugar, dried currants, raisins, sultanas and orange and lemon peel, flavoured with allspice, nutmeg and cinnamon which was traditionally made with minced beef.
2. Small, dried, pink berries from Madagascar used a lot with fish.

STRUDEL TARTE SOLEIL

Here it is, the recipe for my strudel *tarte soleil*. It's fun to do, so give it a go.

Makes 12 twists, plus the centre

Ingredients

375g (13 oz) pack puff pastry
2 tbsp apple purée (alternatively use chestnut purée)
2 tbsp mincemeat. (If you can't get hold of mincemeat, you could use stewed apple and raisins as an alternative.)
A handful of chopped walnuts (alternatively use pecans)
A sprinkling of candied orange and lemon peel (alternatively use dried cranberries or raisins)
1 medium free-range egg, beaten
15 g sachet (½ oz) vanilla sugar

Method

It's essential that you do the following on a baking tray ready prepared with baking parchment.

Thinly roll out 2 x 25 cm (9 in) dinner plate-size circles of puff pastry.

Spread one of the pastry circles with the purée, leaving a 2 cm (1 in) perimeter.

Mix together mincemeat, nuts and dried fruit and spread over the purée.

Brush the edges of the pastry with the beaten egg.

Place the second circle on top and seal the outer edges.

Chill in fridge for 20 minutes.

Place a large glass or small saucer in the centre as a guide and cut the pastry into four quarters up to the glass.

Cut each quarter in three and press the sides of each third together to seal them.

Take each section and gently twist once in a clockwise direction forming 12 individual twists. (Don't worry if a little of the filling shows through.)

Remove the glass and brush the central section of the pastry with the remainder of the beaten egg.

Bake in a preheated oven at 180 C/gas mark 4 for 30 minutes, reducing the heat if the pastry begins to brown too quickly.

Remove from the oven and sprinkle with the vanilla sugar.

Return to the oven for a further 10 minutes at 200 C/gas mark 6.

This is a real showstopper, and people can simply break off a twist to eat.

It can be eaten both hot and cold. If hot, serve with a little brandy cream or vanilla ice cream.

The same principle can be used to make savoury *tartes soleil* with cheese, pesto and pine nuts or salmon and leek. Use your imagination and let me know what ideas you come up with.

A ROSE FOR WINTER

hristmas Day finally heralds an end to the wind and rain and starts with a crisp and fresh winter's morning. I'm outside taking photos. The ground is glistening with frost as if it's been scattered with crushed diamonds. Overnight the spindly rose bush has magically brought to bloom a single bud on its highest branch that looks as if it's been dipped in sugar icing, as it too is covered by a shimmering veil. All is quiet in the hamlet, and I feel a deep sense of peace and happiness. My sense of peace is soon shattered, however. On entering the house, I discover that Mr V has chosen Christmas morning to start rewiring the kitchen. OK, I did complain that I didn't have enough sockets, and the lead on the new toaster is too short to stretch to the existing ones. But, given the fact that I have the uphill task ahead of me of cooking a Christmas dinner on one hotplate and a two-shelf mini oven, the power going off and drill bits the girth of a stick of Blackpool mint rock,[1] descending from the ceiling are something I could do without.

The dinner has been planned with military precision. I cooked a gammon joint yesterday, so this morning I've only got the vegetables to contend with. After brushing up the debris and persuading Mr V to leave the electrics for a rainy day and go and play in the garden, I begin by parboiling the potatoes then transfer them to a tray of hot goose fat to roast. I then do the same to the parsnips. Next I boil and purée the carrots and turnips, leaving them in the pan to keep warm on top of the oven while I use the hotplate to cook the sprouts. During this time I'm frantically looking for something to make gravy out of, as gammon doesn't produce succulent juices as do chicken or beef. I usually rely on Bisto[2] with a couple of teaspoons of cranberry and orange stuffing for added flavour, both of which I've left behind in Paris. All I can find is a beef-flavoured Oxo cube to which I add a glug of red wine. The taste is OK, but it needs something to thicken it up. This is when I hit on the idea of using a spoonful of powdered potato, and the result isn't half bad if you ever find yourself in a similar situation. End result—a delicious Christmas dinner, cooked to perfection. Hopefully the first of many here at Les Libellules, and hopefully many others will be shared with family and friends.

✳ ✳ ✳

The glorious weather is perfect for a stroll around one of the lakes in the pristine sunshine. Perfect except for the fact that we are virtual prisoners at Les Libellules. Today is the most active in the hunting season, and Jacques has advised us to stay indoors, or if we must go out, to visit a town. More dog walkers and ramblers are killed or injured by hunters, fuelled by the previous evening's alcohol, on Christmas Day than on any other day of the year. Heeding his advice, we've decided to stay at home and read in the garden.

Mr V is reading a political biography, and I'm reading a French history book. I don't think I've told you, but I'm going through the procedure to have dual French/British nationality. It's a laborious process, gathering a seemingly endless list of original documents and then having them all officially translated at €28 each, which was extremely cheap compared with what some people have been charged. Then the equally laborious task of trying to make an appointment online to drop off my now 72-document dossier. Finally I've had my file approved and been given a date for my interview in

March, so I'm furiously swotting up on French history, geography, literature, popular culture and politics. I'm now reading all about the Hundred Years' War and the Revolution, but as I love history, this is no hard task. Politics, however, is a different story.

---

1. A hard, stick-shaped boiled sugar confectionery most often flavoured with peppermint or spearmint and commonly sold at seaside resorts in the UK.
2. A popular brand of gravy granules in the UK.

SPECTACULAR, SPECTACULAR!

Today is Boxing Day in the UK. I say in the UK as the 26th of December is an ordinary working day in France, with post and bread deliveries having already arrived this morning, and even our long-awaited, super-powerful TV aerial to put in the loft. So finally I've got a glimmer of hope that we'll be able to shut the tool cupboard door in the living room, which the current aerial is balancing on top of as it's the only place we can get a signal.

After yesterday's clear blue skies and sparkling sunshine, today's sky is laden with snow, hovering like a heavy, leaden duvet over the land. But this duvet will not be shaking out any of its icy feathers, as an afternoon temperature of -3 is forecast. The delicate frosting on the trees and bushes on Christmas Day has been replaced by a dense, white coating, giving them a strangely artificial appearance. The feather tree has a sinister air, with spindly, pure-white tendrils reaching out as if from an enchanted forest. I have to tell you, I've recently discovered the real name of what, until now, I've called the 'feather tree'; it's a tamarisk that I think originates from Africa, according to Fabienne who used to live there. But I've called it the feather tree up to now, and I shall continue to do so.

It's so cold outside that the water in Flaubertine's bowl has frozen solid, and a sheet of crystal blue ice covers the *mare*. Flaubertine has been sleeping on a bed we've made for her in the space between the roof of Mr V's tool store and the roof of the outbuilding. She won't come inside while Pussy Willow is in residence, but I wish she would when it is so cold outside.

✳ ✳ ✳

I'm taking some empty bottles and packaging to the recycle bins. This serves two purposes: one, to get rid of the rubbish; the other, to look inside people's windows to see if they have their lights on. Our power went off about an hour ago, and I want to be sure it's not connected to Mr V rewiring the kitchen yesterday. Loss of power is more than a mild inconvenience, as I was planning to cook a *boeuf Bourgignon* in the slow cooker for dinner. Even worse, no functioning toilet as our flush is powered by electricity.

Flaubertine is trotting at my side. As we reach cat-hating César's house, she hesitates. I reassure her that I won't let anything bad happen to her and point out the field of sheep opposite where she regularly hunts for mice. She tentatively continues until we reach the crossroads. This is the furthest she's ever been, but instead of firmly sitting down as usual, she hesitates again, wanting to stay with me but afraid to leave her comfort zone. This worries me, as although there's never a lot of traffic, the crossroads are wide, and sometimes cars come quite fast from the direction of the main road. If Flaubertine is going to cross with me, she needs to do it quickly and not decide to turn back mid-way. Finally, she plucks up courage and steps forward. I begin to run, as I want her to get to the safety of the other side as fast as possible. She picks up her pace also, staying close to my heels, and makes it to the other side. For all that I'm worried, I'm also touched that she's trusted me to come this far. My fear now is that she won't go the extra 50 metres to the bins but turn around, risking the road alone. I keep encouraging her. She makes it and is rewarded with lots of interesting smells to explore. The journey home is much simpler. I begin to run, and Flaubertine immediately follows me. When we reach Les Libellules, she is rewarded again, with an extra bowl of food.

I've also established that the power cut has affected the entire hamlet as there wasn't a light in sight, and a chance meeting with Fabienne confirms that a tree has come down and cut the power lines. Mr V and I agree that we need to install a generator for incidents such as this, if only to keep the toilet operational... You can all breathe a sigh of relief—the power was returned, and Mr V got his *boeuf Bourgignon*.

It's 4:30 in the afternoon on the 28th of December, and soon it will be dusk. We're driving to Saulieu to combine shopping with seeing the town's decorations lit up in the evening. The trees lining the road are decked out like dancers at the Folies Bergères, concealing their charms behind frosted branches that look like huge, ostrich-feather fans. We pass an open field bordered by a hilltop of trees that now resemble giant balls of cotton wool ready to roll down the slope towards us. This is a unique meteorological phenomenon known as hoarfrost, and I naturally ask Mr V to stop the car so that I can photograph it.

Saulieu is also decked out, with curtains of tiny lights draping the town hall, cathedral and the fountain in the square. There are three enormous trees—one with silver baubles, one with red, and the other blue—as well as countless smaller trees with twinkling golden lights dotted about the town. Garlands of coloured bulbs are strung across the streets, and all the shops have decorated their windows in charming traditional fashion. The effect, with the added splendour of the frost, is that the town looks like a scene from a Dickensian Christmas card. A group of jolly diners spills out into the glow on the pavement outside the Café Parisien, and they call '*bonsoir*' to me and pose for a photograph. I would like to step inside for a *chocolat chaud* (hot chocolate), but Mr V has been to get petrol while I was wandering around the town taking photos, and I have to meet him at the market square as we're going to visit Noëlle to see her reportedly spectacular display.

✳ ✳ ✳

We're now outside Noëlle's house; if you remember, her garden is full of various statues of animals, including a life-size, technicolour horse. This has now been transformed into a reindeer and has wooden antlers on its head and a red harness with golden bells around its neck. Behind it, in a cart covered in fairy lights, is a life-size, but not very life-like, Santa, which is actually a Santa suit stuffed with hay and a ball with a face drawn on it, wearing a red, fur-trimmed pointy hat with a flashing, white pompom. Another Santa, this time more life-like, is on the roof in a sleigh that four neon reindeer are pulling. Everywhere you look there are neon creatures: bambis, snowmen, penguins, and sweet little red and white toadstools lighting the path to the house.

Then, there it is, the pièce de résistance—the nativity crèche. This is what people, including neighbouring priests and curates, have travelled to see. The wooden stable is about four metres long and over two metres high at the apex. There are life-size figures of Mary, Joseph, the Angel Gabriel, shepherds and wise men, plus a donkey, cow and sheep positioned reverently around a larger-than-life baby Jesus in his crib. It truly is spectacular, bathed in a heavenly golden light from a star above. But, and as you would expect with Noëlle, there *has* to be a 'but', on either side of this serene, traditional scene are two less traditional gatherings. On the left there are three Cabbage Patch doll-type figures, one of which is riding a donkey made from logs and another cuddling what looks like a pig dressed as a human. All are wearing woolly hats with large pompoms on the top and have striped scarves around their chubby necks. These are joined by a brightly lit bear, stag and large, fat rabbit. On the right of the holy family is a manic-looking snowman, another Father Christmas and a penguin wearing earmuffs. This is totally bonkers, but as I said, I wouldn't expect anything less.

Noëlle hasn't been well, so we don't intend to stay long. She beckons us into her conservatory to see the indoor display. My jaw drops. On an enormous table up against the wall is a miniature Alpine village displaying what must be over 50 winter scenes. There are enchanting, illuminated shops, houses and churches with stained-glass windows, frozen lakes with animated skaters swirling on their shiny surfaces, and trains and toboggans travelling up and down the snowy mountain backdrop. There's also a magnificent carousel with bobbing, golden-maned horses, and twinkling Christmas trees surrounded by open-mouthed carol singers. Not only are most of these models moving, many of them are also playing music. Tinkly versions of 'Jingle Bells' are competing with 'We Wish You a Merry Christmas' and 'Joy to the World'. It's an assault on the senses. I'm like a child in a candy shop, and I don't know where to look as so much is going on.

Noëlle is rightly proud of her display, and she shows me an article in the same newspaper that came to photograph us on Christmas Eve, with a picture of her standing beside the Alpine village. She encourages me to take photos also, but they can't do justice to the magic of the real thing.

I'm all set to leave, but we're ushered into the dining room where an impressive selection of bottles for an apéritif have been placed on the table. I opt for port as it's one of the least strong, and I'm presented with a large glass that would constitute two double measures in a bar. Next, out come the nibbles. There's France's answer to the sausage roll—mini frankfurters wrapped in crumbly puff pastry that has been brushed with mustard—plus other pastries shaped like stars and crescent moons and filled with goat's cheese. There are also dainty rounds of foie gras topped with fig relish, smoked salmon roulades and cocktail-stick kebabs of lobster and mango. I *was* planning on having duck for dinner, but after this festive banquet, that will have to wait for another day.

Satiated, we say our goodbyes, our breath, warmed by the port, visible in the cold night air. The night sky is studded with stars putting on a display even more spectacular than those in the gardens as we return on foot down the country lanes to Les Libellules to relax by our fireside.

What I've learnt today: The term hoarfrost is derived from the Old English meaning of frost resembling an old man's beard.

FAIRGROUND ATTRACTION

$\mathcal{T}$he time is 6 o'clock on the last Saturday in December. After a dank and dismal day, the highlight of which has been the toilet leaking, we're waiting expectantly for the arrival of Jacques. He's coming to give us a demonstration—of what, Mr V has no idea—and I'm not much the wiser, except for the fact that I know it involves some sort of medical appliance. He arrives at the kitchen door after dark with a handcart covered in a blanket. What he has inside, I will try to describe. It's the prototype of a device he designed to help his aged father put on and take off his tight surgical stockings, but in reality it looks more like a medieval instrument of torture.

It's in three parts. The foot is shaped like a large, green, metal diver's flipper. The middle is even more bizarre with something that looks like half a bicycle wheel in yellow metal and a pink plastic shoehorn attached to a long wooden stick with a pink plastic handle. The top section has a long metal bar with a large clamp attached to it, and a blue metal lever that resembles those used in old railway signal boxes to switch the points. Jacques is visibly excited and chomping at the bit to dazzle us with his ingenuity. I'm questioning why I'm here with a seemingly mad inventor on a Saturday evening when all my friends and family in the UK are probably at a restaurant, theatre or cinema.

This is when it gets really scary. Jacques takes off his shoes, socks and trousers, saying, 'It's OK, Lindy is a nurse and used to seeing men's bodies,' and he's now standing in my living room wearing only a Christmas jumper with penguins on it and a pair of checked cotton boxer shorts. He takes an elastic stocking from his bag and places it over the clamp with all the aplomb of a magician producing a silk handkerchief to cover an about-to-disappear dove. Then he proceeds to pump the blue lever that opens the clamp and therefore the stocking.

I'm beginning to see where this is going, but surely there's a simpler way. He places his foot inside the stocking, and now for the genius part. He turns the wheel, and the stocking rises up his leg. This is worthy of being a fairground attraction like the ones that Caractacus Potts peddled in the film *Chitty Chitty Bang Bang*. Jacques now reveals that the pink shoehorn is an aid to remove the stocking, as it has a small barb at the back that grips it. This part of the device has actually been manufactured and patented and is on sale in France, Germany and Austria, though he tells me he still has to crack the UK market. (I think this is where I come in.)

To make matters worse, Jacques now suffers a wardrobe malfunction as his boxers are a little too liberal around the legs, and nurse Lindy is treated to a sight that she hasn't seen since her time on the wards. Mr V and I are now both trying to maintain enthusiastic interest while stifling the laughter that's bubbling inside us. My shoulders begin to shake as I can't contain it any longer, and I pretend that one of my daughters has just sent me a funny message on my phone. Jacques doesn't seem to notice. He's in raptures in his own world as he now begins to explain the angles and pressure required to make the whole thing function with relative ease. Even mathematically-minded Mr V is lost, so I've got no chance.

Not content with demonstrating himself, Jacques now commandeers Mr V to roll up his trouser leg (Mr V would never strip down to his undergarments in winter—or summer for that matter), and I escape to the kitchen to prepare things for the raclette to follow. Saturday night entertainment Les Libellules style.

What I've learnt today: Never admit that you used to be a nurse.

OYSTERS AND FOIE GRAS

*I*t's New Year's Eve, and my wish has been granted. The TV aerial is working in the loft, and the tool cupboard door is finally closed. I've spent the whole day cleaning and am now fresh from the shower with squeaky-clean hair, wearing presentable clothes. Earlier I looked like a cross between a bag lady and a scarecrow. I've even put on a smudge of make-up, although we're not doing anything special to celebrate other than having champagne and oysters, Mr V's favourite things in the world to eat.

Last year we exchanged presents on New Year's Eve, so this year we're doing the same. I've been a bit selfish and bought Mr V the third boxset of the TV series *Versailles*, which is *not* entirely for him as we both enjoy it. He has bought me a beautiful, padded book with gilt-edged pages, *The Secret Language of Plants*. Each left-hand page has a gorgeous, olde-worlde illustration of a different plant or flower, and the facing page has the history and origins of the plant, its uses and significance. I've learnt that garlic is also known as a *tue-l'amour* (passion killer) due to its strong smell that lingers on the breath. An ancient tradition in the Landes region in the southwest of France was to offer a plate of garlic to a young suitor who came to ask for the hand in marriage of the daughter of the house. If the couple were truly passionate about each other, then she wouldn't be put off by the smell of his breath, and they would be married. To celebrate, the couple were given a bowl of garlic soup to drink on their wedding night.

This is the highlight of our New Year's Eve. As we're both too tired to stay awake, we are in bed by 10:30, and 2019 slips in unnoticed. At least we won't have hangovers in the morning.

New Year's Day has arrived in marked contrast with last year when I was cooking dinner during a tempest while watching the concert from Vienna on TV and fearing I was going to lose the power for both. This year the day is just hanging there, dull, damp and listless, but I lose the power just the same. Mr V has once again chosen a day when I'm roasting a joint of beef with Yorkshire puddings and cauliflower cheese to cut the electricity voluntarily. I'm not as cross as you might imagine. The purpose of this is to have a light at the bottom of the stairs that we can switch on and off from the landing so we no longer take our life in our hands if we get up while it's still dark. It's the little things that make the most difference.

Also, I've got another beautiful book to tell you about. Mr V was cleaning on top of the cupboard after the TV aerial had been taken down, and his hand fell upon a book that had been concealed by the door frame. It's a leather-bound missal of the life of Christ (a daily prayer book), printed in 1948. Like the flower book, the pages are edged in gold, but I imagine that this is real gold leaf. Each page has beautiful illustrations depicting various stories and events in the New Testament. But, best of all, there are a collection of seventeen charming little confirmation souvenir cards dating from 1949–1958, with the majority being from May 1950. Apparently, it was (is) the custom to give these souvenirs to friends and family. Not being Catholic myself, when I first saw them I thought that they were commemorating funerals and wondered why so many young people had died in 1950, until Mr V explained the custom to me. So, I now have seventeen names to research. Confirmation into the church when young Catholics make their first Holy Communion usually takes place most commonly around the age of 13, so their present ages would range from 73 to 82; given the longevity of folks around here, the majority could still be alive. There was also some form of note written by Léa, but I cannot decipher the writing so will have to wait until Mr V has more time to help me.

*　*　*

Noëlle and Pappy Cardigan have just arrived to wish us *meilleurs voeux* (best wishes) for 2019 and brought a present for us—a block of foie gras and a small bottle of sweet Côtes de Gascogne wine to drink with it. They are presented in a basket that, once empty, is the perfect shape and size for the special fig toast that is served with foie gras.

I don't have to wait too long for the basket. As it's almost apéritif time, we open both the foie gras and the wine and polish off the lot. Foie gras is to Pussy Willow as oysters are to Mr V, but she's showing remarkable restraint, sitting on the coffee table and not once putting her paw in the pâté. Her eyes, however, are like saucers, and she is licking her lips, so I cut a small morsel for her, not too much as it's extremely rich and fatty, and she's quite fat enough.

It's always a joy to spend time with Noëlle. Mr V takes Pappy Cardigan off to see the latest developments at Les Libellules, and we girls chat about recipes, as Noëlle loves cooking as much as I. She would like my Christmas cake recipe, but the truth is, apart from the basic flour, butter, soft brown sugar and eggs, it changes every year depending on what I can get my hands on here in France. Last year the cake they sampled was fairly traditional with walnuts, cherries, currants and sultanas brought back from the UK. This year I've gone off piste, and it's all a bit Caribbean. I've replaced the currants with cranberries and the sultanas with the fatter, juicier, golden raisins that are popular here. I couldn't find glacé cherries so have used small pieces of crystalised pineapple then fed the cake with dark, spiced rum instead of traditional brandy. The colour is paler too as I used golden syrup instead of treacle. I have to say, it's remarkably good. Noëlle agrees wholeheartedly, so I've wrapped some for her to take home and set myself a challenge to make an alternative version again next year.

What alternatives have you come up with? Or are you a traditionalist? I'd love to hear your ideas...

THE ICING ON THE CEILING

*J*anuary is my least favourite month. It stretches endlessly between the glamour and decadence of December and the swansong of winter that February heralds. A grey mist clings to everything like a spider's web, and the snow that was threatening to fall now fulfils its threat as lacy flakes drift down from the pumice-stone sky.

Birds perch miserably in the trees, their feathers fluffed up against the cold, and in the little shelter that Mr V built, Flaubertine waits expectantly for me to emerge with a dish of food. The garden has gone into hibernation, giving no hint of what delights are sleeping until spring. Pussy Willow has taken herself off to hibernate beneath our duvet, so I've encouraged Flaubertine inside to sit on a cushion on my knee, but she's on high alert as she knows her adversary is somewhere in the house. Still, she settles enough to pad and suck at the cushion, purring loudly until she hears a noise from upstairs and darts for the door.

The noise is Mr V. He has custom-made and fitted a trap to the entrance of the loft and is now trying to fill in the gaps with plaster—without much success, as the plaster is falling onto his head. I tell him there must be a better solution, and he replies, 'Go and find one then.'

If you know me, as I think you do by now, you'll know I like a challenge, so I run through various options of some sort of pump with a nozzle to insert the plaster into the gap with a block of wood to hold it in place until it's almost dry. I recently watched a programme on TV about the restoration of the medieval Château Guédelon an hour-and-a-half drive from here. I've been fascinated by the techniques that they're using and have put the château on my list of places to visit. It's this sort of thinking outside the box that led me to have my brainwave —an icing bag! This will be strong enough to withstand the pressure of plaster being forced through it and has various nozzles at various widths.

I'm now emptying boxes in the garden room, as I know I have an icing bag somewhere. Ah, here it is. Mr V looks doubtful, but as you all also know by now, this is his usual expression. I tell him I can take the bag away if he doesn't want to use it, to which he replies, 'Oui, I can try.'

To my delight, and his reluctance to admit, it works. The icing bag is of course ruined, but given the fact that I'm years away from having a kitchen in which I could ice a cake, it's been put to good use.

What I've learnt today: Always think outside the box.

We're having a reprise from the damp mist and drizzle. It's the 3rd of January, and the sun has decided to pay us a brief visit. The temperature is forecast to reach a high of -3. But here on my south-facing terrace, it feels more like +10. Granted, I'm wearing leg warmers over my jeans and a padded gilet over my sweater, but I've just had a blissfully simple lunch of a cheese sandwich and a cup of coffee beneath a glorious blue sky. I say blissfully simple as Mr V has gone to Dijon for supplies, and I'm freed from the shackles of cooking a 'proper' lunch and having to wash all the pots and pans afterwards.

I have sheets blowing in the breeze that are actually drying and not freezing. The *mare*, however, resembles an ice rink, and the little puddles that the farm cats usually drink from are frozen solid. I've discovered that milk doesn't freeze as readily as water so have left them a bowl on the garden wall. I know that milk is not generally good for a cat's digestion, but if you saw some of the things that these poor creatures eat and drink, they must have constitutions of oxen. Pussy Willow, whose constitution is more sensitive, is enjoying my presence in the garden and stalking something in the long grass. She emerges with what looks like long, spindly spider's legs dangling and jiggling from either side of her mouth. I hold my breath in case it bites her. But she promptly ejects it back where she found it and gallops for the safety of the terrace. Like me, she is still learning about life in the country.

Sitting here writing at a wobbly little table reminds me once more of how blessed I am to finally have a little patch of earth to call my own. I put down my pen and watch the blue tits feeding on a fat ball hanging on the feather tree. My pots of rosemary and thyme are flourishing in the sunshine, the sight of which reminds me that in six or seven weeks the first sign of spring will once again appear. My feet, however, remind me that it *is* still winter, as the cold reaches through my boots and thick thermal socks and bites my toes, so I fetch a throw from inside and drape it over my legs, not wanting to miss a minute of my moment of peace and tranquillity.

What I've learnt today: Milk doesn't freeze as readily as water.

SAPIN D'HIVER

*T*oday is Twelfth Night, the day when we're supposed to take down our Christmas trees, but mine is going nowhere. I've removed the angel from the top, plus all the heavy or fragile decorations in case the branches droop, but I've left the lighter baubles and little parcels and, of course, the lights. It is no longer a *sapin de Noël* but a *sapin d'hiver* (a winter tree), and it's staying here until March, bringing light and joy into the dark evenings. I'm giving it regular bottles of water, and it's looking decidedly perky. Mr V agrees with me, saying it has more chance of surviving if planted back in the earth in spring than during the frost.

Twelfth Night heralds the arrival of the kings bearing gifts of gold, frankincense and myrrh for the baby Jesus. (They are actually wise men in the Bible, but somewhere along the way they have acquired crowns and been promoted.) Here in France, it heralds the arrival of the *galette des rois*, a special cake made from puff pastry and usually filled with frangipane, but chocolate spread and apple versions are sneaking onto the shelves. Each cake comes wrapped in a golden cardboard crown and contains a *fève* (literally a haricot bean), traditionally a small porcelain figurine of one of those present at the nativity, but I have found a mini Château de Chambord, the planet

Saturn, and even more oddly, a set of miniature Russian dolls inside. The tradition of the *fève* is similar to that of putting a silver sixpence in a Christmas pudding in the UK. It's customary at family gatherings for the youngest member of the party to sit beneath the table while the *galette* is divided into equal parts. The child calls out the names of the people gathered around the table at random, ensuring there can be no cheating as to who finds the *fève* and wears the crown.

The custom of the *galette* dates back to Roman times during the feast of Saturn, which explains the porcelain replica of the ringed planet that I recently found in a slice. A servant from noble households was chosen at random to be king or queen for the day. This was decided in the manner described above, and it was an actual bean that determined who would be the one to enjoy the role reversal and have their master wait on them. The idea behind this was to nurture good relations between the master and his servants. Later, early Christians adopted the tradition to mark the arrival of the magi, replacing the traditional bean with a carved figure of the baby Jesus, who they had long searched for.

During the Revolution, *fèves* and the idea of being a king or queen for the day were banned as they represented elitism and were seen as being against the Republican ideal of equality, though the gâteaux continued to be made and enjoyed. From around 1870, beans were systematically replaced by porcelain figurines, and as I've pointed out, some other strange, unrelated objects. Over the years, I have collected the baby Jesus, Joseph, a shepherd, a wise man and a donkey, and I now use them to decorate the top of my traditional British Christmas cake, bringing the two cultures together.

GALETTE DES ROIS

A *galette des rois* is easy to make, and you often get golden cardboard crowns inside Christmas crackers, so this is a great way to give them a second life. If you don't like frangipane, try stewed apple, creamed chestnuts or Nutella.

Makes 8–12 portions, depending on how much of a gourmand you are...

Ingredients

375 g (13 oz) puff pastry
140 g (5 oz) ground almonds
100 g (4 oz) vanilla sugar
75 g (3 oz) softened butter
2 large free-range eggs, beaten
1 small *fève* (be careful everyone is aware of its presence in case of choking)

Method

Thinly roll out 2 dinner plate-size circles of puff pastry, one 27 cm (10 ½ in) and the other 25 cm (10 in).

Put the smaller circle of pastry in a 25 cm (10 in) tart dish and prick with a fork.

Mix together the ground almonds, sugar, butter and eggs (saving a little of the beaten egg for glazing) and spread over the pastry, hiding the *fève* in the mixture.

Cover with the second circle of pastry, firmly sealing the edges.

Make a herringbone (or other) design on the top.

Brush with beaten egg.

Cook in a preheated oven at 180 C/gas mark 4 for around 25 minutes, checking regularly to ensure the pastry remains golden and not brown (cover loosely with foil if so).

Best eaten warm, with or without a little crème fraîche on the side.

NOW IS THE WINTER OF OUR DISCONTENT

*I*t seems 2019 has got off to a troubled start on both sides of the Channel. The Brexit negotiations are in a shambles, and no one knows if they're coming or going. The longer the process is delayed, the better for me though, as it sees me hopefully closer to obtaining dual nationality. Here in France the situation is even more volatile. Demonstrations by those claiming to be *Gilets jaunes* have turned violent, with the windows of shops and banks being broken, cash dispensers destroyed, police being attacked and cars set alight. There are shocking images on the television and internet of the Eiffel Tower obscured from view by thick plumes of black smoke. It's hard to equate these images with the city I've called home for twelve years; these things happen in other parts of the world, not on your doorstep. A group of protesters almost succeeded in forcing their way into one of the government ministries at the weekend, and thousands of extra police are having to be drafted into the major cities to deal with the situation. Shops are losing business; hotels, restaurants, theatres and cinemas are losing bookings, and the economy is suffering. Plus, ordinary working people are having their lives disrupted by their cars being burnt and premises vandalised. Emmanuel Macron has made some concessions, but I fear it's all too little too late.

Mr V and I have just finished watching the excellent series *Versailles*, and the similarities are remarkable—an angry population revolting against the powers that be, the gap between the haves and the have-nots growing increasingly wider, and mob rule reigning on the streets. There have been calls for the president to resign, and even worse, mock executions taking place, cutting the head off models of him. It's all a bit chilling. At Les Libellules, however, we are in another world, simply spectators to events outside our sphere.

* * *

Despite all the problems the outside world has to offer, it's apparently still the season to be merry here. Another fête is on the horizon—*la Fête des Sapins*. This time it's not to sell, but to burn them; they do like a good bonfire in these parts. It seems not all folks are as ecologically minded as Mr V and I. Their little Christmas trees, far from being planted out for a chance of a second life, are going to be collected and ceremoniously set alight, probably in some Pagan ritual to chase away the cold and dark of winter. Still, I bow to tradition, and we set off into a frosty, moonless night.

The gathering is to take place at one of the nearby villages that make up our commune. It hasn't attracted the hordes that *la Fête de la Saint-Jean* did in June, but a fair number of people *are* here, and the stack of *sapins* is impressive. People from our hamlet are carrying the lit Advent candles in their glass jars to light the way, forming a mystical procession winding towards the, as yet, unlit fire. Many have come bearing the wreaths from their front doors also. The men are having a competition to see who can hook their wreath around the tree that's standing proudly at the top of the pile. There are, as usual, large vats of *vin chaud*, steaming jugs of *chocolat chaud*, plus little cartons of *marrons chauds* (hot chestnuts). There are also hot dogs— half baguettes stuffed with sizzling frankfurters smothered in mustard—and jacket potatoes cooked in smouldering embers in what looks like a dustbin. It all has a British, 5th of November feel to it where effigies of Guy Fawkes are burnt across the country to mark his attempt to blow up the Houses of Parliament in 1605. All that is missing is tomato soup, toffee apples and children waving sparklers.

The evening is bitterly cold, but the welcome is warm. We're approached by many inhabitants of other hamlets and villages, all of whom seem to know exactly who we are, while *we* are at the distinct disadvantage of not having a clue who *they* are. There's even more cheek kissing going on than usual as everyone is wishing each other *Bonne Année* (Happy New Year) and *meilleurs voeux*. Finally the mayor lights a torch and thrusts it beneath the branches. At first nothing happens, then with a whoosh, the flames rise, consuming the trees hungrily. Although I admit I would much rather the trees be recycled, I'm caught up in the atmosphere. I feel that they're having a good send-off and serving their purpose to the community; as we lack facilities such as theatres, bars and nightclubs, we have to make our own entertainment. I might suggest some dancing next year, not only to liven things up, but to warm us up also. The fire burns out quickly, leaving the scent of pine in the air. The night is now freezing cold and pitch black, and it's a good job that Mr V had the foresight to carry a torch in his pocket. It's a treacherous path across the fields back to our own lucky little *sapin*, who is basking in the muted glow from the only fire he is going to be subjected to—the one in our hearth.

I'm in the bathroom, and I notice something that looks like ash floating down from the sky. Within seconds, the ash gathers into flakes larger than a 50-pence piece. The sky is well and truly shaking out her eiderdown of snow. These are no delicate, lacy flakes; it's falling thick and fast—on the day that the old, ineffectual bedroom windows are due to be replaced. I don't know why this surprises me, as experience should have taught me that if it's going to snow, it's going to happen at the most inconvenient time, no matter how pretty it looks—and it does look pretty.

The carpenter, Florian, arrives with enough kit to build a house and sets to work taking out the window in the blue room where we sleep. As expected, half the wall comes out with it, so Mr V is now mixing cement to fill in the gaps while Florian demolishes the wall in the rose room. I'm beginning to doubt my wisdom in spending so much on windows to block the draught and noise from the nearby road, as both will just come whistling through the holes in the wall.

Three hours later Florian has the old windows out and the new ones installed, and both walls cemented and filled with some magic, expanding silicone substance from a spray gun. I stand in front of the one in the rose room in disbelief. A car silently passes on the departmental road close to the house, followed by a van and a small pickup truck, then the real test—two juggernauts travelling in opposite directions pass at the same time. I can hear them, but only as if they were much further in the distance and for a much shorter time. There's not a whisper of air to be felt. Mission accomplished and another task ticked off the indeterminably long list.

Jobs done, it's almost time to leave our little, perfect utopia and take the road back to the metropolis, or return to civilisation as Mr V puts it. But I ask the question: is it more civilised to live with all mod cons but also with violence and civil unrest, or without modern commodities, including the internet, and be at one with nature and have peace and tranquillity?

What would be your answer?

It will be three weeks before we return at the beginning of February, and that means another chapter of life at Les Libellules.

PART IV
THE SPRING OF CHANGE

FEBRUARY AND MARCH 2019

Fair now is the springtide, now earth lies beholding
With the eyes of a lover, the face of the sun;
Long lasteth the daylight, and hope is enfolding
The green-growing acres with increase begun.
'The Message of the March Wind', William Morris

EVERYBODY NEEDS GOOD
NEIGHBOURS

*T*ime seems to have folded like an accordion, and February has almost passed in a blur. Mr V has had an operation for a non-life-threatening condition which is keeping him from driving and doing heavy work at Les Libellules, so we had to postpone our planned visit.

I've been visiting the bridal salons in the swanky 1st arrondissement of Paris, shopping for a wedding dress with my good friend Marie (partner of Vincent, the sneaky sandwich eater). After being shown numerous dresses, none of which inspired either of us, we went to a more *popular*[1] area of the city, where a young, up-and-coming designer had her studio. After some searching, we found a small, black door set in a plain concrete wall, no sign of either studio or shop. We rang the intercom, and the door magically opened onto a quaint street of bow-fronted shops facing each other across a narrow, cobbled road. Their square-panelled windows displayed dusty antiques, gaudy modern art paintings, abstract sculptures, artisan jewellery and vintage clothes. At the end of the street was a leafy courtyard where we found our destination.

We were greeted by the designer, a petite, young woman with glossy, black, bobbed hair wearing an oversized, floral artist's smock with a large bow at the neck. On her wrist was a pin cushion fashioned as a bracelet, and on her feet a pair of oxblood Dr. Martens boots. She welcomed us inside her bijou showroom and asked us to take a seat on a pink velvet chaise longue while she showed us her various creations. The designs were simple, elegant and exactly what Marie had been looking for. After listening to Marie's preferences, the designer began sketching, taking elements from three dresses and fashioning a fairy-tale wedding gown with the top of one, the skirt of another and the sleeves of a third then set to work taking measurements and making notes. She's going to make a toile (a prototype dress made up in muslin) to be sure that the length and dimensions are right before making the actual dress in cotton sateen and lace. I can't wait to see Marie as a beautiful bride, wearing this on her wedding day.

With the dress chosen, we headed back to la Place Vendôme to an expensive, upmarket shoe shop and instantly found what Marie was looking for—T-bar court shoes with a pompadour heel in a blush-coloured sateen, with a leather sole. Shopping over, Marie treated me to lunch at Le Grand Café Capucines near la Place de l'Opéra. A perfect way to end a perfect morning.

✳ ✳ ✳

I've had a visit from a young niece, who is studying French, to immerse herself in the language and culture. I've also been immersing myself in language and culture in preparation for my dreaded interview to gain French nationality. This involves doing gruelling, 90-minute practice language tests online and reading large history books. I'm now an expert on Clovis, Charlemagne, Henri IV and Louis XVI, to name but a few.

One of the frequent questions people are asked during their interview is to explain what 'fraternity' means to them. Our friends and neighbours at Les Libellules have given me the perfect response. On hearing that Mr V isn't his usual fit and active self following his surgery and that we wouldn't be returning as planned, Marcel finished insulating the interior of the fuel store that Mr V had begun and gathered a group of willing volunteers in the form of Jacques, Fifi and Pascal to move the tank inside. No easy task apparently as he told us this involved passing through the now full *mare* (at the shallow end, granted, but still water above knee level), up a wobbly wooden ladder and through a doorway not wide enough for a man to pass alongside the tank. Therefore Pascal and pocket-sized Fifi, being the two smallest, had to go inside to guide it into position while Marcel and Jacques eased it up the stairs and through the door. Our gratitude is immense. I was afraid if we'd been there Mr V would have overdone it and ended up back in hospital.

What I've learnt today: Pompadour heels are medium-high, narrow, curved heels first worn by Madame de Pompadour, the mistress of Louis XV. The style spread from Paris across Europe in the 18ᵗʰ century and is still popular here for wedding or ball shoes.

---

1. *Popular* in French has a slightly different meaning, indicating it's well populated and multicultural, rather than sought-after.

SEASON OF CHANGE

*I*t's now been six weeks since we were last at Les Libellules. The weather has been atrocious during that time, and I fear for Flaubertine. But now, even though today is only the 22nd of February, winter appears to have disappeared in the blink of an eye.

The sky is cornflower blue, and the mercury is set to hit the low twenties all of next week; the only hints that we're still officially in winter are the bare branches of the trees. It was this time last year that our friends PJ and Panda came to stay, and the countryside that was then buried beneath a blanket of snow is now basking in sunshine.

As we arrive at Les Libellules, Flaubertine comes bounding to greet us. She looks a little thinner than when I last saw her, but in good health. I hear that some other neighbours have followed our lead and begun giving her titbits when we aren't here. I think that me giving her a name has distinguished her from the other farm cats and made her more human to the neighbours, if you know what I mean.

The garden is showing signs of spring, and some tiny lemon and mauve primroses have begun to push their petals through the earth. Lila, my lilac tree, has survived the winter also, though she doesn't appear to have grown much since we planted her a year ago. I still think the injury she suffered at the hands of Mr V and his strimmer last summer has stunted her growth, but she *has* sprouted little buds like pale-green seed pearls on the tips of her branches.

The real reason for our visit, apart from the fact that it's been so long since we've been at Les Libellules, is that tomorrow we're signing the paperwork to complete the purchase of our little patch of woodland.

⁂

We're in the *notaire's*[1] office with Jacques to sign the necessary documents to transfer ownership of the woods. The *notaire* looks like a kindly old tortoise with a small, smooth, round head; a broad, flat, aquiline nose and over-full lips that stretch too far around his face. Holey knitwear must be de rigueur with minor officials around here, as like Pappy Cardigan's, the *notaire's* burgundy-coloured jumper reveals patches of his blue and white checked shirt. One of the questions that he asks us, which I hadn't anticipated, was if we were prepared to grant permission to allow the dreaded hunters to pass through our land, to which he receives a resounding '*NON*' from me.

He proceeds to lament the fast-approaching Brexit date and discusses my forthcoming interview to become a French national. This is all very chatty and time-consuming, and, unlike a conveyancer in the UK, time evidently doesn't mean money to a French country *notaire*. Finally out comes the extensive file of documents to be signed. Having already signed for the house, not to mention opening a bank account, I knew this was the part where the pace picks up, and no matter how laid-back he was two minutes ago, he'll be shuffling documents like a croupier in a casino.

One document gets Jacques excited. It's the original one that his maternal great-grandfather, a gentleman by the name of Emile Chalumeau, signed in 1914 when he bought what was then one plot of land consisting of our little woods and the two parcels of woodland on either side. The vendor was a Mademoiselle Madeleine de Balathier-Lantage, a name that carries with it an element of intrigue and romance; my curiosity is piqued...

* * *

Back in the hamlet, I go to Pieter's house to use his internet and see what I can find out about this lady. It seems that the tendrils of the past reach back into the 17th century. I discover that she was a spinster who was born in 1877 and died in 1952 without direct descendants. Madeleine's paternal grandfather was Roger de Balathier-Lantage, a marquis born in 1787, two years before the Revolution, and who died in 1864. He must have seen some turbulent times, especially as he was a member of the nobility. Once more the lines between the past and present become blurred.

The furthest ancestor I could trace was Henri de Balathier de Lantage who resided at the Château de la Chaux from 1670–1722, and who was another former owner of our newly acquired wood. All these discoveries give me such a thrill that we will add our names to such a salubrious list.

The Château de Chaume, as it is now known, is not too far from here and still inhabited, but it's privately owned, not open to the public. We must take a trip there, even if only to see it from the gates.

What I've learnt today: Entries of the family name before Roger de Balathier-Lantage were written as 'de Balathier de Lantage', but as 'de Lantage' indicated a member of the nobility of Lantage, this was probably changed during the revolution of 1789 to 'de Balathier-Lantage'.

---

1. The equivalent of a conveyancer in the UK.

GARDEN OF MORNING MIST

I wake to a garden caressed by a fine veil of mist, and I'm drawn outside while still in my pyjamas. The ground beneath my feet is cushioned in a deep carpet of sage-green and silver-grey foliage, as if I'm walking on damp sponge. I take care not to step on the heads of the yellow and mauve primroses peeking above the virgin grass. I'm filled once again with the sense of wonder that spring never fails to deliver, and I thank God for giving me the privilege of knowing this wondrous place. I wish I had the gift of writing poetry as prose doesn't have the power to capture the essence of the morning. The mist forms tiny pearls of moisture on my hair, soaking it like rain. Anyone passing would think I was a mad woman standing half obscured in the garden in my nightclothes, but with the sight of the silvery morning sun piercing the mist and falling in little pools of light on the *marc*, it's I who think anyone *not* standing here is the mad one.

Mr V is up also, but he is dressed in his gardening clothes and boots. He's brought some fledgling fruit bushes to plant along the wall where the tomatoes were last year. It wasn't an ideal spot for them, as they didn't have sun all day, and many of them ripened too late, but it's a good spot for raspberries and black and red currants. He's also planting some potatoes that I found sprouting in a bag in the kitchen. It's a little early to plant potatoes, but we'll give them a go.

We're waiting for a gardener with a rotavator to turn the earth in front of the terrace to create a *potager* (kitchen garden), but three weekends have passed since his promise to call at the weekend— apparently it's just *any* weekend! I've put some herb seeds in pots, so we'll see what shoots up. If they don't thrive, we've found a super little garden centre on the road leading into Arnay-le-Duc that has some which are already established. Mr V has also planted the *sapin d'hiver* in the small woods at the back of the house. Yes, it has finally left the building and been returned to the earth.

We are planning the *potager* as we're not sufficiently advanced in the plumbing department to install a new septic tank, so we're going to use that part of the garden to grow our fruit and vegetables. The mayor was not entirely happy about this, but Pappy Cardigan had a private word, telling him how much progress we'd made in preparation, and how much actual work there is to be done here. He has also approached the mayor on my behalf to ask if he could write a statement on official paper to add some clout to my bid to have French nationality, saying how well integrated I am within the community and how I actively take part in all the local cultural activities. I, for my part, have put together a little album of photos showing me joining in at various events.

The postponement of the septic tank installation has cleared the way for visits by two friends in June and July, one of whom, Ang, is a keen gardener, so she'll be put to good use. The trouble is Les Libellules is so soporific that although people come here full of good intentions, eating, drinking, reading and just generally sitting around chatting seem to take over everyone, me included.

The soporific effect seems to have extended not only to Mr Rotavator but to Marcel as well, as we haven't had sight or sign of him for the past three weeks and are waiting for him to render the outside of the new fuel store and fit the door. This is the problem with relying on people who are working to a different agenda; as a result we haven't advanced nearly as much in two years as we'd anticipated.

Extreme patience is required, and as Mr V put it, 'This is the country. No one is in a hurry here. The problem is that *we* are Parisians.'

I would love to embrace my new-found country lifestyle and take time out to go for a leisurely walk or explore more of the surrounding area, but Mr V is hanging on to his Parisian mindset, and all work and no play are making him a dull boy. I have, however, put in an early request to visit a local town of historical interest on my birthday in May, so he can hardly refuse me that.

ALMOST FRENCH

*I*t's the 15th of March, and we're passing fields gleaming with the first green shoots of wheat pushing through the earth—signs of new beginnings. Changing your nationality is certainly a new beginning; you're even presented with a new birth certificate. Preparing for the dreaded interview has hung over me like a lead cloak for the last three months, but today my mood is light as the ordeal is finally over. I had my interview yesterday; it was both better and worse than I anticipated. Better in that the man who conducted it was pleasant and smiley. Worse in that I had no history or culture questions whatsoever, just a lot of political and administrative ones and numerous dates and statistics—frankly, my worst nightmare.

He began by opening the sealed envelope and going through all my documents and asking me for additional ones, some of which were on the official list, some not, but I'd been forewarned about this so was well prepared. He then asked the standard questions: How long had I been in France? Did I mix in French or British circles? What language did we speak at home? Did I still have relatives in the UK, and how often did I visit? Next he asked what societies I belonged to, what interests my husband and I shared and where we went on holiday last year. I told him that we no longer take holidays as all our time is spent at our house, to which he replied, '*En Bourgogne alors.*'

'Yes, in Burgundy then, I suppose.' I felt like now was the time to produce my trump card, so I showed him the letter from the mayor, which he seized upon with glee and added to my file.

He then went on to the more general stock questions: What is the National Day of France? Name three symbols of France. Give examples of *Liberté, Egalité and Fraternité*. What are *les droits et les devoirs* (rights and obligations) of French citizens? Who are the president and prime minister? What republic are we in? Name all the presidents in order...

All that went without a hitch, and I was encouraged by the frequent use of the word *parfait* (perfect). But then it all started to go awry. He asked me how many regions there are. I know there are eighteen, of which five are overseas, but out of my mouth came one hundred and one. This is the number of departments. He threw me a lifeline asking me how many departments there are. At this point the penny should have dropped, but it didn't. My brain scrambled about in panic amongst various statistics and came up with 577. This is the number of deputies. I told him figures weren't my strong point, so he threw in another question, asking the number of overseas departments, which I got correct. Then he asked me to name them, which I did, but by this time I hardly knew my own name. When the final question of why I wanted to become French came, all my well-rehearsed answers flew out of the window, and I rambled on about my husband being French and having three French step-children and liking the wine!

On verra as they say—we'll see. I now have an eight- to eighteen-month wait to see if I've been successful or not.

⁂

We're having a little celebratory dinner to mark the fact that I can now relax, and I'm making one of my favourite starters— *huitres chaudes* (hot oysters). Mr V almost had apoplexy when I first suggested that I served oysters hot, but after tasting them, he came around to the idea and now enjoys them equally cooked or served raw with lemon juice, brown bread and butter and a glass of chilled white wine.

After the oysters we're having coq au vin, followed by cheese and one of my go-to desserts—*fondant au chocolat*, a warm chocolate sponge with a gooey middle. But you'll have to wait a little longer for these recipes. I feel exhausted after the stress of yesterday and want nothing more than to do nothing. But in the words of that wise bear Winnie the Pooh, 'Doing nothing often leads to the very best something.'

So here is the recipe for the hot oysters.

HUITRES CHAUDES

Serves 2

Ingredients

1 small banana shallot, finely chopped
Knob of butter
100 ml (3 fl oz) white wine
1 tbsp lemon juice
2 tsp fresh (or 1 tsp dried) French tarragon
2 tbsp crème fraîche
12–16 oysters
1 tbsp fresh breadcrumbs
1 tbsp freshly grated parmesan cheese
Freshly ground sea salt and pepper to taste

Method

Gently sauté the shallot in the butter over a low heat until soft, taking care not to brown.

Add the wine and lemon juice and reduce to half the volume.

Add the fresh tarragon (but add halfway through reducing the wine and lemon juice if using dried).

Remove from the heat and stir in the crème fraîche.

Put a heaped teaspoon of the mixture onto each of the oysters.

Sprinkle with a pinch of breadcrumbs, then the parmesan and seasoning.

Cook under a moderate grill[1] for around 5 minutes until the top is browned.

Serve immediately.

---

1. Broiler.

DOWN THE HATCH

J have another opportunity to demonstrate my integration into the community. There's to be a *dégustation de vins* (wine tasting) this evening, hosted by the daughter of one of our neighbours who works for a vineyard near Beaune. It's to take place in the *salle des fêtes* (village hall), and there will be charcuterie. As you may know by now, I'm not over fond of the array of processed meats and dry-cured sausage that charcuterie entails, but Mr V assures me that he'll eat my share. Thankfully there will also be cheese and dessert and, if I'm lucky, some salad.

I've opted to wear camel trousers and a navy, boat-neck top as I'm never quite sure how to dress for these occasions, but everyone else appears to have gone full-on formal. Valerie, looking nothing like a farmer's wife, is floating around in a multicoloured, chiffon maxi dress, and another neighbour, Marguerite, is wearing a white, lacy top and black, velvet maxi skirt. A couple of the men are sporting dickie bows, and the mayor is even wearing his tricolour ceremonial sash, so I'm erring on the casual side.

Celine, Fabienne and Solène are at a table with their husbands. Solène comes and asks us to join them, which I'm glad of as they look by far the least formal group. There are cards on the table with a list of wines and their prices, and two vouchers for each person, as apparently two complimentary glasses are included in the €10 ticket price. I was expecting a small taste from each of the bottles on sale or, at the very least, a talk about the vineyard and the various wines it produces. But people are already queuing up at the counter to get their first free drink like tourists at an all-inclusive hotel in Benidorm.

The food has arrived, and it's not as bad as I anticipated. There are various cooked hams and chorizo-style sausage plus baked *Epoisses*, a local cheese, with crusty baguette to dip into the gooey centre. The cheese is giving off a strong, pungent aroma, but the flavour is nutty and the texture creamy, so I dig in.

Mr V and I are still on our first glass, a Saint-Joseph red from Côtes du Rhône, not normally one of my favourite wine regions, but this is surprisingly excellent. Solène's husband, Jean, tells me it was originally called *vin de* Mauves and is mentioned in Victor Hugo's *Les Misérables*. Celine, however, has downed her two free glasses and is up at the counter buying a bottle, not to take home, but to drink now. The others have also sent their complimentary drinks down the hatch, and the table is filling up with bottles. This isn't at all what I was expecting. As I look around, I see all the other tables are sipping their samples and discussing their merits, while ours is getting more raucous by the glass, and the ambience begins to resemble that of a pub in Liverpool city centre on a Saturday night. Mr V and I don't want to appear to be party poopers, so we buy a bottle to drink also, and after four glasses of wine, I'm feeling as well-oiled as the others, and my command of the French language seems to have flourished with the popping of every cork.

Now Christophe, the expert willow wreath maker from the workshops, has come over from another table that's also beginning to show signs of raucousness. He's carrying a bottle of champagne. I don't know where this has appeared from as it is not on sale at the 'bar'.

'Drink up,' he says. We all drain our glasses and hold them out to be filled with his bubbly nectar. I have to say, as wine tastings go, this is up with the best.

'We need something sweet now,' says Celine. Christophe nods knowingly and goes back to his table, returning a few minutes later with a packet of delicate rose wafer biscuits especially for champagne. This is obviously not a happy accident—this has been planned.

The rest of the evening passes in a blur. Everyone from the hamlet has driven up the hill to the village, but no one is in a fit state to drive back, especially under the watchful eye of the mayor, so we all stagger down in the dark, some staggering more than others.

It's been an interesting evening, a good excuse for a drinking session under the guise of a wine tasting. Given there are no licensed premises in either the hamlet or the village, I see that this is a way of getting around the sale of alcohol. Personally I can't wait for the next *dégustation*.

What I've learnt today: Mauves is a small village in the heart of the Saint-Joseph wine region in the Rhône Valley, which lent its name to Saint-Joseph wine throughout much of its history. The wines of Mauves were highly regarded throughout the centuries, and the emperor Charlemagne is said to have been an admirer.

⚘ ⚘ ⚘

All this talk of wine is a good opportunity to give you a wine-based recipe, so without further ado, here is my recipe for coq au vin.

COQ AU VIN

Serves 4

Ingredients

4 large free-range organic chicken thighs
2 medium/large carrots cut into 2 cm (1 in) rounds
2 bay leaves
1 sprig of fresh rosemary
1 sprig of fresh thyme
1 bottle of red wine. (Burgundy is great, not too heavy and not too fruity. For a more rustic flavour, try a Côtes du Rhône.)
A good glug of olive oil
200 g (8 oz) smoked lardons or smoked streaky bacon, cut into fine strips
2 shallots, very finely chopped
1 tbsp cornflour, seasoned a little with salt and pepper
1 tbsp sherry vinegar (or brandy if you prefer)
25 g (1 oz) 70% cocoa solids chocolate. (This gives the sauce a lovely silky texture.)
12 baby (pickling) onions
30 g (1 oz) salted butter
A good pinch of brown sugar
200 g (8 oz) chestnut or button mushrooms, quartered
Extra salt and pepper to season if required

Method

Marinade the chicken, carrots, bay leaves, rosemary and thyme in the red wine and leave in the refrigerator for 24 hours before cooking.

Remove the chicken from the marinade and drain.

Heat the olive oil in a heavy-bottomed casserole and brown the chicken on all sides to seal in the juices, then remove from the pan and set aside. (This is best done two at a time so that the meat seals quickly; if you put too many pieces in the pan at once, they will create steam and not brown.)

Add a little more olive oil to the pan if necessary and sauté the lardons/bacon over a moderate heat for three minutes until beginning to brown, then add the shallots and cook for a further minute, taking care not to burn.

Drain the carrots and herbs from the marinade, saving the wine.

Gently sauté the carrots in the saucepan with the bacon and shallots.

Return the chicken to the pan and add the cornflour, making sure all the meat is coated, then add the sherry vinegar, stirring well to form a paste with the flour.

Add the wine and finally the chocolate, stirring until the chocolate has melted and is incorporated into the sauce.

Bring to the boil then reduce the heat to the lowest possible and gently simmer for at least 2 hours (the longer the better), stirring from time to time.

Fifteen minutes before serving, sauté the pickling onions in half of the butter with a pinch of brown sugar until they are caramelised, then add to the casserole.

Just before serving, sauté the mushrooms in the remaining butter until golden, add to the casserole, and simmer for a further 5 minutes.

Season to taste.

I serve this with mashed potato that has been crisped in the oven, but it is equally good served with just a warm, crusty baguette to soak up the sauce.

EVERYTHING'S COMING UP
ROSES

J'm in the kitchen at the rickety, makeshift worktop preparing vegetables to make soup. Suddenly, a shower of small stones, grit and earth begins to tumble from the ceiling, striking me on the head and landing on my freshly peeled carrots and parsnips. Clouds of choking dust follow, covering all the cooking utensils, jars of spices and bottles of oils and vinegars on the shelves above. Then another shower of grit and larger stones begins raining down on the plates and glasses unprotected in an alcove.

Mr V is directly above in the rose room. Either there's been an earthquake, or he's *not* cementing the wall beneath the window as he told me he was going to do. I yell upstairs for him to stop and ask what he's doing.

He responds with one of his stock answers. 'I am working.'

'Well, whatever you're *working* at, stop,' I reply. 'There's a terrible mess in the kitchen.'

His routine response to every disaster follows. 'It is nothing.'

I run upstairs to see exactly how much 'nothing' he's doing. As I approach the rose room, the dust is getting thicker and catching the back of my throat. I open the door, and a great gust of it escapes. I can hardly see Mr V who is covered from head to foot in a fine grey powder; only the skin around his eyes, protected by goggles, is visible. He's got a hammer in his hand and is smashing away at the layer of cement on the floor. This is something we'd planned to do, but not before clearing the rooms below and putting protective sheeting across the ceiling beams to limit the mess and prevent damage to the unprotected freezer and washing machine, not to mention injury to me.

I can't risk going into the room as shrapnel is flying everywhere, and he's oblivious to the fact that I'm standing at the door, so I throw a chunk of cement, which hits him on his shoulder. *Now* I have his attention. He turns angrily, about to retaliate, but sees how angry *I* am so meekly follows me downstairs.

'*Oh putain*,' (I won't translate!) is now his response, followed by the classic, 'Why did you not move things?'

I explode, as if he'd told me what he intended to do when I specifically asked this morning, then I would have done so, and I certainly would *not* have been merrily chopping vegetables in the direct line of fire.

Mr V now starts tacking great swathes of polythene to the ceiling, while I am moving all the items from the shelves and worktops and putting them in the garden to clean. I then brush all the debris onto the floor, which is now an inch deep in grit. Using a brush is sending even more dust into the air, so I suck it all up with the nozzle of the industrial vacuum. Finally I tackle cleaning the floor, once with the mop then again with the steam cleaner, as there's so much residual dust, it's turning to mud.

Two hours later, all is clean and sparkling. The reason that there was so much mess has become apparent. Beneath the cement were *tomettes*, the ancient, red square tiles found in all old French houses, then beneath them were the floorboards, thick planks of wood like roughly hewn railway sleepers with four or five centimetres of uneven spaces between them packed with earth, grit and stones. It is this that had been falling through some seriously large gaps in the ceiling below, which weren't visible before as they were covered with tiles and cement. This packing is an ancient method that preceded the use of *tomettes*. The *tomettes* themselves were laid in 1835. I know this is the precise date as Mr V uncovered a tile with the name Jean Pitoche and this year engraved on it, so now I have another mission to see what I can find out about him.

This is not the only find. The floor level is now a good twelve centimetres below where it was, revealing part of the exterior wall not previously visible. Embedded there we have found a rifle bullet that looks as if it has been shot from the outside in the direction of the upstairs of the house. Again, I would like to find out where this originated, the most likely explanation being that it came from a German gun firing at Resistance fighters who may have been using Les Libellules as cover; the floors and walls are certainly beginning to talk. Alas, they haven't revealed the whereabouts of any hidden treasure—yet.

✳   ✳   ✳

The fact that I was making soup indicates that although the weather is fine and dry, the temperature is still fresh, so it's *fondant au chocolat* weather. This is one of Mr V's favourite desserts—you'll see why.

This recipe was given to me by my Parisian friend, Marie, and, as everything that I cook in my make-do kitchen, it's incredibly simple but incredibly impressive. The recipe is for two generous portions, but don't be tempted to stretch it to three as it doesn't work; just make sure you have left plenty of room for dessert.

MARIE'S FONDANT AU CHOCOLAT

Makes two generous individual portions

Ingredients

30 g (1 oz) caster sugar
1 tbsp cornflour
1 medium egg, beaten
100 g (4 oz) dark cooking chocolate
60 g (2 oz) mascarpone

Method

Mix the sugar with the cornflour.

Add the egg and whisk with a small hand whisk until the mixture pales.

Melt the chocolate and mascarpone in a medium-power (400–500 watts) microwave, 30-second bursts at a time, stirring well each time.

Add the chocolate to the egg mixture a spoonful at a time until completely blended and free of any lumps.

Put into crème brûlée dishes (if you don't have any, use ramekins, but I find a wider, flatter dish works better, giving a larger, crisp shell and gooey middle).

Bake in a preheated oven at 160 C/gas mark 3 for ten minutes until the top is firm.

Allow to cool for two minutes before serving and eat from the outside, dragging the hot chocolate sauce out from the middle.

This really is an amazingly simple dessert. I always have all the ingredients measured out in their basins ready to prepare it at the last minute.

What I've learnt today: Preparation (and information) is the key to everything.

SHIPSHAPE AND BRISTOL
FASHION

*I*t seems to have become fashionable in the hamlet to invite us into people's homes. Today we're out for a before-dinner stroll and are beckoned into the house of Maurice and Josephine, a rather reserved couple in their mid-seventies. It is an impressive, double-fronted building on the edge of the hamlet that used to be the *gendarmerie* (police station) but now more resembles an elegant stately home. We go up the steps leading to the imposing front door and enter into what I would describe as a salon, a sort of entrance hall-cum-sitting room. A pale-yellow and green striped Regency-style sofa with matching chairs are grouped around a low, cream-coloured table with Queen Anne legs. The floor is highly polished chestnut parquet, and the almost floor-to-ceiling windows are draped with heavy brocade curtains held in place by barley-twist tiebacks the same colour as the sofa. On the walls hang what I believe are original paintings, many with a Russian theme, one being a charcoal sketch of Tolstoy. The Russian influence continues to dominate the room with an enormous, 19th-century silver samovar that Maurice tells us came from a Russian retirement home in Paris.

We are led into another room that is also filled with elaborately framed oil paintings, but a really unusual bed with an intricately carved wooden frame dominates the space. The headboard and footboard have rolled tops that curve outwards, putting me in mind of a sleigh.

'This is a traditional Norman bed,' explains Josephine.

Mr V, who is Norman by birth, tells her that his grandmother had an almost identical bed that he remembers from childhood. The couple are looking to downsize, and I would love to buy this from them, but it's only three-quarter size and not wide enough for two people. This leaves me yearning for a third bedroom, and I'm even considering putting the bed in the garden room, but at the moment there is simply no space.

We go back through the salon, and Maurice takes us into his study. He was a naval officer, and the room is full of maritime paraphernalia. At the side of the window is a mirror made from a porthole, and next to the door a large brass floating compass like something from the *Titanic*. Sextants and telescopes and other nautical instruments are displayed on shelves and small pedestal tables; there's even a bosun's whistle, which Maurice demonstrates. This makes me feel a stab of nostalgia for my former job as a theatre[1] nurse, as it's the exact same sound that the anaesthetic machine makes when the oxygen supply to the patient is running low, and it is indeed referred to by this name. The walls in this room are full of paintings of ships and seascapes, and maps and charts in wooden frames. Large, fragile-looking models of sailing ships sit landlocked on the top of tall cabinets, and to my delight, something that has always enthralled me, ships in bottles act as bookends on an upturned rowing boat that has been sawn in half and is serving as a bookcase.

It's here that we meet the family pets: a white pug, also with Queen Anne legs, that looks as if it's about to pee against my boot, and a nut-brown sausage dog with a bark ten times greater than its size. The pug is growling now and pulling at the hem of Mr V's trousers. I think it's because to them we must smell like an entire cattery has just walked through the door. Dogs snapping at our heels, we enter a sunny, dual-aspect drawing/dining room. The drawing room area has views over the large, beautifully kept garden. Lilac and magnolia trees are already in full bloom, and a wisteria bine gracing a wall to the side is heavy with flowers forming a lavender-blue canopy around the windows.

Inside there's a dresser displaying a fine bone-china dinner service with ladies and gentlemen lounging on the grass in 18th-century attire similar to those on the music box that Mr V gave me for a New Year's gift last year. But the most striking feature of this room is a cherry-wood, double-turned staircase which is wide enough for a lady in a crinoline dress to descend.

As the French are not generally in the habit of showing people around their houses, although we're delighted that they're doing so, we feel a bit confused as to why we're here. Heaven forbid they think we are potential buyers; this place must be worth at least ten times Les Libellules…

We're now drinking tea in the drawing room from equally elegant bone-china cups to those on the dresser. Mr V's fingers are far too big to thread through the harp-shaped handle, so he takes the cup in his hand like a beaker, almost dropping it as it burns his fingers.

'You like the tea set?' Josephine asks.

'Yes,' I reply. The cups are as fine as eggshells; too fine to be fully white, they filter the muted colours of all that is behind them. They're decorated with tiny sprigs of blue flowers, whose imperfections show that they've been painted by hand.

'Would you like them?'

I hesitate, not sure what is being offered. They look as if they're worth a fair amount of money, more money than we have to spend on cups with a hundred and one other things to buy.

'I would like to give them to you as a present.'

Again I hesitate because we have absolutely nowhere to put them, as Les Libellules is still a virtual building site. I see disappointment begin to cloud Josephine's face.

'I would love them, thank you very much,' I say.

So, here we are, each carrying a box of antique, hand-painted crockery. I have the cups and Mr V the saucers and cake plates. I'm not sure why Josephine wanted me to have them, but she obviously did. If only she'd offered me the bed...

What I've learnt today: Many members of the Russian aristocracy fled to Paris during the Russian Revolution, which is ironic when you think that it was inspired by the French Revolution 130 years earlier.

———————————————

1. Operating room.

DANCING IN THE MOONLIGHT

*C*eline has just called out of the blue to ask me if I'd like to go to a local farmers' market with her. I find this as odd as the offer of the tea set, as although we're now friendly, we're not what I'd consider friends. The market is held every Wednesday and Friday at the nearby village of Marcilly-Ogny, and as today is Friday, it's an evening market beginning at 5:30 and closing at 7:30, or when everything has been sold.

The village is nearer than I thought, and I wonder why we've never ventured up here before. But there's no sign of the bustling street market that I was expecting. Celine parks the car on a grass verge at the side of the road, and we walk twenty metres towards what look like double garage doors. And there is the market—in a garage, a large one granted, but still a garage.

There are only seven stalls, three each side, and the renowned bread stall taking pride of place stretched across the back. Everything on sale is locally produced, but it's the bread that's the big crowd-puller. Most people telephone their advance orders, but I have to take pot luck on what's left. The bread is made with flour milled from wheat grown by the family that bake it. Celine fills her basket with her pre-ordered baguettes and *petits pains* (an assortment of rolls). I select a rustic granary loaf from the dwindling basket of 'extras'.

Bread secured, we browse the other stalls. The first has a selection of seasonal salad and vegetables. The day has been unseasonably hot and the late evening sun warm and mellow, but we're still only at the end of March, so the choice is limited. There's Swiss chard, spinach, leeks and the most enormous radishes I've ever seen. I buy a bunch and am warned to be careful, as they're extra hot. But for someone brought up on extra-hot curries in the UK, extra-hot radishes hold no fear.

Next is the egg counter. I buy a box of six feather-laden eggs of assorted shapes and sizes. I'm being drawn by what looks like pizza with a base as thin as a crêpe. I ask what the toppings are. One is goat's cheese and red peppers, which looks delicious. I do wish I liked goat's cheese. The other is duck with mushrooms. I'm not sure how duck will go down on a pizza, but I buy it anyway; it will save me from cooking later. The base, like the bread, is made with home-milled flour, so that at least should be good.

We're now at the cake stall. There are various tempting tarts, but my attention is caught by individual tiramisus made with lychee and raspberry. I buy two, so that's the starter, main and dessert. Now I just need cheese which is, as I expected, *fromage de chèvre*, from their own goats, naturally. Once again, I really wish that I liked it. It looks amazing—little, fluffy rounds like truffles rolled in fresh herbs and spices, others drizzled with honey and studded with chopped hazelnuts. I buy one with honey for Mr V, as he has a very sweet tooth.

'Are you in a rush to get back?' asks Celine.

With dinner literally in the bag, I say I'm not.

'Good. There's somewhere I'd like to show you.'

We return to the car and head back the way we came, but at the point where we would have turned right, we go straight ahead through picturesque villages of russet stone and fields of wheat the colour of pea soup. We pass under a low-arched bridge and mount a steep, tree-lined road that becomes narrower the higher we climb. Narrower and darker, not just due to the trees whose branches almost meet above us.

The heat and sun have disappeared with the passing beneath the bridge, and it's as if we've entered another kingdom. A wall, the same russet stone as the village houses, runs along the road on our right, behind which is, I presume, a vineyard. Celine makes an abrupt right turn down an even narrower lane lined on both sides by tall trees kept in check by a similar wall.

It's begun to rain, and the gloom enveloping us is really eerie now after the bonhomie of the market. The car comes to a halt in front of a grey stone wall with an open gateway leading to an isolated clearing bordered on three sides by pines and spruces. The fourth gives views across a sweeping landscape of meadows with grazing cattle.

Alone in the centre of the clearing is what I first think is a stone hut or dwelling, but as we walk closer, I see it's a tiny chapel.

'The Chapel of St Martin,' says Celine. 'This site is protected by a foundation created to safeguard French art and heritage. It's interesting not just because it is very old, having been built in the 12th century, but also because of the roof which is made of *lauze*[1] tiles usually associated with Périgord Noir in the southwest of France.'

I look up at the roof; the tiles really are distinctive, overlaying each other in an almost scallop-shell pattern. Celine, it seems, is a bit of an aficionado.

The ancient building looks forlorn in the centre of the vast clearing.

'Is it always this deserted?' I ask.

Celine explains that people still come here on *la fête patronale*, a fête day when homage is paid to the patron saint of the village—in this case St Martin. She can't remember when this is but tells me we must come as there are fireworks and other festivities. But other than that, yes, it's always deserted.

Behind the chapel a natural spring flows like a fountain, swelled with the recent rain. The water trickles away to join a stream that descends towards the farmland. I wander off, taking photos. The rain has stopped, bringing a freshness to the air which carries the scent of ferns. At the edge of the clearing are large, rectangular stones that resemble tombstones, lying under eons of moss.

'This was a cemetery in the 12th century,' Celine confirms. 'But I think the last burials took place here during the 15th.'

There's a heavy sense of presence, and it's not all good. Unlike the nurturing presence of the past that exudes from the stones of Les Libellules, there is something slightly sinister here.

'This was a place of pilgrimage long before there was a chapel, a Pagan place of worship,' says Celine.

There's a large, flat stone set apart from the tombs, older and elevated slightly like an altar. I can imagine maidens in oatmeal-coloured, homespun gowns with flowers in their hair doing a ritualistic dance in the moonlight. I feel a chill even though the sun has returned. Ankle-deep steam rises from the damp earth. Celine looks as if she is floating. I suddenly have the urge to leave. I don't think I'd like to be here alone at night.

As we emerge from under the arched bridge, all returns to how it was. Rosy-roofed *pigeonniers* rise like friendly giants above cottages with invitingly open, sage-green shutters and gaily coloured geraniums spilling over window boxes.

I breathe a sigh of relief. I've seldom had such an overwhelming sense of disquiet in a place.

What I've learnt today: Duck breast goes surprisingly well on a pizza.

⚰ ⚰ ⚰

As it's been such a warm evening, more like May than March, I'm outside listening to the sounds of the night. An unpleasant, rasping scream rises above the crickets and cicadas—a fox's mating call, two foxes in fact.

The sound is both harsh and haunting and sends a chill through me. I gather up my things and head indoors. We're leaving tomorrow, and when we return it will be April and the real start of spring—my favourite time of year.

---

1. A traditional roof covering made from finely cut stones overlaid in a scallop shape.

PART V
THE PASTEL PALETTE OF PRINTEMPS

APRIL AND MAY 2019

While human ingenuity may devise various inventions to the same ends, it will never devise anything more beautiful, nor more simple, nor more to the purpose than nature does, because in her inventions nothing is lacking and nothing is superfluous.
Leonardo da Vinci

SPRING CLEAN

*T*oday is the first of April—April Fools' Day to you and me—
and indeed the French have their own version—*la Fête du
Poisson d'Avril* (the April Festival of Fish). I don't know how I've lived
in France almost thirteen years and this has escaped my notice.
Boulangeries up and down the land are baking bread in the form of a
fish; patisseries are making little, seafood-shaped pastries, and the
freezer shop is selling fish-shaped choc ices. There's a report on TV
showing school children painting brightly coloured paper fish to hang
like garlands around their classrooms and then playing April Fools'
tricks by sticking them onto the backs of unsuspecting classmates and
teachers. You can even download printable fish from the internet. No
one seems to be able to tell me why; it's as big a mystery as the
chocolate fish and lobsters sold here at Easter.

Today is also Monday. We've stayed an extra night to deep-clean
the house. My daughter Kate is coming to Les Libellules at the
weekend for the first time, and she's allergic to dust and cats, both of
which we have in abundance. All the bedding, sofa throws and
cushion covers have been washed, and Flaubertine banned from the
house. I've removed the cobwebs from between the rafters and pulled
out furniture to harvest *les moutons* (dust balls—literally 'sheep')

gathered underneath, which is fortunate as the nursery cupboard in the living room was harbouring a dead mouse behind it. Kate has a great love of animals, so I will keep this particular snippet of information from her, until of course she reads this.

What I've learnt today: I've discovered a possible explanation for the April Fool fish. One theory is that the fishing season in Brittany begins in April, but only foolish fishermen go out in their boats this early as the catch is small and not worth the trouble. But this is just one of numerous theories, so who knows?

Kate has arrived, and Les Libellules has cast its spell over her in a heartbeat; even Flaubertine has seduced her and is cooing at her feet. I'm so relieved that Kate feels at home here despite all the renovations. She's outside now, photographing everything, but notably cats. Flaubertine, who's usually the most difficult subject to capture unless she's asleep, is posing like a pro for Kate.

Thankfully the weather has held, and we're able to have lunch on the terrace, accompanied by a symphony of bees busy in the Japanese azalea. I've made a red pepper and feta cheese quiche, and we're enjoying a chilled glass of rosé. It has made me complete to have my daughter here, and I long for the day when both of my girls can be here at the same time, all three of us cooking and eating together around a large table.

Lunch over, we're on our way to visit the woods. The last time Mr V and I were there with Jacques, we must have taken the long way around, as it was at least twenty minutes by car. This time we're here in just under ten. The woods are not so picturesque as when I first saw them in all their autumn splendour, as most of the trees are still in bud, but Kate is enchanted and happy that she's the first visitor to come here. We're tramping through the overgrown paths, searching for good places to make secret clearings and mentally mapping out narrow, winding trails leading to them. I'm imagining tiny feet following signs to find the hidden treasures. Brambles are snatching at our jeans, forcing us to stop and disentangle ourselves, with every stop presenting a photo opportunity.

Mr V has his woodman head on. Dressed virtually all in green, he's disappeared into the trees to dig up the earth to plant some of his saplings. The only clue that he's here is the thwack of soil beneath his spade and the crack of twigs beneath his boots. Job done, he emerges, striding like a dryad from amongst the mossy trunks, carrying armfuls of deadwood for the fire.

Kate grasps my arm and says, 'Just look at him, Mam.'

I understand what she means. It fills me full of joy to see him in his element; after so many years of not even having a small garden, he now has his own wood.

* * *

It's 7 p.m. at the end of Kate's first day here. We're sitting on the terrace, sipping Kir Royales and dipping baguette into the remains of the feta cheese marinated in olive oil. The sun is low in the west, casting a golden glow over the garden, and insects float like motes of dust in the haze. Mr V joins us on the terrace for a Kir. The evening is too pleasant to waste precious time cooking, so I leave him talking to Kate and go indoors to prepare an extended apéritif. Kate is vegetarian, so I rustle up some homemade hummus with carrot and pepper batons, a dish of preserved red bell peppers stuffed with olives, another baguette, cheese and a large bowl of green salad leaves with sliced avocado. To keep Mr V satisfied, I add slices of dry-cured sausage, *cornichons* (tiny gherkins) and one of his favourites—rillettes *de thon* (tuna rillettes) with crispbread rolls. A veritable al fresco feast.

Rillettes *de thon* is one of my most popular apéritif dishes. It's incredibly simple to make, and there's never a scrap left in the dish for Pussy Willow. Here's the recipe if you'd like to try it.

RILLETTES DE THON

Makes 2 flat 8 cm (3 in) diameter crème brûlée dishes full

Ingredients

160 g (5½ oz) can of tuna in sunflower oil (you can use tuna in water, but oil preserves more of the vitamins from the fish and is tastier)
1 tbsp crème fraîche
1 tsp English mustard (less vinegary and stronger than French mustard)
2 tsp capers
Cayenne pepper to taste

Method

Drain the tuna of all excess oil (or water) and mix in a basin with the crème fraîche and mustard.

Add the capers and transfer to serving dishes.

Cover with cling film and chill in the refrigerator for at least 30 minutes.

Sprinkle with cayenne pepper and serve with warm toast or crusty French bread.

That's all there is to it.

GOING PAST THE APRICOTS

*K*ate and I have been walking in the hills behind the hamlet and are now in the village close to Jacqueline's house. Jacqueline must have a hidden antenna to detect when I'm approaching, as once again she appears out of her front door like the little woman in a German weather house. Her face lights up when she sees me, making it impossible to refuse her invitation to come inside. Kate is hesitant as she doesn't speak French, but the warmth of the welcome surpasses all her misgivings, and she's now installed at the opposite end of the oval dining table from me while Jacqueline puts the kettle on and produces a tin of her homemade, crumbly fruitcake. I chat away, translating the gist of the conversation for Kate, who finds that she can understand a lot more than she thought she would be able to, even if she can't talk back.

Then Jacqueline decides to call her nephew and his wife who are working in her garden to ask them to come in as they both speak a little English. This is such a thoughtful gesture, though Kate was perfectly happy just us three.

Now there are five of us around the table; the nephew, whose English is *not* that great, is sitting next to me, and his wife, whose

English is excellent, is sitting next to Kate. They discover that they are both teachers, so they're discussing education.

Jacqueline's neighbour Janine has just arrived and sits the other side of Kate. She hasn't come alone, however; she's brought a 'nice young man' in tow—her grandson, who's visiting from Strasbourg for the weekend—who Jacqueline seats between her nephew and his wife. We're now all practically elbow to elbow, squashed together in a bizarre, franglais tea party. The intention of the two elderly ladies is clearly to try their hands at matchmaking as they are bristling with anticipation, their tiny, dark eyes sparkling in their crumpled faces. The young man is around 22 years old; Kate is 31 and married. No one has cottoned on to this fact. Jacqueline asks the young man what he is studying at university; the answer naturally is engineering—the go-to subject for young French men. She then turns to Kate and asks the same question. Kate looks embarrassed and says that she's not studying anything and that she is in fact a teacher. Now it's the turn of everyone else to look embarrassed. Jacqueline asks her age, and when Kate replies, they all gasp, having thought that she was about 18, and that I, of course, was far too young to have a daughter aged 31...

The young man, however, looks relieved, as he probably realised he was being set up as bait. It transpires that, like Kate, he's done a fair amount of travelling, and his English is reasonable, so the two of them strike up a stilted conversation about various places around the world that they've both visited.

Meanwhile I've struck up a conversation in French with the nephew, who proceeds to speak about the history of the house and how a box of letters was found after Jacqueline moved in. The letters had been written by a Napoleonic soldier who was on both the Italy and Egypt campaigns and wrote every week to his sweetheart who lived in the village. I would dearly love to get my hands on these. I imagine an epic story of love and war written around their contents and see myself as a latter-day Tolstoy. But it's his brother who has them now. The nephew tells me that he'll try to have them photocopied for me. He also tells me that this soldier's grave is in the cemetery at the top of the village.

*   *   *

Kate and I are scouring the cemetery for an ancient grave that has a bridge chiselled on the headstone, the problem being, all the graves in this part of the cemetery are so old and worn it's difficult to make anything out. We're almost about to give up, thinking that we must have missed it, when I remind myself of my motto to 'go past the apricots'. This originated from spending a good twenty minutes in a wholefood store looking for something, I can't remember what, but I got as far as the dried apricots then gave up and left the shop. I discovered later that whatever it was that I was looking for was right next to the apricots. If I'd not given up, I would have found it within seconds. This is now my rule of life, so we press on until we're almost at the gate leading out of the cemetery where I see an old, dilapidated grave, its headstone worn smooth by time and the elements.

It's set a little way back, so we have to weave our way between other graves, stepping over urns of dead flowers to reach it. The inscription has been completely weathered away, but there in the arch of the headstone, I can clearly make out the form of a bridge. My arms break out in goosebumps, thinking of the life that the man lying to rest beneath this tomb must have led, what sights he had seen. Had he actually met Napoleon? I think also of his love for the young woman he wrote to each week. No doubt they were married when he returned, probably in this very church. As I don't have a name to research, my questions go unanswered. I wish I could get my hands on those letters.

What I've learnt today: Always follow my own advice and go past the apricots.

A RAINY NIGHT IN DIJON

he weather hasn't held, and clouds are gathering in the east as we head in that direction for a mini sojourn in Dijon. Mr V is going to drop Kate and me in the small city centre then continue to drive back to Paris. We're staying in a *chambre d'hôte* for the night then taking the train to the Gare de Lyon tomorrow.

We pass through numerous vineyards of baby vines no higher than a dandelion, laid out in neat rows full of hope and anticipation of a good harvest come autumn. The imposing rocks of *les Roches de Baume* loom grey and foreboding on our left, blending with the bland, colourless sky. Without sunlight to brighten it, the Burgundy Canal is like a dull sliver of mercury. Still, I'm happy that Kate has been able to spend quality time in the garden at Les Libellules and visit the woods without sinking ankle deep into mud. I'm happy also to be finally visiting this historic city after almost two years of being confined to DIY and furniture stores which form a concrete fortress between the vineyards and the town.

※ ※ ※

The *chambre d'hôte* is situated in the old town on a cobbled medieval street of half-timbered houses whose upper storeys overhang a graceful colonnade of stone arches, behind which bow-windowed shops display antiques, luxury goods, stylish ladies' fashions and the most delightful children's garments. But as it's Sunday, all are closed, plus it's begun to rain, so we go straight to our destination.

We arrive at a nondescript door with disappointingly plain windows either side and are greeted by a diminutive Japanese lady who introduces herself as Yuka, speaking French with a soft, oriental accent. Yuka takes us down a narrow hallway with a colourful tiled floor and heavy, wooden doors along the right-hand side bearing the room names on small, porcelain plaques. At the end of the hallway is a pleasant courtyard garden, and here is the door to our room. It has a much older appearance than the others we've passed, framed by large, angled stones in the shape of a Gothic arch, giving the sense of entering a cathedral or castle. Yuka turns a large key in an equally large keyhole, presses down on the latch, and the door swings open onto a scene straight out of a fairy tale.

A sumptuous four-poster bed with heavy brocade drapes and golden canopy dominates the room. Kate and I gasp; we both agree that this would be the ideal place for a romantic mini break, rather than an overnight stop for a mother and daughter.

The floor is laid with Versailles-style herringbone parquet, which Yuka tells us was once gracing the rooms of a Norman château. The door to the bathroom came from the same château and is also surrounded by large stones which she says are between twenty and thirty kilogrammes a piece. The walls, which are painted a barely detectable shade of pistachio, have Rococo-style panels and mock-Grecian columns. Angels bearing candle-shaped light bulbs are on three of the walls, the fourth being hidden behind an enormous wardrobe with wooden cherubs adorning wide, barley-twist poles either side of the doors. One door is set with an elongated oval mirror, the type that makes the reflection of the room behind seem as if it stretches into another world.

We do indeed feel as if we've entered another world, or another time, to be precise. A Regency-style chair is next to a little, kidney-shaped writing desk tucked away in a corner, and beside the window overlooking the tiny garden, there is a table and two chairs, where tomorrow's breakfast will be served.

＊ ＊ ＊

We have a table reserved for 7:30 at one of the few restaurants open on a Sunday evening offering a vegetarian option. The fact that Kate is vegetarian made my task of making a dinner reservation doubly difficult, as we're in the land of beef and snails, and even fish is hard to come by.

The restaurant is in a residential area in the opposite direction to the city centre, and, though little more than a café with Formica tables and hard-backed, wooden chairs, it's almost full when we arrive. The owner, Christophe, a larger-than-life character who speaks excellent English with a Cockney accent due to his years working as a chef in the southeast of London, leads us to a table by the window, overlooking a block of flats. Not ideal, but we were driven here through lack of choice. There's no menu, hence no prices, but the other diners are made up from a mixture of mainly locals and a handful of tourists, which is a good sign. I have a choice of steak, duck and the dreaded *tête de veau*. I opt for the duck, much to Kate's distaste. The vegetarian option is just a plate of rice, chips and mixed veg, albeit fresh and seasonal. We're presented with complimentary Kirs and order a bottle of local Gamay.

Then the cabaret starts with Christophe putting on a one-waiter floor show, telling jokes, teasing customers, swirling cocktail shakers and whipping out an enormous, flame-throwing blowtorch to caramelise the crème brûlée, which we also order. Christophe has taken a bit of a shine to me. He pulls up a chair at our table, opens another bottle of wine and pours all three of us a glass, again allegedly on the house. I think he would like us to stay drinking with him, but most of the other diners have left, and I don't want to be put in a compromising position (he's already given me his phone number), so we say our *au revoirs* and assure him next time we are in Dijon, we shall return. Although this may not have been one of the best meals we've ever eaten, we were warm, dry and well fed in good company, plus the bill was remarkably reasonable.

The rain has stopped when we leave the restaurant, but the pavements are still glistening in the dark, reflecting the lights and colours of the city. We wind our way through narrow, cobbled streets where the roofs of the buildings are straining like separated lovers longing to meet in the night sky. We find ourselves in la Place François Rude,[1] a quaint square surrounded by steep-roofed, half-timbered houses, more German than French in appearance. In the centre of the square is a sleeping fountain, with the statue of a rather well-proportioned naked youth in the centre. Next to the fountain is a forlorn-looking carousel, its gaily painted horses half hidden under green tarpaulin. Apart from us, the place is deserted and slightly creepy. I'm half expecting the Child Catcher from *Chitty Chitty Bang Bang* to appear and offer us lollipops. We're not sure of the way back to the *chambre d'hôte*, but the strikingly tall tower of the Tour Philippe le Bon, which is bizarrely floodlit in candy pink, acts as a beacon to point us in the right general direction.

The tower leads us to la Place de la Libération and the fabulously illuminated Palais des Ducs. La Place de la Libération is a sweeping, semi-circular piazza surrounded by an elegant arcade of shops, bars and restaurants. Miraculously, one of the bars is open, so we go for a nightcap. We're now seated outside under the benevolent glow of a heater, with soft, red blankets to warm our shoulders and knees, sipping glasses of soft, red *vin de Bourgogne* to warm our insides. The *palais* is stretched out in front of us like a panorama bathed in warm, golden light. Jets from fountains set into the pavestones are rising and falling in sequence in an elegant water ballet. Inside the almost-empty bar, a pianist is playing some laid-back jazz melody, and the notes come drifting out to reach us, a completely different kind of floor show from the one we've just left. We take our time sipping our wine, savouring the moment. A classy way to end a not-so-classy evening.

---

1. François Rude is the name of the sculptor who created the detail on Porte Guillaume, Dijon's 18th-century Arc de Triomphe.

THE TRAIL OF THE OWL

*A*fter a blissful night's sleep in the four-poster bed, I'm awakened by a gentle knock on the door. I open it to find Yuka there with a tray laden with what I imagine is breakfast for two. She sets it down on the table by the window then disappears to return with a second, almost identical, tray. I honestly don't know where to begin. I start by savouring a dish of fluffy scrambled egg and a platter of ham and cheese. Next, I'm faced with buttery croissants, lightly toasted baguette and pains aux raisins, spirals of flaky pastry filled with custard and raisins. The croissants are melt-in-your-mouth crumbly and the pains aux raisins finger-licking delicious. This is all served with little pots of homemade pineapple and red currant jam and rolls of pale-yellow butter. There's a jug of freshly squeezed orange juice, and pots of fragrant fruity tea and milky coffee, plus a yogurt I'll save for later. A feast fit for a Burgundy duke, after which we set off to explore the town in daylight.

We follow the trail of the Owl of Dijon, a tiny stone figurine carved into the wall of the church of Notre Dame. Legend has it that if you stroke the owl with your left hand then your heartfelt wish will come true; as a result the owl has been stroked as smooth as a pebble. The trail is marked by little bronze owls embedded into the pavement, guiding visitors to all the important sights in the city. Even on a damp Monday morning in early April, the town is full of tourists, mainly French, American and Japanese, all holding maps at various angles, trying to follow the trail. Kate and I, being a pair of maverick tourists, are vaguely following the trail in the opposite direction.

As we're a stone's throw from the church, we begin here. It is this church, or rather its clock tower, that really ignited my interest in visiting Dijon after discovering the legend of Les Jacquelines[1] on an old confectionery box in the *pigeonnier* last year. I wanted to see, or rather hear, for myself the four automatons who in turn strike the hour, half hour and quarter hours. The 13th-century church is a Gothic masterpiece with a facade of 51 foreboding gargoyles. In fact only the ones on the sides originate from the 13th century. The story goes that a young man coming to the church to be married was crushed to death by a falling gargoyle, so they were all removed to be replaced by lighter, less dangerous copies in 1880. Still, they look spectacularly authentic when viewed from the ground.

Dijon is so small, you stumble upon the next historic building almost as soon as you have left the last. We're once again at la Place de la Libération and le Palais des Ducs to visit the fabulous chamber of the tombs. The stone likenesses of Jean sans Peur (John the Fearless), his wife, Margeurite de Bavière (Margaret of Bavaria), and his father, Philippe le Hardi (Philip the Bold), are laid out in splendid royal regalia on plinths supported by exquisitely carved ivory clergy and mourners. Guarded by golden-maned lions at their feet and golden-winged cherubs at their heads, the figures are clothed in celestial blue and white robes and equal anything I've seen at the Basilica of Saint Denis in Paris.

Philip the Bold is a renowned figure in the wine world and is considered the father of Burgundy wines. He introduced the Pinot Noir grape to the region in 1395 and wrote an edict banning the more robust, but bitter-tasting, *Gaamez* (Gamay) variety. Hence Pinot Noir was established as the only grape recognised in Burgundy. This edict became the origin of mono-grape cultivation and was way ahead of its time, preceding the AOC (appellation d'origine côntrolée) by 600 years.

The white Chardonnay grape joined the red Pinot Noir, bringing Burgundy wines world fame, and bringing me much pleasure.

＊　＊　＊

The rain has begun again, so we shelter in a snug little crêperie within the sound of the bells of Notre Dame until it eases off, then go in search of mustard. You can't think of Dijon without thinking of mustard; it's what the town is famous for. We don't have to look far; there's an abundance of shops, their windows displaying colourful jars of it in more flavours than I could ever imagine: pale-green tarragon, bright-green basil, nut-brown walnut, deep-yellow curry, earthy-red *piment d'Espelette* (a fiery condiment made from peppers that grow in Espelette in Southwest France), earthy-orange *pain d'épices*, dark-pink cassis, pale-purple lavender and even a dark-purple Pinot Noir. We're spoilt for choice. I buy a selection of six miniature jars to sample some of the more unusual flavours like *pain d'épices* and a large jar of the traditional wholegrain.

＊　＊　＊

Next stop is an entire shop dedicated to the local, gooey ginger loaf, *pain d'épices*, again in more flavours than imaginable: honey, walnut, orange, almond, and chocolate, to name but a few. As it's almost Easter, there's an Easter tree in the window with sugar icing-coated gingerbread decorations hanging from its branches, surrounded by a woodland scene of gingerbread biscuits shaped like rabbits, bells, chicks and lambs. In fact, all the shops appear to have gone to town with their Easter windows, displaying springtime flowers and decorative eggs nestling in baskets on beds of powder-pink, lilac and pale-green tissue paper. I buy a honey-flavoured loaf for Mr V and Kate an orange one to take back to the UK.

We wander through the streets towards Jardin Darcy, a small park with a replica of the François Pompon[2] polar bear, as we have at Saulieu. The park is a lovely little oasis in the city with balustraded terraces and shady areas to sit and watch the world go by. An array of spring flowers carpets the lawns, and an elegant, Italian-style fountain cascades into a turquoise pool. I would love to linger and take more photos, but time is running short, so we head in the general direction of the station.

On the way, we pass the Cathédrale Saint-Bénigne, which looks bland and nondescript compared to Notre Dame church, then we look up and see the fabulous polychrome-tiled roof and towers that this region is famous for, with zigzag and diamond patterns in red, green, black and gold. Once more I marvel at the craftsmanship it has taken to produce these magnificent structures.

It's now started to rain heavily again, so we make our way to the station to have a coffee before taking the TGV back to Paris.

We have both fallen in love with Dijon; in a nutshell, it has everything that you could need, and I can't wait to return.

What I've learnt today: The TGV (train à grande vitesse), France's high-speed train service, travels at speeds up to 320 km per hour (200 mph). Our train back to Paris clocked an average speed of 297 km per hour.

---

1. The collective name for the four automated figures in the bell tower of the church: Jacquemart, who strikes the hour; his wife, Jacqueline, who strikes the half hour, and their children, Jacquelinet and Jacquelinette, who strike the quarters.
2. A French sculptor born in Saulieu, known for his animal sculptures, notably a polar bear.

GARDENING BY NUMBERS

*M*r V and I are taking a leisurely drive down to Les Libellules with Pussy Willow, who is standing on my knee like a small dog, admiring the countryside as it drifts past. It's a glorious spring morning, and as we've left at the crack of dawn, we've missed the Easter holiday rush.

The fields are once again startling yellow with rapeseed flowers, but the sky is still the milky blue of early morning. The hill of happiness looks as if it's been divided in two. The top, where it's bathed in gentle sunlight, is the colour of pale apples, while the bottom, remaining in shade, is the deep blue/green of a dense pine forest.

Today is Good Friday. It's only been five days since we were last here, but so much has changed in the garden. The Japanese azalea has been drunk dry by the bees, and although still charming, has lost much of its former glory. The grass is a mass of dandelions, but without the abundance of rain we had last year, the wild primroses are much thinner on the ground. The bluebells haven't materialised either, and only one solitary tulip is poking its head above the long grass.

Maybe the good weather has tricked me into thinking it's later in the season than it really is. I'm sure the apple tree was in blossom this time last year, but hopefully it will bless me with blossom next weekend. One little tree that hasn't disappointed though is Lila. She has not only survived both the winter and the injuries that she sustained last summer at the hands of Mr V's strimmer, but though still not tall, seems to be flourishing, and the buds that appeared in February have burst into an abundance of healthy leaves. I don't know how long it takes for lilac trees to flower, but if she keeps this progress up, maybe she will reward me with some next year.

I'm gardening by numbers again. In the absence of really knowing what I'm doing, I'm making it up as I go along, pruning the bush at the end of the terrace that went totally out of control last summer. I'm now snipping branches off at an angle just above a bud and hoping for the best. Last year I thought I'd killed the spindly rose bush, and that came back with a vengeance, so I hope to have a similar result. I'm also pulling up lots of dead, dried stems from another unidentified plant. I'm tying these into bundles with green gardeners' twine to provide kindling for the fire—nothing's wasted here.

I plan to stay for 23 days. Mr V must go to work from Tuesday to Friday next week, so this will be the first time I'll be at Les Libellules without him. As I'll be alone and the evenings are still chilly, I want to make life as simple as possible, so each bundle is the right size to light one fire. When I say alone, of course you are never alone here. Apart from Pussy Willow, who's staying with me, there's the ever-present Flaubertine, who I strongly suspect is pregnant again. Then there's the latest member of the cat clan, Gus, so named as he resembles the fat mouse in the Disney version of *Cinderella*. For all his size, Gus is the most timid of all the farm cats and remains behind the gate like a prisoner behind bars. You can see by the look on his face that he's dying to come into the garden with the others but just isn't brave enough.

DING DONG BELL

e're fighting a losing battle with the algae in the *mare*, so next weekend we're going to buy some plants to oxygenate the water. Sadly we've not heard the mating calls of amorous frogs; maybe this is due to the algae or maybe it's the below-average temperatures for the time of the year. We *have*, however, seen two tiny newts, so pond life has begun to return there after we drained it in the autumn. Speaking of the *mare*, I suppose it was bound to happen given her curious nature—Pussy Willow has fallen in. Like Narcissus, she was admiring her reflection and slipped on a rock, and in she tumbled. Fortunately she was able to scramble out, leaving a trail of water and algae across the terrace. Poor Pussy now looks like a scraggy kitten and seems to have lost half of her bulk. I, as usual, have been given the blame for this and have been slapped by a wet paw. Mr V has just exacerbated the situation by trying to dry her with a bright yellow bathmat, using the novel technique of throwing it on top of her. Pussy Willow now wants to get into the house, notably our bedroom, but she has to remain outside in the sunshine until she's dry.

Mr V says we'll have to get her a little boat, to which my response is naturally to recite:

The Owl and the Pussy-Cat went to sea
In a beautiful pea-green boat,
They took some honey, and plenty of money,
Wrapped up in a five-pound note.
The Owl looked up to the stars above,
And sang to a small guitar,
'O lovely Pussy! O Pussy, my love,
What a beautiful Pussy you are,
You are,
You are!
What a beautiful Pussy you are!'
'The Owl and The Pussy-Cat', Edward Lear

This conjures up an image of a little, pea-green boat and two small landing stages made of (non-slippery) rock on either side of the small stretch of water. I begin to fantasise again about the children who will go on treasure hunts in the wood, picturing them being ferried across the *mare* by Mr V in their own little boat. I voice my ideas, and hey presto, Jacques arrives right on cue. Naturally he knows two people who have little boats and might be willing to sell. I ask myself why not only one but two people in the vicinity of landlocked Burgundy would have a boat, and then I remember our proximity to the lakes in the Morvan National Park and make a mental note to visit again soon.

*　*　*

Pussy Willow is giving water a wide berth now, which is disturbing the crows, as in order to circumnavigate the *mare*, she is passing directly under the tall trees where the birds have built no less than seventeen nests. The crows have been noticeably quieter than last year, when I couldn't hear myself think for their constant cawing. I have a theory on this. The house having been empty for around three years, they had no one there to disturb them. The first year we arrived, it was the month of August, and their young were no longer vulnerable in the nests. Last year, however, we were resident when they were hatching their eggs, and I think this alarmed them. Now we're all just part of their extended family, all except for Pussy Willow; she is a cat and therefore a predator. Every time she slinks beneath their trees, they take to the air, flapping and cawing, but she just nonchalantly goes about her business, refamiliarising herself with her domain.

*   *   *

In contrast to the crows, the other birds who were sadly silent last year have rediscovered their voices, and their melodious tunes ring through the air as I write. The swallows have also returned in greater numbers and soar high in the sky, their fork tails black against the cerulean blue. The crows are not the only ones nest building. I have seen a number of sparrows, their beaks bulging with pine needles, passing under the gutter beneath the rose room, and I wonder if Mr V's recent demolition work has opened up a passage for them. There's a flurry of activity in the feather tree also, which is, as last year, the domain of the blue tits.

The one thing that has really taken me by surprise is that although we're surrounded by droves of farm cats and kittens, they seem to have little or no interest in birds. I think this is because mice are in such abundance and much easier to catch. The birds seem to sense this lack of feline threat. Yesterday two blue tits were pecking at the remains of a fat ball that had fallen from the tree onto the roof of Flaubertine's little shelter while Flaubertine dozed inside oblivious.

What I've learnt today: The old English word for mare *is* mere, *meaning a small lake, marsh or pond.*

EASTER LAMB

*L*ambs are once more bleating in the fields, though I haven't been lucky enough to see one being born this year. Today is Easter Sunday, and nor have I been lucky enough to receive a chocolate bunny, or anything chocolate for that matter. Mr V says it's to help me to fit comfortably back into my summer clothes for an early holiday that I've got planned in the Italian lakes with my daughter Kate—a treat from her for my birthday —but quite frankly this excuse is just adding insult to injury, and I've a good mind to bite the ears off the chocolate bunny that I bought for him.

Instead, to celebrate I'm going to make a typical Easter meal, with spring lamb, some early new potatoes, baby carrots and spring cabbage. I've made mint sauce with fresh mint picked from the garden mixed with a little sugar and some Chardonnay vinegar and added a teaspoon of this to the meat juices that I'm reducing to serve as a *jus* (a light gravy made from the meat juice). I've also speared the meat with some freshly cut sprigs of rosemary. The joy I feel cooking with fresh herbs from the garden is immense; this is all I've ever longed for, and I count my blessings. As I don't have a real oven at the moment, it's not possible for me to cook a whole leg of lamb, so I've bought two more manageable shanks, but the following recipe is for a leg joint.

SPRING LAMB

Serves 4 with meat enough for 8

Lamb
Ingredients

A 2–2.5 kg (4.5–5.5 lb) leg of lamb
1 heaped tsp sea salt
1 tbsp light olive oil
2 large cloves garlic, sliced longways into 8
4 small sprigs thyme or rosemary
Zest and juice of two unwaxed lemons
500 ml (1 pt) white wine (I prefer something more fruity than dry)
Warm water
8–10 whole baby carrots (scraped)
4–8 small new potatoes per person (depending on appetite)
Half a small spring cabbage, shredded
Freshly made mint sauce for the *jus* and to serve

Method

Rub the lamb lightly all over with the salt.

Heat the oil to a hot temperature in a deep, ovenproof dish and brown
the lamb on all sides, including the ends, to seal in all the juices.

Remove from the dish, make deep cuts into the fat and insert the garlic and sprigs of thyme or rosemary.

Add the lemon juice to the pan to deglaze, then add the wine.

Return the lamb to the pan and add enough warm water to come halfway up the joint.

Cover with foil and cook in a preheated oven for 3 hours at 180 C/gas mark 4, basting regularly.

Add the carrots and potatoes and sprinkle everything with the lemon zest.

Return to the oven and cook for a further 2 hours at 200 C/gas mark 6 until the vegetables are cooked and the meat tender.

Remove the meat and set aside to rest.

Steam the cabbage for around 10 minutes until beginning to soften, but retaining some bite.

Remove the carrots and potatoes and keep warm in a low oven of around 100 C/gas mark ¼.

Put the meat juices into a saucepan and add a teaspoon of the mint sauce. Bring to a simmer for 10–15 minutes until the juices have reduced then pour into a gravy boat.

Mint Sauce
Ingredients

Makes just over 60 ml (2 fl oz), enough for two generous servings

2 tbsp fresh mint leaves (stalks removed), very finely chopped
1 tbsp hot water
50 ml (1¾ fl oz) white wine vinegar
½ tbsp caster sugar (adjust to your own taste)

Method

Put the mint leaves in a basin and sprinkle with the sugar.

Pour over the hot water and pound the mint until the sugar is dissolved and mint softened but keeps its leafy form.

Pour over the vinegar and leave to stand for at least an hour before serving.

Any excess can be stored in a clean 40 g (1.5 oz) or similar spice jar with a lid for up to 3 days in the fridge.

Serve the lamb and vegetables on warm plates with the lightly steamed cabbage and *jus*.

This is a real crowd pleaser and one of Mr V's favourite British dishes, and the smell while cooking is incredible.

I'm serving it with a crisp, chilled Chablis and a *tarte au citron* (lemon tart) for dessert.

NOT SO HOME ALONE

*M*r V has just left for Paris, so Pussy Willow and I are alone at Les Libellules for the first time. I, being someone who likes her own company, am excited about this. I set to, cleaning the bathroom, brushing, hoovering and steam-cleaning the floors, and dusting and polishing all the surfaces. With no one to walk in with muddy boots or begin smashing up a bedroom floor, I can have three days of something resembling a clean home. Chores completed I make myself a cup of tea and sit outside in the sunshine.

No sooner have I sat down than a car pulls up. It's Noëlle with a dozen eggs and an offer of dinner. I gratefully accept the eggs, but decline the dinner, telling her I've already prepared something and I've got a lot of writing to catch up on. She stays for about half an hour, telling me to call her anytime, night or day, if there's anything I need. The dust on the road hasn't settled from Noëlle's car when my neighbour Valerie calls with the recipe for the tuile biscuits I enjoyed at the Christmas decoration workshop last November. She also tells me, as she lives just behind, to knock if I need anything.

Time for another cup of tea and getting down to some serious writing. That would be if Jacques hadn't arrived asking me if I wanted to go with him to photograph some toads that he's just found in his barn. Well, *there's* an offer I can't refuse. Jacques is a little sad. Poulette, his seventeen-year-old pet hen, has just died, and though she must have been about a hundred and fifty in hen years, he was very fond of her, and she was more like a dog with feathers than a chicken.

The toads are very cute—tiny, brownish-grey creatures with greenish-grey bellies and large, though not protruding, eyes. Jacques takes me into the garden and shows me where he's buried Poulette deep beneath a large crop of rhubarb to stop foxes or cats digging her up. He walks me back to Les Libellules, and Pieter's wife, Eva, comes out to greet us, asking me if I'd like to go for an after-dinner walk in the hills behind the hamlet; actually, would I like to come to dinner? This is getting ridiculous. The way people are cosseting me, you wouldn't think that I was the mother of two grown-up daughters and held down a responsible nursing job for many years, but I feel blessed that we've had the good fortune to have found such a supportive, close-knit, caring community. I accept the walk as I did the eggs, and graciously decline the dinner.

Back in the garden, I'm just about to sit down when a troop of eight or nine neighbours, out for a leisurely ten-kilometre hike, stops by. The word is out that I'm alone, and they ask how the *jeune célibataire* (young singleton) is doing and if I would like to join them on their ramble. As I'm already fully booked for walking later, I once again decline but say that I'll go next Tuesday, as this is a weekly event apparently.

Now at last, as you can see, I'm finally getting some writing done.

I've passed my first night and blissfully tranquil morning at Les Libellules. A storm blew in overnight, so all the shutters have stayed closed to prevent the wind from driving the rain through the doors. This, coupled with the weather, has served as a deterrent to going out, and I've spent the morning washing my hair, making yogurt, reading local guidebooks to decide on a day out for my birthday in two weeks and making my first-ever fire for this evening—let's hope it lights.

The rain has stopped, and the sun is shining. It's brought all the colours out, and the field opposite is once again the same shade of green that I've only ever seen here and in the Austrian Tyrol. Set against a cobalt sky, the effect is breathtaking. The first caller of the day has arrived. It's my neighbour Eva bearing gifts: a dish of homemade pesto which is just begging for pasta, and an edible plant that I can't identify. The leaves look like those of lily of the valley, but Eva says it belongs to the spinach family. The taste is like a peppery spring onion with a slight citrus tang. She only knows the name of the plant in Dutch, which is the most unfathomable language in my book. The pesto is incredible, even better than what I make, more like a dip. We sink some freshly baked baguette into it while sitting on the terrace with a glass of chilled rosé. I have to say, as much as I love Mr V, I'm loving my time alone here.

It's now 8:40 in the evening. The sun is going down behind the screen of poplars in the west. I've put a match to the crumpled paper beneath my carefully stacked kindling and wood. They catch fire instantly. The kindling begins crackling, and then the larger branches burst into flame with a whoosh. My day is complete; all I need do now is select a book to read by the firelight. Good night, everyone.

I've passed another tranquil night without Mr V snoring at my side. He's due to return this evening, however, and as lemons and limes are in abundance at the moment, I was going to make *tarte au citron* to welcome him home. But I've found this recipe in a French cookery magazine, and it's much less complicated, so I'm going to make that, using limes instead of lemons, and hope it tastes just as good as mine.

LIME AND GINGER TART

Serves 6 to 8

Ingredients

9 ginger biscuits, crushed into fine breadcrumbs
30 g (1 oz) unsalted butter, softened
4 egg yolks
3 or 4 limes
400 g (14 oz) can sweetened condensed milk

Method

Mix the biscuits and butter in a food processor and spread the mixture into a 20 cm (8 in) tart dish.

Bake for 15 minutes in a preheated oven at 180 C/gas mark 4, taking care not to burn.

Whisk the egg yolks with the zest of the limes until the mixture becomes pale.

Add the condensed milk and the juice of the limes and whisk a little more.

Pour the mixture into the tart dish and bake at 160 C/gas mark 3 for

15-17 minutes or until the top is just set and beginning to turn slightly golden.

Allow to chill at room temperature then refrigerate for at least three hours before serving.

This was so quick and simple to make and exceptionally tasty.

I think it would work just as well with lemons, but I love the taste and smell of limes.

What I've learnt today: I showed Jacques my mystery plant, and he told me it is oseille—*sorrel, in English. Sorrel is rich in vitamins A, C, B-6, B-1 and antioxidants, can improve eyesight and aid weight loss, so I'm looking forward to adding this to my cooking.*

DINING WITH THE VIANDIERS

*T*oday is our wedding anniversary. Mr V has bought me a wonderfully thoughtful gift—the book *Dining with the Durrells*. We both loved watching the boxsets of the British TV series about the family's adventures on the island of Corfu in the 1930s. I've always had a love of Lawrence Durrell's writing. Having been inspired by his memoir *Prospero's Cell*, I called my house in Wales 'The White House' after his home in Kalámi. You can probably understand why Gerald Durrell has become a bit of a muse of mine with his love of nature and animals, and his astute observations of not only them, but also his human friends and family. This latest addition to my Durrell literary collection is based around recipes that their mother, Louisa, made while living in India and Corfu, with some historical background and snatches of prose from Gerald's *The Corfu Trilogy*.

This is all close to my heart, as my books also contain observations of nature, anecdotes of friends and family, historical facts and feature many of my recipes. I've discovered that as I had to create a franglais style of cooking, adapting English recipes to French ingredients and tastes, and spicing up French ones to suit the adventurous English palate, so too did Louisa to her many curry dishes, using what ingredients she had available on Corfu.

This evening, as I don't want to be a slave to the kitchen, I've opted for a ready-made apéritif of snails with parsley butter in dainty pastry shells, followed by ready-to-cook frozen duck confit with fine slices of potato sautéed in duck fat with garlic and parsley, and a raspberry meringue dessert, all from Picard. My one concession is one of Mr V's favourites, and the dish that persuaded the sceptical Vincent that an English woman could cook—*soupe de moules* (which sounds so much more appetising than mussel soup). We also have champagne and have opened one of the bottles of Saint-Joseph that we bought at the wine tasting. So, it's time for me to put my glad rags on and celebrate three years of marriage with our usual toast—*toujours ensemble* (still together).

SOUPE DE MOULES

Serves 4 as a starter

Ingredients

30 g (1 oz) salted butter
2 medium shallots, finely sliced
1 large clove garlic, crushed
1 level tbsp cornflour
800 ml (1½ pt) light fish stock
2 tsp rouille[1]
450 ml (15 fl oz) dry white wine
A generous pinch of saffron
Freshly ground sea salt and black pepper to taste
200 ml (7 fl oz) double cream
10–12 mussels per person (to allow for wastage) or 6–8 per person if
frozen/ready-prepared, shelled mussels are used.
(You can use frozen/ready-prepared mussels if you are scared about
cooking fresh ones, but defrost/cook them thoroughly according to
the packet instructions before adding to the soup and reduce the
amount of dry white wine to 150 ml (5 fl oz.)
Flat leaf parsley to garnish (alternatively the feathery tips from a
fennel bulb add colour and a slightly aniseed flavour that works well)

Method

Melt the butter over a low heat in a large saucepan and gently sauté the shallots for 2–3 minutes until softened, taking care not to brown.

Add the garlic and cook for a further minute.

Remove from the heat and add the cornflour to form a thick paste.

Loosen the paste with a tablespoon of stock and blend in the rouille.

Using a hand whisk, add the rest of the stock (and the wine if using frozen/ready-prepared mussels), until the soup is smooth and lump free.

Stir in the cream.

Cover and simmer for around 20 minutes, until it has lost its floury taste.

Add the saffron and season as required with the salt and pepper.

Prepare the mussels if using fresh.

Serve the dish in pre-warmed shallow soup bowls and decorate with 6–8 mussels per person and a sprinkle of flat-leaf parsley.

Serve immediately.

Preparing fresh mussels

Rinse the mussels under running water in a large colander.

Bring the dry white wine to the boil in a large saucepan over a high heat.

Add the mussels and cook for around 6 minutes until they're completely open.

Discard any mussels which don't open.

Drain the mussels in a colander, reserving the wine liquid.

Pass the liquid through a fine sieve into the soup.

When the mussels have cooled a little, remove them from their shells and use immediately.

---

1. Rouille is a fish essence that comes in a smooth, salmon-coloured paste and can be bought in most UK supermarkets. It adds a hint of heat to give a little kick to the soup without being obviously spicy. If you can't find this, add a drop of Tabasco sauce.

RADIO GA GA

*T*oday is the annual *vide grenier* in the hamlet, and the Sunday before my birthday. But the weather is in sharp contrast to last year's scorching heat. The temperature during the night dropped to -2 and only managed to reach the dizzy heights of +2 during the afternoon. This morning the mercury has managed to crawl up to +3 degrees. It's still only 8 a.m., and I've just got out of the shower. I haven't yet had my breakfast, but Jacques is already at the door with Mireille, the wife of Christophe, who gave us champagne at the wine tasting. I've christened Jacques 'Monsieur Alouette' (Mister Lark) as he's always up at the crack of dawn. Mireille has set up a stall for the first time, and I think she's regretting it as she's frozen stiff. I give her a cup of hot tea, eat a hasty piece of toast, and we all set off down the road.

It was this time last year that I first met Jacques as he passed on his way to this annual event. The road in front of Les Libellules was then already jam-packed with parked cars. This year the cold weather has not only deterred visitors, but stallholders too, as only a handful have braved the elements. In a way I'm relieved as we simply have to stop buying stuff. I do, however, find some elegant tiebacks for curtains that we don't have, to put in a dining room that doesn't exist.

I also find a selection of *National Geographic* magazines I've no time to read.

Mr V, to my dismay, has discovered another vintage radio that Mireille and Christophe are selling. The one he bought last year now sits on top of the spare chest freezer and has to be moved every time I need to take something from inside. Today's specimen is smaller and doesn't resemble something used by the Resistance, but rather something that families gathered around to listen to General de Gaulle making his rousing address to the nation from London.

I've picked up some little vintage items myself—a selection of rather racy glasses with ladies in various 1930s attire stencilled on them. Not so racy, you might be thinking; that is until you look inside the glass, and there is the rear view of said ladies baring their derrières. Christophe is selling these also. He has no idea where they originate from, but the ladies have a South American air about them with a touch of Carmen Miranda. He seems reluctant to part with the glasses, but Mireille hastily wraps them in newspaper, puts them in a bag and gives me them for free.

I also acquire an attractively shaped blue and white metal wall plaque, which was awarded to the Blonde d'Aquitane cow who won a bovine beauty contest in 2009, the year that I arrived in France. I was going to put it in the kitchen or dining room when they are finished, but Mr V said the eventual downstairs bathroom is the place as it's the right colour, and I have to agree. So, if you come to visit and spend a penny in the downstairs bathroom when it's renovated, now you know why there's a prize cow award on the wall.

⁂

Although the weather is icy cold, the sky is a crystal-clear blue, and the rain during the night has freshened the colours and aromas of spring. The scent of bluebells infuses the air, their dainty bells almost the same shade as the sky. The feather tree is laden with pastel-pink blossom; wild primroses, the colour of buttermilk, have sprung up along the garden wall, and the field opposite is once again a profusion of shimmering buttercups. All is pure and delicate in the frail sunshine. We're immersed in the pastel palette of *printemps* (springtime).

* * *

Mireille has abandoned Christophe to man the stall alone and invites me to take a coffee with her in her sunny garden. It is on a slight rise at the rear of the house, and from the outside you'd never guess it was there. At the top of the lawn sits a wooden pavilion with an open porch. Christophe uses this as his workshop, but I see a wonderful entertaining space. It's just begging to have coloured lanterns hanging from its roof and to be filled with the sound of popping corks, lively conversation and laughter. Mireille agrees, saying we can turn the workbench into a large table in the summer when her daughter and grandchildren are visiting and have a little get-together.

I love the garden at Les Libellules, but it's not entirely private, and any get-together there would attract everyone who happened to be passing. Mireille's garden is lovely and secluded. It reminds me of one in the Conwy Valley, where I spent all my childhood summers. The henhouse, where I collected the eggs for breakfast every morning, was situated where Christophe's pavilion stands; there's even a stone-walled well in exactly the same position as the one that was the only source of water.

An abundance of cornflowers is growing in the borders, one of my favourite flowers. Mireille gets a spade and digs up armfuls for me.

I take them home to Les Libellules to plant amongst the bluebells at the back, and the primroses at the front of the house. Mr V and I work as a team, me plotting out the plants, Mr V digging holes and planting the flowers, and me banking down the soil and watering them. All this is taking place under the watchful eye of Pussy Willow, who is sitting on the garden wall. I hope she's not planning to dig them up when we're not looking…

* * *

My world is shrinking. My boundaries are more and more within the house, the garden and the hamlet. After living in the hustle and bustle of a major city, it's strange to be content with this, but I am. The City of Light has a darkness hanging over it. Notre Dame Cathedral has been struck by a devastating fire that saw its Gothic spire fall to the ground in a crumbling mass of ash, and many of its beautiful, stained-glass windows destroyed as the intense heat melted the lead that held them in place. I watched these events unfold live on TV, and like many people all around the world, I was deeply saddened. The gardens behind Notre Dame were my comfort and refuge when I first came to live in France, and anyone who has ever visited me in Paris will know that this was my go-to place whenever I was in the city. The beauty of the building never ceased to touch me, but it was not only its beauty; the cathedral had a magic, healing quality about it not dissimilar to that at Les Libellules.

Alas, this is not the only dark cloud on the Parisian horizon. The *Gilets jaunes* movement is in its 25th week. Last week events turned particularly ugly when an angry mob blockaded Pitié Salpêtrière, the hospital that Princess Diana was taken to following her car accident, and where I myself have worked, teaching medical English to specialist anaesthetic nurses. It has both saddened and shocked me how quickly, like the spire of Notre Dame, society can come tumbling down. I pray that our little corner of the world can remain in the light.

What I've learnt today: Buttercup in French is a renoncule, *which doesn't sound very pleasing to the ear, but they are commonly known as* boutons d'or *(golden buttons), which I think is much more lyrical.*

A DAY TO REMEMBER

J wake to the sound of logs crackling in the room below. It's my birthday, and Mr V has silently sneaked out of bed to open the shutters, light the fire and make a steaming pot of tea—such pampering and luxury as I've never known. I'm woozy with sleep and sit on the sofa nursing my cup, watching the flames dance in the grate and the sunlight seep through the lace curtains. The day is clear and bright, but the temperature remains well below the seasonal average, and it's still cold enough to light the fire every morning and evening.

I pull Mr V's big, chunky sweater over my pyjamas and go out into the garden. The air smells like burning dung from the still-smouldering dried ferns he burnt yesterday evening. It's a strange, fusty smell, but not entirely unpleasant. The sun is beginning to warm the ground, and a pungent aroma of damp soil rises from it to mingle with the remnants of the smoke; the bluebells are no match for this morning's earthy perfume. My friends the crows bid me good day then get back to their business of tending to their chicks. All the other birds are in full song, a joyous chorus of a multitude of sounds.

Gus is at the gate, waiting for his breakfast; he hisses and growls at me from the ground as I leave his bowl on the wall but leaps up and gobbles down the food as soon as my back is turned. Flaubertine, who is lazy with a belly full of babies, lounges beneath the feather tree, comfortable in the knowledge that if she's patient, she'll be fed in good time.

I take my tea and some toasted baguette to the table on the terrace. I'm joined by a particularly friendly sparrow who regularly sits on the edge of the guttering above the table while I write. He informs me every time the fat ball needs replacing, which is frequently. This morning it is full, so my little companion just cocks his head from side to side, listening to me as I whistle to him.

I'm being whistled to also by Mr V. He's ready to leave to go to Semur-en-Auxois, as I've requested for my birthday treat, so I'll see you there later.

✳   ✳   ✳

The road to Semur-en-Auxois runs alongside the Burgundy Canal on the left. On the right are sweeping fields of yellow rapeseed flowers, pale shimmering barley and vivid-green wheat. The sky is the colour of mother of pearl, with some patches as bright and shining as silver, and others as dark and dull as pewter. The sun breaks through little troughs of blue in the cloud and sweeps across the fields like a searchlight, turning the wheat and barley into an exotic carpet of more shades of green than I have names for. Every so often we pass through a hushed hamlet of honey-stoned houses sleeping beneath red-tiled roofs, many having *pigeonniers* similar to ours. Distant villages cling to hilltops, and distant châteaux with polychrome spires rise above the treetops.

We see a sign for the Lac de Pont so leave the road and park the car at the top of a steep bank. Lac de Pont is a long, narrow, man-made lake that serves as the reservoir for the canal Densely wooded banks rise steeply on either side with only a narrow path that clings to the lakeside. We're walking on a carpet of dried ferns, much like those that Mr V burnt in the garden yesterday; they crunch and crackle underfoot. Occasionally we disturb a bird in the nearby undergrowth, and it rises in panic into the tops of the tall pine trees. The sun comes out, turning the water a bright pea green, the effect of which makes me feel so peaceful and calm. The weather has been terrible for the past two days—cold with wind and rain—and although the sun isn't exactly cracking the flags, the weather is mild and dry. We've planned to eat lunch in the medieval town of Semur-en-Auxois, so we leave the lake and pick up our route.

✳ ✦ ✵

Semur-en-Auxois is a *village perché* (hilltop village), tumbling down towards the River Armançon. The skyline is dominated by the twin towers and spire of the Gothic church of Notre Dame, and the wide round turrets and ramparts of the 14th-century fortress. The view from the river looking towards the romantic, dual-arched Pont Dinard is world class, and I dearly want to return to capture this with the guidebook blue sky behind it.

Walking through the town is like walking through history with the eclectic jumble of architectural styles: the medieval ramparts, Gothic churches, half-timbered houses, polychrome roofs and elegant, 18th-century facades. We head towards the picture-book cobbled square in the centre, which is almost deserted as we've arrived at lunchtime, and all the shops are closed, so I have the perfect conditions to take some great photographs in the medieval quarter. There's a disproportionate number of hairdressers, end-of-line clothes shops and jewellers. There's also a tempting choice of pastel-painted patisseries, their windows brimming with dainty cakes and pastries, plus an excellent array of restaurants for such a small place. We make our choice—a traditional *Bourgognoise* brasserie next to the Porte Sauvigny, the ancient principal gateway into the old town.

✳ ✦ ✵

I'm here now, sitting at a table by a window looking out over the quaint square. We've ordered a *pichet* (jug) of Nuits-Saint-Georges and are sipping it in anticipation of our *boeuf Bourguignon*, the aroma of which pervades the room. The atmosphere is relaxed and friendly, the decor simple and traditional, plus most of the other diners seem to be regulars, so I think we've chosen well. The beef arrives in a steaming red wine sauce that is so rich it's almost black. It is melt-in-your-mouth tender and garnished with sliced carrots, button mushrooms and tiny pearl onions. There's a stack of creamy potato dauphinoise to complete the plate and a basket of bakery-fresh baguette to mop up any remaining sauce. Now for dessert. We're spoilt for choice but finally both opt for the same—a traditional pear and chocolate tart called *tarte aux poires belle Hélène*, served with crème brûlée ice cream.

After a leisurely coffee, we stroll around the ramparts. The views are spectacular, looking down on the red roofs of the town in one direction and the green landscape lying beyond the semi-circular curve of the river hugging the town in the other. We come across an unexpected restaurant with a terrace facing the hills to the west. I imagine enjoying a meal here in the presence of a magnificent sunset. I would like to linger a little and savour the view and a glass of wine, but we still have our dinner with Marie-Claude to look forward to this evening. I only hope that I haven't eaten too much…

＊ ＊ ＊

We're now standing outside Marie-Claude's house, having knocked at various French doors without reply. We're wondering how we are going to get inside when Jacques pops his head out of an upstairs window and calls to us that he's on his way down to let us in, as Marie-Claude is talking on the phone.

Mr V and I exchange glances, and he whispers to me, 'What is Jacques doing in Marie-Claude's bedroom?'

All is revealed. Marie-Claude has an upside-down house. Jacques, it turns out, was in the living room. The ground floor is the newly kitted out *gite*.[1] The house used to be the station in the days when the railway passed through here. Later it became the post office. Now it's been tastefully transformed into a comfortable and stylish home. The upstairs living/dining room opens onto a large, half-moon terrace with stunning views across open farmland, and Marie-Claude tells us that Mont Blanc is visible in the distance on a clear day. The room is bright and airy, and to my astonishment, the walls have been expertly covered in a warm, Sahara sand-coloured fabric, which has been mounted on a frame, giving them a slightly cushioned effect, adding extra heat and sound insulation. The only other time I've ever seen this done is on the British TV show *Escape to the Chateau*, and I thought it was a bit bonkers, but I can now see its merits. Mr V tells me that this is his idea for covering the insulation on the ceiling of the *pigeonnier*.

The table is set with a white, bone-china dinner service and four crystal glasses each: one for the champagne with the apéritif, one for the Chablis with the main course, another for the red Burgundy with the cheese, and a water glass. We've brought a local sparkling rosé, *Crémant de Bourgogne*, to serve with the dessert, so this will share the champagne glass. A white, embroidered, fine-linen tablecloth with matching napkins and an array of highly polished cutlery set the scene for a stylish evening. I'm installed in the best seat at the table, overlooking the terrace and beyond. The apéritif arrives: little rolls of Bayonne ham, balls of melon and mozzarella, cherry tomatoes and green olives, accompanied by a flute of champagne. The mood around the table is convivial with Marie-Claude and Jacques enjoying some friendly banter. Mr V chooses this moment to give me my present (I thought the box of Mon Chéri chocolates that he presented me with at breakfast was it). He hands me a long, slender box with a golden bow, that *he's* obviously not tied. Inside is a beautiful silver bracelet, a delicate chain spaced with tiny filigree spheres. I traditionally don't have much luck with bracelets, so I hope I don't lose or break this one.

There's a 'ding' from the timer on the oven to indicate that the main course is ready. Marie-Claude won't accept any assistance and disappears to return with a large dish of cod fillets baked with rose-pink prawns, carrots, fennel and shallots in a cream and wine sauce flavoured with tarragon. The Chablis is served, and the obligatory basket of bread is passed around the table. It's now that the banter between Marie-Claude and Jacques starts to get a tad heated. What began as a discussion about workmen has turned into an argument about people working 'in the black', without declaring taxes. Now the whole *Gilets jaunes* subject has reared its ugly head, and it's clear that they're standing on different sides of the political fence. I swiftly gather up the empty plates and head for the kitchen. Marie-Claude even more swiftly follows me, as the dinner is supposed to be in my honour; hence bringing the argument to an abrupt halt.

The atmosphere is still a little charged, then we're saved by the cheese, a particularly tangy *Epoisses* and a *Bleu de Bresse* served with the red wine, and the argument is forgotten. I'm not sure about mixing all this wine, but Marie-Claude assures us that she will put a spoonful of bicarbonate of soda in our coffee. This has the opposite effect on me than I think she intended. Still, the wine is excellent, so I'll let tomorrow's hangover take care of itself.

Last up is the dessert, homemade *mousse au chocolat* served with warm brioche and the sparkling rosé. Chocolate desserts are my forte, and this doesn't come up to my mark, so I discreetly pass my serving to Mr V, who is commonly known as *mange tout* (eat all), and I concentrate on mixing even more wine and put my faith in the bicarb.

The evening has had its moments but on the whole has been thoroughly enjoyable and a much-appreciated gesture by Marie-Claude, who put so much time and effort into it.

It's after midnight when we leave into a clear, starry night and watch with bated breath as Jacques wobbles home down the road on his bicycle.

*   *   *

I've woken this morning feeling refreshed, with no sign of a headache. The wind and rain are back again, so we were indeed lucky yesterday. Tomorrow we leave after more than three weeks here at Les Libellules, and we don't return for four weeks, by which time it will be the beginning of June, and I hope that summer will be upon us.

What I've learnt today: A spoonful of bicarb helps the alcohol go down in the most delightful way.

---

1. Self-catering holiday accommodation, usually in a separate annex of a private home, or part of the home itself.

PART VI
THE SEASON OF FRIENDS

JUNE AND JULY 2019

*We carried cut hay from the heart of the rick, packed tight as tobacco flake,
with grass and wild flowers juicily fossilized within—a whole summer
embalmed in our arms.*
Cider with Rosie, Laurie Lee

JUNE IS BUSTING OUT ALL OVER

*M*eandering strands of morning mist are still lingering in the air as we drive down to Les Libellules, past fields tightly packed with dense, green sprouts of sugar beet. Mr V informs me that sugar beet, or *betterave sucrière* as he calls it, is one of the most prolific crops grown in the country, and the principal source of sugar. In the UK, sugar primarily comes from cane that grows in the Caribbean. During the early 19th century, British merchant ships protected by the Royal Navy controlled sea routes, effectively blocking French trade. Napoleon Bonaparte hit on the idea of planting this sweet white variety of beetroot for France not to be reliant on imported sugar cane. Ironically it was one of my ancestors, Francis Fryer, who prompted this action. He was the captain of a privateer, a privately owned ship commissioned to patrol the Atlantic, capturing French vessels, seizing their guns and cargoes and imprisoning their officers. Mr V told me that my ancestor captured French ships, and I had captured a French heart...

The expanse of green gives way to fields of what at first glance resembles lavender, but as we get closer, I can see the flowers are sparser and more forget-me-not blue. I once again benefit from Mr V's knowledge as he tells me that this is *phacélie*, known as lacy phacelia or blue tansy in English, which is grown to rest the soil in between crop planting. It's breathtakingly beautiful and not something that I remember seeing last summer. I didn't know that my husband was such an expert.

*　*　*

June certainly is busting out all over when we arrive at Les Libellules. The garden is swollen with an abundance of flowers which have blossomed in our absence. Pastel-pink and milky-white peonies struggle to support their heads, weighed down by flowers as big as rosettes. Shy little fuchsias peek out from beneath the shade of the raspberry bushes, where they're protected from the sun. Hot-pink and deep-mauve valerian sprouts from the seams between the house and the borders, tenfold the amount of last year, spilling onto the paths, attracting a host of busy bees and butterflies. The ancient roses surrounding the terrace are in such profusion that you can barely see their leaves, and the spindly rose bush, amass with blood-red blooms, no longer lives up to its name.

What I've learnt today: My ancestor changed the agricultural landscape of France.

SOWING THE SEEDS OF LIFE

*W*e're at the Saturday morning market armed with a long list of things we want to plant in our little *potager*. We have two wooden crates that we're filling with an assortment of seedling plants: lettuces, tomatoes, cucumbers, radishes, courgettes, squash, peppers and leeks. We're in such a hurry to get home and start planting that I even forgo my ritual coffee at Café Parisien.

Back at Les Libellules, I give the plants a good sprinkling of water and put them in the shade while Mr V rakes over the soil and begins to mark out rows with string and wooden pegs. It's all looking expert and orderly, and I have to admit, I wouldn't have known where to start. Now it's time for planting. The tomatoes are first to go in, forming a natural border separating the *potager* from the garden. We're not 100% sure what varieties we've bought, but as last year, we'll have a surprise. Next we plant some more potatoes that I'd forgotten I had and that have now begun to sprout. Jacques says it's a little too late in the season, but as they're going to seed anyway, nothing ventured, nothing gained. We plant them along the path that separates the garden from the former garage next to the house, having already planted raspberry, blackcurrant and redcurrant bushes against the wall. Now we position the lettuces in two straight rows, and behind them the radishes, carrots and leeks, which are all easily identifiable. But we've hit a stumbling block. All the other plants look pretty much the same, and we haven't a clue which are cucumbers, which are courgettes, which are peppers and which are squash.

'*Ce n'est pas grave*' (It doesn't matter), says Mr V. We'll have even more surprises.

But it *does* matter, as the squash will take up far more space in the garden than the courgettes and cucumbers, which in turn will take up more space than the peppers. We take pot luck and hope for the best, planting what we think might be the squash in a space of their own behind the ancient roses and tomatoes, filling any gaps with what's left. Next year I'm going to make little labels on cocktail sticks to identify each plant as we buy it and have a proper garden plan in order to be able to crop rotate effectively.

Marie-Claude has given us a tub full of black beans, which will be great for stews and chilli come winter. I've soaked them in water overnight in readiness for planting this morning, and Mr V has now added a row of canes to support them when they begin to sprout. Being new to this gardening game, I harbour sneaking doubts of anything coming to fruition. We do, however, have a fine crop of tiny *fraises des bois* (wild strawberries) nestling beneath the peonies. I pick them, popping one in my mouth; it is fragrant and floral, tasting somewhere between a strawberry, a raspberry and violet-scented sweets—delicious.

禾　禾　禾

Marcel has just arrived. He sees me in the garden and says, '*Ah, la Reine Soleil*' (the Sun Queen). When I ask why he has given me this name, he says it's because I bring sunshine into everyone's life; he's such a smoothie. He's come to measure the floor of the rose bedroom to level it so we can finally start working there.

Gus continues to sit at the gate, and he's been joined by a small tabby female with startling, sage-green eyes. I'm determined not to get attached to her, so I simply call her the cat with no name. She, however, is determined to worm her way into my heart and runs to greet me in the garden, rubbing her silky, little body against my legs and head-butting my outstretched hand. Unlike Flaubertine, she is silent and doesn't purr. The cat with no voice.

A LITTLE NIGHT MUSIC

*T*oday is officially the hottest ever recorded in France with
the mercury rising to 46 in some parts, and even in Paris it
has topped 42. It's the day of *la Fête des Voisins*, the annual neighbours'
get-together. The party was planned to start at seven o'clock, as last
year, but due to the heat has been postponed until after the sun has
gone behind the poplar screen at around nine. I've made what's
becoming my speciality, rillettes *de thon* and twenty *verrines* of
gazpacho: ten red, made with tomato, red pepper, cucumber and a
hint of chilli, and ten yellow, made with melon, yellow pepper,
cucumber and a hint of ginger. I'll give you the recipe for the yellow
gazpacho at the end of this chapter.

* * *

The heat has made me feel drained, so I've taken advantage of the late
start to the festivities and gone to bed for a nap.

I'm woken by the booming voice of Marcel as he clinks glasses
with Mr V in the room below. He's been rendering the outside of the
fuel store in this insane heat. I think he's driven by the fact that he
goes on holiday tomorrow, and our payment for the work will come

in handy. The way I feel, I could honestly just stay in bed. I'm definitely not in the mood for dancing, but I stagger downstairs and into a cold shower. I emerge marginally refreshed but still not ready to face the world, so I fix myself a glass of my latest 'special'—a limoncello spritz, first sampled on my recent holiday treat to Lake Garda with my daughter Kate. If you're tempted to try it, and I fervently recommend that you are, it is limoncello over ice, topped up with equal measures of a light sparkling wine and sparkling water.

I'm now sitting concealed by the rose bushes and am astonished to see everyone arriving by car. The hamlet is only 900 metres from end to end, and we are more or less in the centre, so it amounts to walking the distance of two Parisian train station platforms. The result is it now looks like a Parisian train station car park in front of the house. I wonder if they all plan on driving home if they knock back the vino with the same gusto that they did last year.

Suitably fortified, I go inside to make up my face and head out to join the gathering in which Mr V is already mingling. It's far too hot to erect the marquee, plus it would be stifling inside, so the tables and chairs have been set out like a horseshoe in the open air. Small glass jars holding citronella-scented tea lights run in two rows down the centre of each table to give light and ward off the inevitable invasion of mosquitoes once the sun goes down. There's an ongoing feud between Monsieur Mouton and Fifi, and each has stayed away in order to avoid the other. I breathe a sigh of relief at the absence of Fifi whose fancy footwork on the dance floor last year got a bit out of hand. Everyone else has already arrived though, and I pride myself on remembering each and every name correctly, which is no easy task as many of the men look like clones. Last year I was the only woman wearing a dress; this year, whether due to the heat or whether I've set a trend, most of the ladies are wearing them. I, however, have upped the ante in a black, wrap-over number with a yellow leafy pattern; gold, dangly, leaf-shape earrings and yellow, wedged-heel sandals. Maybe a little too Saint-Tropez for the occasion, but I hardly ever get the chance to dress up these days.

At past events my offerings have been met with a degree of

suspicion until someone takes the first bite and declares them delicious. Tonight, however, the rillettes *de thon* and mini gazpachos haven't even made it to the table as I'm surrounded by a flock of men eager to sample the delights of my cooking, or maybe it's the dress, which is, now I look down, a little on the revealing side. Mr V dips his chin and raises his eyebrows at me. I'll have to go and find a pin before the dancing begins, or I could reveal more than my cooking skills.

I deposit my empty tray on the table and take a little pastry swirl filled with green pesto and pop it into my mouth. Now for something to drink. There are two vats of iced punch, one light and refreshing, not dissimilar to my limoncello, the other made with rum from the Antibes and packing far more of a punch (excuse the pun). Mr V is on his third plastic cup of the latter and already getting in the party spirit. I opt for the lighter iced variety. Marie-Claude is seated and waving a bottle of top-notch champagne at me, but I'm not ready to be pinned down, as now that I'm here, I too would like to mingle.

Jacob, our Dutch neighbour who has a holiday home behind Les Libellules, tells me that he, his brother and his son, Jann, are going to provide the music. My mind flashes back to Jean-Pierre and his less-than-impressive accordion last year and the frenzy of fancy footwork that followed, and I'm anticipating a similar performance. Three chairs are placed between the open ends of the horseshoe of tables, and Jacob, his brother (whose name I can never remember, let alone pronounce) and Jann go to get their instruments.

I'm totally unprepared for what happens next. Jacob is first to take his seat, carrying a cello; Jann follows with an electric keyboard, then Jacob's brother arrives, carrying a far more impressive accordion; no perching on stools for this trio. They settle themselves down and begin to play, or rather Jacob and Jann begin to play, a movement from Mahler's quartet for piano and strings. The melody is sad, uplifting, haunting and beautiful all at the same time, and the tone is set for a genteel, relaxed evening to come. Silence falls like the flick of a light switch, and everyone takes their place at the tables. All are transfixed as the music drifts on the warm evening air. I much prefer this. The fête is turning from something I dreaded into something I will cherish the memory of.

There's a brief pause while everyone fills their plates from the buffet, and it's now the turn of the accordionist. I brace myself, expecting rousing folk tunes, but instead the distinctive, quirky music from the French film *Amélie* comes flowing from his, I must say, enormous instrument, again in complete contrast to last year.

I've not told you about our neighbours at the table. Apart from Marie-Claude, there are Maurice and Josephine from the nautical house, and Marie-Claire and her husband, Serge, the former *gendarme* who nearly swirled me into orbit last year, but no one has taken to the floor this evening, so I'm safe, yes? Apparently not. Serge is on his feet, offering me his hand. I protest, but as you all know, to protest is futile. Here comes another surprise; he places a firm hand in the small of my back and leads me gently around the floor in a restrained waltz. Jann has now joined in, playing the haunting piano melody from the soundtrack of the same film. It's beautiful. I feel as if I'm floating, and it's not the punch. I catch a glimpse of the faces of my friends and neighbours smiling benevolently as I glide serenely past like Cinderella. Dance over, Serge gallantly kisses my hand, and people at the tables applaud us as we make our way back to our seats.

* * *

Suddenly the spell is broken. The short, swarthy husband of one of the ladies I met in the Christmas decoration workshops takes to his feet and begins singing in an exceptionally loud voice, drowning out the music. It's some sort of revolutionary song, which must be well known as others join in, and the accordionist picks up the tune. I'm now in for another shock. He's singing in French, but the words are about the potato famine in Connemara, Ireland, and the struggle for independence against the English. It's as bloodthirsty as the Marseillaise. Mr V sees the astonishment on my face and pays more attention to what is being sung. All the others are oblivious to the political implications and are swaying from side to side like drinkers in a German bierkeller; all that's missing are the steins.

It's too dark now for the little orchestra to see to play. Valerie asks if she can use the power in our garage to put some music on a CD player. The strains of chilled, smooth jazz swing the mood back to its former ambience. She comes around the tables, lighting the tea lights that flicker in the gentle breeze. Up above, myriad stars flicker in the vast blackness of the sky. People converse in little clusters, some drinking coffee and others a glass of port.

Ella Fitzgerald is singing 'Ev'ry Time We Say Goodbye'. All too soon it's time to say goodnight. It's now 1:30 in the morning, and people are beginning to drift away, leaving their cars and finding their way home by torch light, looking like fireflies as they disappear into the darkness.

Here is the promised recipe.

MELON, YELLOW PEPPER AND GINGER GAZPACHO

Serves 2 as a starter or 6 to 8 as an apéritif

Ingredients

¼ of a cantaloupe melon, diced into small cubes
¼ of a large cucumber, diced into small cubes (I leave the skin on for more fibre)
1 medium yellow pepper, diced into small pieces
A little finely chopped fresh ginger (this really needs to be super fresh so that it's juicy and fragrant, not dry and woody)
1 tbsp olive oil (I use Oliviers & Co Olive Oil with Mint)
1 tbsp white wine vinegar (I use Maille Vinaigre de vin Chardonnay—a bit pricey, but worth it—but if you cannot find this, then use a good quality white wine vinegar)
Freshly ground salt and pepper to taste

Method

Blend the melon, cucumber, pepper and ginger in a food processor.

Add the oil and vinegar.

Taste and season as required.

Pour into individual *verrines* for an apéritif or into serving dishes and add a small ice cube to cool and thin it down a little for a starter.

Chill in the refrigerator for at least 2 hours.

I often serve this as a starter garnished with tiger prawns and sprinkled with a tiny pinch of cayenne pepper.

TOP GEAR

*I*t's the day after the night before, and again, in sharp contrast to last year when the place was like a ghost town, the hamlet is all a hubbub with people coming to collect abandoned cars, tables and chairs, and forgotten crockery and glasses. I, as you can see, am trying to write in the garden, but everyone who passes feels obliged to stop and say *'bonjour'*, then I feel obliged to offer them a coffee. I think that next year I'll just fill up the percolator, put extra chairs out and cancel all plans for the morning.

Pieter has asked me if I'd like to go to Saulieu to the market and Café Parisien at 11 as he knows Mr V is busy. I *did* want to get some serious writing done, but with all the interruptions, it now looks like I'll barely have time to brush my teeth. Another problem is that we've been invited for apéritifs tomorrow lunchtime just before we're due to leave. What a problem to have, I hear you think. No problem at all if it was just one invitation; but Mr V and I have received one each, and both of us have accepted. One is from Mireille and Christophe, who I'm friends with, plus Mireille has promised Mr V some dwarf palm-tree cuttings, so I accepted with pleasure; the other, that Mr V has accepted, is from Maurice and Josephine who kindly gave us the tea set. We don't want to upset one couple by telling them that we are

267

going to another, so we decide to go to both. As no specific time was arranged with either couple, Mr V tells me it will be acceptable to go to Maurice and Josephine's house from 11:30 until 12:30 and then Mireille and Christophe between 12:30 and 13:30. Problem solved, though personally I think that 12–13 and 13–14 would be more suitable times, but who am I to argue?

⁕ ⁕ ⁕

Pieter has come to get me. I'm expecting to go to the market in his minivan with Akemi, a young Japanese ceramics artist who is staying at his place, but he leads me in the direction of an exceedingly small and yellow car that has appeared at the side of his house overnight. The vehicle belongs to Tillman, a German artist who arrived early this morning to check out Pieter's facilities and the local area with a view to coming to stay later in the year. He's wearing a top to rival his car: bright yellow with rather feminine-looking puff sleeves and Peter Pan collar. The top has been matched with blue and white check trousers, white golf shoes, a large, white belt with lacy holes punched in it and a white straw hat. To top it all, he's about 6'3" with wiry, orange hair and a goatee beard. The overall effect is comical, but he seems charming.

Tillman folds himself into the driving seat and offers Akemi the front seat next to him. Pieter and I are squashed into the back that's made more for parcels than people, especially when accommodating Tillman's legs in the front. Everyone except me is talking in broken English, and I have to bite my tongue to keep the teacher in me from correcting tenses and past participles. Goodness knows how they can understand each other as I'm struggling. I only hope my French doesn't sound as bad as this.

I now understand the significance of the chequered-flag trousers— Tillman drives like a madman. He comes hurtling down the hill from the hamlet and straight onto the departmental road, paying no heed to the stop sign at the bottom or even glancing to the left to see if anything else is coming. He then proceeds to jump the red light at temporary traffic signals and engages in conversation with Akemi while feeling the need to look at her like an actor in a black and white American movie who is not actually driving.

On entering the town, we make a left-hand turn on two wheels, almost taking a pedestrian with us who was on the zebra crossing. Finally we come to an abrupt halt in the car park, though not actually in a parking space, but a small strip of concrete separating two ornamental flower beds. Akemi, being Japanese and the size of a glove puppet, has no difficulty extracting herself from the yellow peril without trampling the floral display, but I'm interested to see how Tillman and his seven-league legs will negotiate it. He's obviously done this before. Drawing up his left knee until his leg is practically under his chin, he places his foot with precision on a foot-sized patch of concrete. He then holds onto the doorframe to steady himself as he swings his body out, bending his right leg like a flamingo and placing his right foot heel to heel with his left in what should be an impossible ballet position. Pieter is next to go but can't quite master the manoeuvre and ends up flattening a patch of marigolds. Now it's my turn. I manage it but twist my ankle in the process. Still, here we are and all still in one piece. Pieter turns to me and says he thinks he'll give coffee a miss and have a glass of Chablis. I think I might join him.

＊　＊　＊

The market is buzzing. The wine bar is packed, the wine tasting van also. An accordionist in a Breton top is playing typical French music, adding to the ambience, and corks are popping in abundance. Along with the usual fruit, vegetables, plants and flower stalls, there's one selling olives: huge, shiny black beauties; smaller purple ones like oval amethysts; tiny, brownish-red varieties; large, green ones that are almost silvery grey, and ones the size of beans and as green as frogs. There are stalls selling artisan jams in unusual combinations such as apricot and basil, cherry and lavender, and strawberry and poppy, and others selling honey in just as many flavours. Tillman is darting from stall to stall like a pinball, filling his backpack with goodies to take home with him tomorrow. We dissuade him from buying cheese in this heat as the smell coming from the stall is already pungent. I purchase some eggs, and we all make our way down the narrow streets to Café Parisien, clinging to the sliver of shade on the pavement.

We're lucky enough to get a table under a parasol outside the café. Pieter and I order our glasses of Chablis; Akemi asks for a café au lait and Tillman two espressos. This he definitely does *not* need. I'm already dreading the Formula One drive home and am seriously considering calling Mr V and asking him to pick me up. Then the Chablis kicks in, so we all squeeze into the canary-yellow bean can, which has been baking itself in full sun for the last hour or so, and whose air con consists of a little, plastic fan fixed to the dashboard. I shut my eyes and hope for the best as we hurtle off at breakneck speed towards the hamlet.

As you can see, we safely made it back, but now I'm off to lie down in a darkened room to recover.

THE EARLY BIRDS

J'm decidedly unsure about turning up on someone's doorstep at this hour in the morning for an apéritif. Mr V, who eats lunch at the office at 11:30 every day, assures me, 'It is good,' (one of his stock phrases) but Josephine and Maurice are retired, and for me this is more the time for a morning coffee. Still, here we are outside their grand residence with no sign of life inside, confirming my fears.

'*Coucou*' (Hello). It's Josephine in her gardening clothes, wearing a large pair of green rubber gloves with a bunch of freshly picked radishes in her hands. She wipes the hair from her eyes with her arm and beckons us to follow her.

I'm all apologies for arriving at such a *bonne heure* while flashing Mr V an 'I told you so' look.

'No problem,' says Josephine, calling Maurice from inside. The usually formally dressed Maurice emerges in shorts and T-shirt that look suspiciously like pyjamas. He'd been in the kitchen preparing the apéritif. I think of the 101 things that I could be doing with an extra half an hour back at Les Libellules instead of feeling awkward while our neighbours scurry around, graciously making out that they were expecting us at this time.

Mr V is oblivious. He's gone off into the garden and is oohing and aahing over the fabulous array of trees and plants. I follow him with Josephine who tells me that it is they who have planted all the trees and bushes. The path is lined with scented, ancient roses and leads to an enormous water feature, like a scaled-down version of the terraced fountains found in Italian gardens. Water in a raised central pond is cascading down rocks on either side into a smaller basin, which in turn tumbles into another pond at lawn level where huge, orange goldfish are weaving their way between pads of water lilies. Two narrow paths lead up to the main pond that's shaded by cherry trees and also has goldfish meandering around in it. There are raspberry, blackcurrant and redcurrant bushes, and huge beds of lavender, rosemary and tarragon. One of two large greenhouses has peppers and melons ripening inside; the other has tomatoes. We descend to the original path and return to the house, where Maurice is ready for the apéritif in a crisp, white shirt and smart, beige trousers.

As it's so hot, we eat indoors in the formal dining room. The table has a splendid selection of little *tartines* (small toasts) topped with smoked salmon, sardines and aubergine caviar. There are also cubes of cheese and cherry tomatoes on cocktail sticks, thankfully not too much if we're expected to do it all again in an hour's time. Maurice goes down to the cellar and comes back with a bottle of champagne. I shoot a warning glance at Mr V not to drink as he has to drive us back to Paris, but he says that he's allowed one glass. One glass becomes three, and I doubt we'll be hitting the road this afternoon. Then Josephine says that if we're not going back, why not stay for lunch?

We really have no good excuse apart from saying, 'Oh no, it's very kind of you, but we don't want to impose.'

We will not be imposing, it seems; there's rabbit in a mustard sauce waiting for us in the oven. This is Maurice's speciality, and they were hoping that we'd stay to sample it. I feel as if we've been lured into a honey trap; by plying Mr V with champagne, they've secured us as luncheon guests. I'm frantically thinking about Christophe and Mireille expecting us in around twenty minutes, but Mr V appears to have forgotten all about our second date as he's tucking into the excellent rabbit which is served with sautéed field mushrooms, onions and potatoes. I can't eat rabbit on principle, having kept them as pets, so I skilfully slide mine onto Mr V's plate while Maurice has gone to get a second bottle of champagne and Josephine a basket of bread.

It's now 13:20, and I'm feeling more than a little bit stressed. We've managed to pass on the cheese, but there's still dessert to get through. I hope Christophe hasn't also got a rabbit in the oven, or it will be decidedly dry by now. I discreetly send Mireille a text message to apologise for being so late, saying we've been held up.

She replies, 'Ce n'est pas grave. It's only an apéritif.'

Thank goodness. I relax and enjoy the excellent strawberry mousse with, yes, more champagne.

✳ ✳ ✳

Mireille opens the door with a welcoming smile and leads us into the garden where the table is laid with more tasty goodies than I really want to see. There are little puff pastry horns filled with cream cheese and smoked salmon, miniature kebabs with cubes of grilled chicken and courgette, a savoury cake with ham and olives and a huge tortilla cut into squares. As if that wasn't enough, there are glasses filled with breadsticks, dishes of olives and pistachio nuts, small orange and yellow tomatoes and grilled red peppers in olive oil on slices of baguette. Plus a crystal bowl brimming with strawberries. And, of course, more champagne.

The tables are turned; this time it's Mr V tipping his champagne into my glass, having already polished off more than half a bottle. I, who have paced myself a little better, and also passed on the rabbit, am better placed to enjoy all this table has to offer.

We're joined by Christophe's mother, Adèle, an elegant Parisian lady in her 80s who worked as a demonstrator for kitchen appliances in the 1960s. She was one of the first of her kind working in the *grands magasins*, the large Paris department stores such as Printemps and Galeries Lafayette, giving presentations on how to use the latest food mixer or coffee machine. She had to be immaculately turned out to sell the fantasy of domestic bliss to the housewives eager to buy into it, and wore a uniform of sorts: a black dress with a white apron and a little, gaily coloured silk scarf tied in a bow at the neck to soften the look. She still looks exactly like that, minus the apron. Her hair is dyed coal black and cut into a soft bob that she has tucked behind her ears, revealing oversized pearl earrings. She sits with her feet to one side like the Queen, and shuns Mireille's offer of slippers, keeping her black, square-toed court shoes with a small Cuban heel. I like her instantly.

She pats the chair next to her for me to sit down. I feel decidedly underdressed, though I'm overdressed by Mireille's standards. Adèle speaks excellent English and wants to practise. She has a voice and face like the actress Leslie Caron, with impossibly high cheekbones and a wide mouth that is emphasised by carefully applied red lipstick. I feel as if I *am* in the presence of royalty. She tells me that sometimes she would be asked to demonstrate equipment in private homes, often bulky items like vacuum cleaners, so she had to learn to drive, and the company gave her a small car. Few women drove at that time, so she was truly emancipated; that was until she met Christophe's father and joined the throngs of housewives herself, swapping demonstrating kitchen equipment to becoming a slave to it, as she told me, not without a twinkle in her eye.

'Adèle is an excellent cook,' says Mireille.

Christophe nods in agreement.

Adèle looks demure but nods also.

'A perk of the job was that they paid for me to attend the Cordon Bleu Cookery Institute in Paris once a week. They thought that if I improved my culinary skills, then I would persuade the housewives of Paris that the gadgets I was demonstrating would improve theirs.' She laughs. 'I became an expert in preparing dishes such as coronation chicken, lobster bisque and crab soufflé, without getting as much as a splash on my white apron,' she says proudly. 'The next time I am here, I will teach you how to make some classic dishes.'

This thrills me, as food like this is all far too fancy for me to prepare at the moment. Maybe when I finally have a kitchen, I can write a recipe book revealing little glimpses of life at Les Libellules. What do you think?

What I've learnt today: Cordon bleu means 'blue ribbon' (literally translates as blue cord). Marthe Distel, a French journalist, published the cookery magazine La Cuisinière Cordon Bleu *in January 1895 and opened the cookery school in October that year. The American celebrity chef Julia Childs attended courses there in 1950, graduating in 1951.*

THE GOOD LIFE

$\mathcal{M}$y good friend Ang has come to stay for a week. This is the first time she's seen Les Libellules, but she takes to life here instantly. She's a keen gardener; hence she's at this moment rigged out in gardening gloves and Australian bushman's hat, armed with spade, trowel and secateurs. She's been at it all day apart from a pause for breakfast and lunch.

Ang has cleared and edged paths, tied back wayward valerian, pruned and dead-headed roses and trained the Virginia creeper to wind itself around the gate. She's also discovered what looks like the beginnings of two wasps' nests. She's really making a difference. I wish she could stay for a year to help me through the seasons, as although I've made some advances, watching her, I can see that I'm still virtually a complete novice.

Jacqueline has just popped by to see the garden. She's so happy that we've begun planting fruit and vegetables here again and has her eyes on my melons, counting seven and asking coyly will I eat them all? She's also in raptures about the cherry tomatoes, as she tells me that the first time she had ever tasted a cherry tomato was in this very garden when she was four or five.

Some of the radishes are ready, so I ask Jacqueline if she'd like to join Ang and me for an early apéritif to try them. She accepts my invitation willingly and settles herself under the shade of the parasol on the terrace. I pull up two bunches, wash off the soil and give one to her to take home. I trim the stalks and whiskers from the other, and we eat them dipped in salt with slices of fresh crusty bread and butter. This is the usual way of eating radishes in France, but I have to admit, the first time a hostess presented me with a bowl of radishes and a basket of bread in the centre of the table, I was a bit nonplussed and wondered where the rest of the salad was.

The radishes are delicious, crisp and hot and slightly sweet, burning our tongues in a pleasant way, far more flavoursome than any I have ever bought in a shop or even at the market. We wash them down with cool, sparkling Perrier water flavoured with fresh mint and lime. Who could ask for more?

*　*　*

I haven't exactly been idle in the garden. I was swotting up on taking care of pumpkins (that's something I never thought I'd hear myself say) the last time I was in Paris, or rather, watching fascinating videos on YouTube made by a real authority on the subject. Ours, I discover, have powdery mildew—as the name suggests, powdery white patches all over the leaves—which blocks the plants' photosynthesis and stunts the growth of the fruit. Really badly affected leaves must be cut off and burnt to prevent further spread, but The Pumpkin Man assures me that those not too badly affected can be treated by spraying the leaves on both sides with a mix of milk and water, and that this should also be sprayed on new, healthy leaves as a preventative measure.

Here I am now with the sun burning my arms and shoulders, spraying away. Easier said than done; the garden is a mass of pumpkin leaves that seem to have invaded the most inconvenient places. I'm climbing over molehills and treading gingerly through tomatoes and peppers trying to reach them. I've used the best part of a litre of milk, and my hands are aching from the constant pumping action. I wish I'd known this when we planted them, as I could have nipped it in the bud, but you live and learn.

I've also been learning how to cure pumpkins in order to be able to store them for up to six months to use over the winter period (again courtesy of The Pumpkin Man). You must cut them when the stalks have gone dry and the fruit sounds hollow when tapped. Then you have to brush off any soil and place them in a warm, dry place such as a greenhouse or on a sunny window ledge for two weeks, then turn them upside down and leave them for a further two weeks. After this, their skins should have hardened, which allows them to be stored for a longer time without drying out, and this also intensifies the flavour. Next you polish the skin with olive oil to prevent it from splitting, and then the fruit is ready to store on a raised wooden or metal rack covered with a deep cushion of straw or newspaper in a dry, frost-free, well-ventilated shed or store room (at a temperature of around 20 degrees if possible). The pumpkins should be checked regularly for signs of becoming soft and, if so, used immediately.

The courgettes and cucumbers, however, cannot be stored in this way and have to be eaten as soon as they're ready or kept in the fridge for up to a week, so I'm making a lot of recipes using both. As it's so hot today, I'm going to make a refreshing soup using a freshly cut cucumber and mint from the garden. This is quick and simple to make and a perfect way to hydrate and cool down after all this hard work.

CUCUMBER SOUP WITH
FRESH MINT

Serves 4 as a starter

Ingredients

2 medium cucumbers with the outer skin removed, but leaving a layer
of the darker green flesh
8 fresh mint leaves
4 tbsp crème fraîche
A pinch of salt to taste
1 tbsp olive oil (I use Oliviers & Co Olive Oil with Mint)
1 tbsp white wine vinegar (I use Maille Vinaigre de vin Chardonnay)

Method

Cut the cucumbers in half and carefully remove the seeds with a
spoon (these can be planted to have another crop next year).

Chop the cucumbers and mint and mix together in a food processor
with the rest of the ingredients.

Divide the soup between individual dishes.

Add an ice cube to each dish then leave in the fridge until ready to
serve (at least 30 minutes). What could be simpler?

THE LANGUAGE OF FRIENDSHIP

*O*nce again, it's *la Fête de la Saint-Jean*, and the wooden sacrifice has been a closely guarded secret. I've told Ang all about last year's spectacular windmill complete with Wicker Man figure, and the haunting hurdy-gurdy music, so we're full of high expectations. We've both opted to pass on the meal, as I've also told her about my 'everything I hate on a plate' experience last year, so we've eaten a tapas-style apéritif, but Mr V is saving himself for the raw steak and Camembert.

The French language has always been a bit of a mystery to me, and although I knew it was *la Fête de la Saint-Jean* and not *la Fête du Saint-Jean*, I was unsure why. There was only one person to ask—the fount of knowledge who is Jacques. He explained that it is *not* the celebration of Saint John the Baptist, but rather of his saint's day, which lasts the entire day—*une journée*, in French, which is feminine—hence '*de la*'. Confused? To put it simpler, it's the fête of the day of the man, not the man himself. Each day in France is affiliated to a particular saint, and Saint John the Baptist's day is the 24th of June. The fête was originally called *le Feu de la Saint-Jean* (Saint John's Fire) as beacons were lit on all the hillsides, hence our bonfire. In the past, this would have been on the actual day. But now it's celebrated on the

Saturday after the 24th, to be sure it takes place after the summer solstice.

✳ ✳ ✳

Noëlle is already here when we arrive and tells us not to hold our breath before going to see this year's pièce de résistance. It's just as well she warned us...

We're faced with a giant, wooden squirrel and a smaller, 'baby' model. When I say giant, yes, it *is* big, but nothing like last year's proportions, let alone the cockerel and wild boar of former fêtes. All in all, a bit of a let-down.

'What's this all about, love?' asks Ang.

'I've no idea,' I reply. As far as I know, squirrels are not particularly significant to the area, and I find the fact that these are meant to be a mother and baby not entirely fitting to be set on fire. The music is not the same either; no fit firemen spinning the dulcet tones of Christophe Maé on the turntable. Tonight we have a local farmer playing 1970s disco, and there's a lot of Boney M going down. The dance floor *does* look much more stable though; farmers are obviously better than firemen for building platforms even if their taste in music is a bit cheesy.

Then Village People comes blasting out of the speakers. Ang and I cannot resist; we take to the empty boards and start waving our arms in the air to the sound of 'YMCA'. The French are dumbfounded, but the DJ looks thrilled that at last someone is appreciating his sounds. Noëlle jumps up next to us and soon picks up the moves, then some children join in, thinking it's hilarious. Mr V shakes his head from the sidelines, but his dimples give his amusement away.

'YMCA' fades into 'Rasputin'. Ang and I are now singing along at the top of our voices in our own personal karaoke.

A few other French people drift self-consciously onto the floor and begin dancing as if this is serious, but the DJ has a trump card up his sleeve—'Spinning Around'. Ang and I are in full Kylie Minogue mode now; all that's missing are our gold lamé hotpants. More people venture onto the dance floor, and the DJ, seizing his chance, puts on 'Cotton Eye Joe'. A small, wiry farmer grabs my hands and raises my arms to form an arch with his. The other dancers cotton on and begin selecting partners to duck under the arch, forming two lines, clapping and stomping in time to the music as each couple takes their turn. Ang and Noëlle hook up together and pass, giggling, beneath our arms then form their own arch. The music changes to a line dance, which is still popular in rural France. I personally haven't danced like this since the group Steps released '5,6,7,8' twenty-odd years ago and am completely lost. The French are tucking their thumbs into the belts of their jeans and forming orderly lines; obviously there's no place for amateurs here, so we make a hasty retreat back to Mr V and the rest of the men.

It's time to eat, or in Ang's and my case, time to drink. We definitely made the wise choice of not taking the set meal as it's virtually the same as last year except for a soggy-bottomed apple pie taking the place of the murky-grey chocolate mousse. Litre carafes of local wine are on sale for €5, which I'm sure are good, but there are also bottles of Nuits-Saint-Georges for €10 that I know will be excellent. Ang buys a bottle, and we share it with Noëlle. The three of us are now all talking and laughing together with me acting as translator, although they seem to be making themselves understood with tone of voice and gesticulation. Ang and Noëlle both have the same wicked sense of humour, and despite the language barrier, they're getting on like a squirrel on fire. It's great to see my two friends, who can't speak a word of each other's language, hitting it off so well together. The language of friendship is indeed universal.

Night is beginning to fall, and clouds have started to gather in the distance; a storm is brewing. There's an announcement that the fire will be lit in five minutes. We don't fight our way to the front as we did last year, as a burning squirrel just doesn't have the same appeal as a windmill with fireworks shooting from its sails. The firework display that follows, however, more than makes up for the disappointing bonfire; it is spectacular, on a par with any I've ever seen on the 5th of November in the UK. Rockets soar into the air, bursting into multicoloured fountains of tiny stars that come raining down from the night sky. Galaxies of silver and gold evaporate in mini explosions to sounds of 'ohhh' and 'ahhh' from the crowd. Starbursts of pink and purple, and flashes of red and green light up our faces in the dark. Behind us the sky is also lighting up with spectacular flashes of lightning beyond the hills in the distance. The storm isn't forecast to reach us for a couple of hours yet, so when the fireworks have finished, we buy another bottle of wine, sit back in the warm night air and watch the show that Mother Nature is putting on for us. Ang says she finds this more thrilling than the fireworks, and I have to agree.

※　→　※

All this wine and accompanying glasses of water have made me desperately need to *faire pipi* as we politely say in France. I ask Mr V where the toilets are as he'd gone in search of them earlier. He tells me there aren't any, and I'll have to go in the bushes at the side of the car. I say he must come with me to keep a lookout. He has a trick where he opens the front and back doors of the vehicle, forming a little chamber in between the two where you can't be seen. I must add that I'm not in the habit of relieving myself al fresco, and on the couple of occasions when I've done this, it's been in broad daylight. Mr V assures me that no one will be around as the fireworks have only just finished, and the disco will be starting up again soon, and even if people decide to leave early, by the time everyone kisses goodbye, I'll be done and dusted and on my way back.

So here I am in full flow when it becomes like a scene from the film *The Truman Show* where as soon as Truman leaves the house, the previously empty streets are full of people. It seems some of the revellers have left early, and they arrive just in time to find me peeing at the side of the car. I call to Mr V to open the car doors to shield me, and something not visible in daylight happens— the interior light comes on, drawing attention to the car and me crouched in an undignified manner beside it. A family with young children appears from nowhere. The mother sees me and swiftly looks away, distracting the father, but a small girl asks in an incredibly loud voice, 'What is the lady doing?' The mother replies that I am looking for something, and her little brother says, 'Has she lost a kitten?' and lurches towards the car to help me find it. The father has now seen my dilemma (I have actually stopped peeing, but I have to stay crouched 'looking for my kitten' until they go). Thankfully he drags the child away, and I hastily pull up my pants before another troop arrives.

I'm feeling uncomfortable as I haven't arranged my underwear properly, and something else—I have been bitten on the bottom. Some opportunist little beastie has attacked my derrière while it was in the long grass, and it's itching like mad.

ABBA is now booming out of the turntable, and everyone, it seems, is a dancing queen. There's hardly a place to shuffle your feet, so all earlier arm antics are out of the question. I'm happy just to wriggle around and alleviate my itch. Ang and 'Nolly', as Ang has taken to calling Noëlle, are belting out 'Fernando'.

Well I don't know about there being something in the air, but there was certainly something in the grass. I seriously need to get some after-bite lotion on this itch and fast.

My salvation comes in the form of large drops of rain suddenly splashing onto the dance floor; it is soft and hot like a gentle shower. I've never felt rain like it. It feels pleasant on my skin and evaporates almost instantly. Under different circumstances I would like to stay to experience this, but it's a signal that the storm is coming, plus, as I have more pressing matters, we head off for the car.

We arrive at the house at the same time as the first clap of thunder. The rain has become cooler and sharper and not so pleasant on the skin. We hurry inside, and I rush to the bathroom, but where I've been bitten is not easy to see, so I have no option but to ask Mr V.

'Oh là là,' comes his response.

'What? What is it? Is it a mosquito sting?'

'Nooo, I don't think.'

'Well what then?'

'I don't know. Maybe *un serpent*.'

'A snake! I've been bitten by a snake?'

'I think... Only a little one. It is nothing.'

'It is *not* your backside.'

I soak a cotton wool pad in TCP and ask him why he thinks it's a snake bite.

'I don't know... There are two little 'oles. We have to see on the net.'

I take an antihistamine tablet in case I get a reaction and do what I do best. Write about it.

What I've learnt today: Don't lose your kitten in the grass; you could attract an audience, or even worse, a snake...

CAT CHESS

We're down at Les Libellules for a long weekend and have Pussy Willow with us. She is *not* happy, as Gus has finally decided to pluck up courage and enter the garden. At this moment he's stretched out on the patio in front of the living room, and Flaubertine is lying like a doormat across the kitchen step. Gus runs away when I come out with a bowl of food for him and hisses at me from behind the garden fence. I push the bowl through a little gap and try to engage some cat communication, screwing up my eyes at him. I'm rewarded with him screwing up his eyes back at me, then he hisses again, but he takes the food just the same. The cat with no name has also arrived, but she is afraid of Gus and wary of Flaubertine, so I call her to come and eat on the step by tapping my thigh. I realise that not having a name is somewhat of a hindrance when trying to call a cat, so the inevitable happens. I'm sure you all knew that it was only a matter of time; the cat formerly known as the cat with no name is now Princess.

* * *

Gus has progressed from hissing at me as I approach to making a token lip curl like a tomcat Elvis Presley, often doing this and screwing up his eyes at the same time. He's not a handsome cat by any stretch of the imagination, and was a bit unkempt to say the least, so he's not easy to warm to. I suspect that his appearance has led him to be treated unkindly by humans; the way he used to flinch leads me to believe that perhaps he's been kicked in the past. Everyone who sees me interacting with him looks at me as if I'm mad, but my kindness is evidently paying off; he's even begun to wash himself and has a remarkably white and black coat beneath the grey patina. He's now sitting on the far right-hand corner of the patio. Pussy Willow is on the near right-hand corner, Flaubertine the near left, and Princess on the far left. Every so often one of them moves to a different square, and the others adjust their positions in a bizarre game of cat chess. Pussy Willow stays in the squares closest to the front door, guarding her territory, and Princess stays where she can make a quick getaway should a fight break out. They all seem perfectly content as long as no one invades another's personal space...

What I've learnt today: Even the most untrusting animal will eventually respond to a little human kindness.

A FÊTE TO REMEMBER

*T*oday is one of the most important dates on the French holiday calendar—the 14th of July, *la Fête Nationale*—Bastille Day to you and me. For once our little commune is going to mark the anniversary of the storming of the Bastille prison that heralded the start of the Revolution on the actual day as opposed to the nearest Sunday (as this year the 14th is a Sunday). Normally the occasion is marked by an evening hog roast and fireworks, but as traditionally a big firework display takes place in Saulieu every year, the mayor has decided to host a lunch in the *salle des fêtes*, paid for from the commune coffers, aka our taxes.

A dozen or so cars are already outside the *mairie* when we arrive. Monsieur Mouton is perched on the stone wall separating the car park from the graveyard and is smiling and waving at me, calling 'Lola'. I've only just got used to being called 'Lydie', and now I have another name to grapple with. The mayor has just arrived, informally dressed in a pair of stone-coloured shorts and a white shirt that has clearly just come straight out of the packing. He proceeds to shake the hand of each and every man and plants a kiss on both cheeks of each and every woman. In fact, a lot of kissing is going on, and it's proving difficult to have a conversation, as there seems to be a permanent queue lined up to kiss me.

The mayor is ushering us all to tables beneath the trees where corks are popping like party streamers, and glasses containing thimblefuls of the blackcurrant liqueur *crème de cassis* are being filled with champagne to make Kir Royale apéritifs. This is no frugal affair. The mayor and a couple of helpers are going around topping everyone up, and Noëlle and another lady are passing around plates of canapés. No one seems to be in a hurry to eat, and it's 1:30 before the gong sounds, and we drift into the *salle*. All the ladies are handed an eco-friendly shopping bag as a gift from the mayor. There's a photograph of the principal village printed on the front, and four smaller photos of the three hamlets and other village that make up the commune on the back. The tables have been set out beautifully for eight, with white linen cloths and glass jars filled with wildflowers. Each has two bottles of chilled, white Burgundy wine and two large jugs of iced water. My hopes rise that maybe the meal won't be so bad.

Celine steers us towards a table at the back of the room that's away from the sun streaming in through the windows and benefits from a breeze fluttering in through an open door that leads to the garden. I sit with my back to the door, giving me a good view over the rest of the room. The others at our table apart from Celine and her husband, Luc, are Fabienne and Solène and their husbands, Benoît and Jean.

The *entrée* has arrived. There's a platter with a meat terrine, salami and *jambon de Bayonne* (cured ham from Bayonne in Southwest France), plus a large basket of freshly baked, crusty bread. I take a piece of the ham and a chunk of bread, so far so good.

Now for the main course. Again, I'm pleasantly surprised. Carafes of chilled rosé appear on the table, droplets of water dripping from the frosted glass. There is perfectly edible, finely sliced, raw fillet steak and a sort of turkey-ham served with a mixed vegetable salad, pasta and tomato salad and another salad with diced ham. I take a slice of the turkey, some pasta salad and a generous dollop of Dijon mustard. For a free meal, this is not bad at all. Mr V is on form, and he has a generous helping of everything on offer.

The cheese follows with another excellent wine, this time red. Then the pièce de résistance, the dessert. It's more like a *café gourmand*, a selection of mini coffee tiramisu, raspberry framboisier and chocolate opera desserts, all accompanied by an excellent bottle of the local sparkling wine, *Crémant de Bourgogne*.

The conversation is flowing as freely as the wine. Mr V is rather well lubricated by now and not pausing for a breath. I, however, feel the need to stretch my legs after all that food and drink so take myself outside into the garden. There to my astonishment are two elderly ladies wearing 1950s-style floral dresses and peep-toe crossover sandals from the same period, seated at two trestle tables that have miraculously popped up out of nowhere. The tables are laden with pots and pans, dishes and vases and an assortment of bric-à-brac. These two ladies have politely refused the mayor's invitation to the fête in order to take full advantage of those who've been taking full advantage of the free refreshments. I'm impressed at the speed with which they must have moved to set up their stalls. I've not taken as much advantage of the refreshments as others, but as I'm a sucker for a table full of knick-knacks, I'm easy pickings for them.

Fabienne has had the same idea and come outside to take the air. She buys a large, white porcelain salad bowl edged in a lacy, blue pattern, an assortment of napkin rings and *porte-couteaux* (knife stands) that are used regularly in France. I'm instantly attracted by a straw basket similar to those changing hands for €29 at the market, but a retro version with large, straw flowers on the front. Now that my Provençal basket is full of Christmas baubles, I need another for fruit and vegetables, so I ask how much they want for it, being prepared to go up to €10.

'Four euros,' is the reply. Bargain, done deal. My eye is now caught by a rectangular ovenproof dish with a basket-weave design. It's neither the dish nor the design that attracts me but the colour. It's the same shade of green as the pottery in the house of my late great-aunt Matty, not quite sage or jade enough to be fashionable today, but it strikes a chord with me. Again, I ask the price, not wanting to pay over €5 as this is something that I do not need.

'Three euros, *madame*.'

'Right, put it in the basket.'

*   *   *

I return to the *salle des fêtes* to find the plates and cutlery cleared away, candles being placed on the tables, and bottles of champagne being taken from the fridge. The mayor is certainly pulling out all the stops as there are rumours in the commune that he's not the favourite to win the upcoming elections. Who is remains a mystery, as everyone I ask just shrugs.

I think it's time for us to leave before we get involved in another round of drinking and conversation. I need to type up my notes; Mr V needs to water the garden, and the presence of the candles indicates this could go on into the night. I thank the mayor for his hospitality, and he in turn says, '*Non madame, c'est moi qui vous remercie.*' (No *madame*, it is *I* who thank you.) How jolly civil of him.

What I've learnt today: Bastille Day is commonly known as 'Le Quatorze' (The Fourteenth) by the French.

HOME ALONE TWO

*I*t's the summer holidays. Well, it is for me, as I only work during school term time, and French schools break up earlier than those in the UK. We're driving down to Les Libellules with Pussy Willow for what will be, for both of us, a five-week stay. Mr V must return to Paris early Monday morning until his holidays begin on the second of August.

Last week France experienced record temperatures for the second time this year. The mercury in Paris reached a staggering 43 degrees and only dropped to 35 at 3 in the morning. I for one shall be glad to arrive at the house with its thick stone walls and narrow windows after a week in the apartment, which has been like a greenhouse.

The scene we pass is a pastoral idyll. Most of the hay has already been harvested and is rolled into bobbins like giant cotton reels. Each bobbin seems to have a bird of prey perched regally on the top, scanning the surrounding fields. A little further down the road, the scene is not so picturesque, and the reason that the birds are on top of the haystacks is all too apparent.

A combine harvester is at work, sending a cloud of hay-laden dust into the air, and sending the creatures that had made their homes in the fields scurrying for cover as their safe haven is mowed down. The birds are circling and swooping, sweeping up these poor creatures with ease. I'm once again reminded of the cruel, dual-edged sword of nature, as without this furry bounty, the birds would probably starve; it's a question of survival of the fittest.

You all know of my aversion to mosquitoes, but a Christian friend gave me an answer I had never considered when I asked her what purpose she thought they had on earth, as all they did was spread discomfort and disease.

Her reply was simple. 'To provide food for the swallows,' she said without hesitation.

I'll look at mosquitoes in a different light from now on.

✳   ✳   ✳

Mr V has left, and I'm alone at Les Libellules for a second time, but it's a different ball game from last time when I simply had to close the shutters and put a match to the fire. This is summer, and there's the *potager* to tend to. As I spend more time photographing the *potager* than working in it, this shall be fun.

Mr V, being Mr V, has rigged up a remote-controlled device whereby water can be pumped from the *mare* into a gigantic hosepipe that will stretch the length and breadth of the garden. I'm not good with technology, and the handset to operate this has a multitude of buttons, not just simply an 'on and off' option. I'm already blinded by the science of it all; coupled with the weight of the hose pipe, I'm not off to a good start.

The recently turned earth is as soft as Sahara sand, and my feet immediately sink almost to my ankles. The hose pipe is not only heavy, it's filthy and unwieldy, with a mind of its own, like a giant, muddy python, twisting and turning in unexpected angles.

Operating it is another matter. It's impossible for me to hold the remote control as well as direct the hose, so I have to keep this in the pocket of my trousers. I need to cut the flow of water each time I drag the hose to another patch of vegetables and must put it down to retrieve the remote control. This results in the hose transforming into a fountain, giving me an impromptu shower.

Thirty back-breaking minutes later, I'm covered in mud and soaking with both perspiration and water from the *mare*. Now it is time for an actual shower.

What I've learnt today: It helps if you spray water on the soil in order to bank it down a little before walking on it.

∗　∗　∗

I'm showered and sitting on the terrace with a glass of chilled rosé, and Madeleine Peyroux crooning on the stereo. Steam is rising from the freshly watered ground that's been basking in the sun all day. The spicy smell of tomatoes, intensified by the heat, rises also. Newts in the *mare* amble to the surface, creating large ripples that merge together, giving the water a blurred effect like a painting by Monet. I shut my eyes and inhale deeply. Along with the aroma of damp earth and its fruits, I breathe in the peace and solitude. Sometimes it's good to be alone.

I spoke too soon. Jacques has arrived to check if I'm OK and to offer me a hand watering the garden, which has come too late, but I eagerly accept for tomorrow. He also asks if I'd like him to get me some bread in the morning when he cycles to the bakery for his two daily baguettes.

I don't think I'll ever understand the French obsession with bread. Scrumptious as it is, and it *is* delicious, I can live without it. My French friends and neighbours, however, cannot. When I posed to Mr V this question of why it is so important, he told me to cast my mind back to a christening we attended earlier in the year where the bread delivery had not arrived. I was ravenous, but everyone refused to begin eating until there was bread on the table. I also heard on the grapevine that there were grumblings amongst the French contingency at our wedding that took place in the UK, as no bread was served with the main course, and cheese was an 'option' in place of dessert, not as well as. This was a cultural faux pas on my part. I should have asked the caterers to provide baskets of bread to soak up their excellent sauces, but frankly it never entered my head. When I told Mr V that I found both these reactions excessive, he gently reminded me that I was living in a country where a revolution was ignited due to bread shortages.

Jacques isn't my only gentleman caller. Pieter has noticed that I'm alone in the garden and has called to see if I'd like to go to the market to buy fresh fruit and vegetables, which are more in my line than bread. But I decline, pointing to the *potager*, which has gone bonkers, and tell him he's welcome to take whatever he needs from there.

I feel like Alice after having eaten a 'shrink me' cake. I'm dwarfed by the size of everything. It all looks like prize-winning entries at a summer fayre. A lot of the courgettes have grown into marrows the size of draught excluders. The beef tomatoes are like cricket balls. The lettuces look like green parasols, and the mint has literally gone wild.

Everywhere you look, things are sprouting and pushing their way to the surface. The forest of cherry tomatoes is so dense I fear they will never ripen, as the sun can't reach their shadowy depths. The bell peppers also are obscured by the vast leaves of the giant pumpkins that are spreading over the garden like Cinderella's coach, their tendrils curling into coils resembling its wheels.

Ironically, after waiting almost four months for the man with the rotavator to come to turn over the land so we could begin planting, gardeners now appear to be dropping out of the sky when we evidently have no further need for them.

As the courgettes have gone out of control, I'm using them every which way I can. Here's a lovely warm salad that also gives me the opportunity to use up some of my wild mint. We really do need to think before we plant next year.

WARM COURGETTE AND
AVOCADO SALAD

Serves 4 as an accompaniment

Ingredients

1 tbsp light olive oil for frying
1 large courgette, washed and finely sliced
A good handful of pine nuts
1 tbsp white wine vinegar
1 tbsp lemon juice
1 large, ripe avocado, cut into small slices
1 tbsp olive oil (I used Oliviers & Co Olive Oil with Mint)
About 12–15 decent-sized fresh mint leaves, rolled and finely sliced

Method

Heat the olive oil in a large, heavy-bottomed frying pan and sauté the
courgette slices until slightly charred on both sides.

Add the pine nuts and stir for 2 minutes until golden.

Add the white wine vinegar and lemon juice and reduce until only
half the liquid remains.

Transfer to a warm serving dish and toss in the avocado.

Drizzle with the olive oil and sprinkle with the mint leaves.

Serve immediately with either grilled fish, chicken or lamb cutlets.

For a veggie option, serve with grilled haloumi.

This is also great cold with feta cheese crumbled over the top before you drizzle the oil.

SKIES OF STARS AND STORMS

*T*he former cat with no name has progressed from Princess to Princess Tam-Tam. Princesse tam.tam is the name of a French lingerie brand inspired by the words on a poster for a concert by Josephine Baker, who used to dance to the sound of the tam-tam drums, expressing freedom in the movement of her body. The brand was one of the first to take men's boxer shorts and redesign them for women, coming up with the concept that underwear can be both comfortable and feminine.

Our Princess Tam-Tam is tiny and lithe and silky. She burrows between my knees when I bend to stroke her and nuzzles my ankles. I know she's going to break my heart. She already has as she doesn't purr, and I find this really sad.

Flaubertine, by contrast, purrs like a motorboat. She's also the size of a boat, with her sides bulging like saddle bags, and I'm expecting her to have her next batch of kitties any day now. I do hope that they arrive in time for my final friend of the summer, Jayne, to meet them.

Flaubertine appears to be going head-to-head with Gus in the 'Glo Cat' competition as both are now so clean and white they would glow in the dark. This isn't the only head-to-head contest taking place between them. Gus has installed himself in Flaubertine's shelter and is sitting there now. Every time I look at him, he lifts his paw in an endearing, cat-begging fashion, but I know that if I approach, his lip will rise instead.

Pussy Willow, resembling a stripy tiger, is camouflaged in the long grass under the apple tree. She must have telescopic vision as she's lying in wait for lizards to appear on the wall of the *pigeonnier* a good twelve metres away. On seeing one, she launches herself with the speed of a projectile missile. She never catches one of course, as they're too far up the wall. She tries singing her little 'yang yang' song to them as she does to the pigeons at the apartment, but they are not to be cajoled, so she returns to take refuge from the sun beneath the shade of the tree.

* * *

The temperature has suddenly dropped. An expanse of slate-grey cloud looms low in the sky like a damp dish cloth, making the air below dank and oppressive. It has forced down insects and pollen from their dizzy heights, delighting the birds, but irritating my eyes. I have a headache, and my lips feel charged with electricity—a storm is coming. I gather up my things from the table, collapse the parasol and take in my chair then close the shutters to prevent the rain from entering the house and go upstairs to watch from the bedroom window.

Fork lightning is raining down from the clouds like a biblical painting of Judgement Day. The flashes are so close together that the room is almost permanently lit up. It's thrilling but also a little scary here on my own, and I pray that none of the trees within crashing distance of Les Libellules are struck. Pussy Willow is agitated and has gone behind the sofa, as she does when there are fireworks.

Usually storms blow over quickly here, but this seems to be going on for hours. The thunder is so loud, it sounds as if it's right here in the room. I go back downstairs where the shutters block out most of the light, and I'm less likely to receive a tree on my head.

I wake on the sofa. It's five in the morning. The storm has passed. I make a coffee, put on one of Mr V's fleecy jackets and sit outside to watch the sun rising through the trees, which thankfully have survived. The birds that fell suddenly silent last night are twittering and chirping at the top of their voices, happy to have survived the night also. Pussy Willow puts a tentative paw out of the door and sniffs the air, her little, pink nose twitching as it sweeps from left to right, analysing all the new scents after the rainfall. But even though I lack her feline sense of smell, the air is fragrant with the aroma of damp earth, grass and freshly watered vegetables. I cradle my coffee cup in my hands and inhale.

It's almost midnight, and I'm walking in the lanes behind the hamlet with two of my Dutch neighbours. The night is cool and fresh after the day's heat, and a welcome, gentle breeze caresses my arms and face. A sliver of crescent moon is suspended above the crest of the hill, just waiting for a cow to jump over it.

We've seen a shooting star. It's a little early in the year for them as we're not yet in August, which makes the sighting doubly thrilling, as it is unexpected. We walk craning our necks, looking up at the sky in the hope of seeing another. But it was a unique experience; still, there are plenty of other marvels to hold our attention. There are so many stars that the sky looks like a piece of Lurex fabric with just hints of darkness breaking up the brilliance. I've never seen the Milky Way so dense. I now understand why so many people come to this area simply to stargaze, and my dream of having a telescope in the *pigeonnier* is reignited.

We barely talk, as we're so enthralled and captivated by the beauty of the sky. I relish the peace and tranquillity. Tomorrow Mr V returns, and my little solo sojourn at Les Libellules comes to an end. The day after, work begins on laying the cement to level the floor of the rose room, so my peace will be well and truly shattered.

MICRO BREAK IN AUTUN

$\mathcal{W}$e're having a holiday, well, a day out. As this is our summer vacation, we've allowed ourselves a day of rest and are finally going to visit the Roman remains at Autun.

The weather is fine and dry with clear blue skies and a light wind, so perfect for sightseeing, but first we have a spot of shopping to do, and maybe a spot of lunch. Mr V wants to buy some coloured glass to put into a lantern that he picked up at one of last year's *vide greniers*, and there's an artisan glass shop here that will custom-make it to size; all I have to do is choose the colours. We find the premises tucked away between a second-hand book shop and an art gallery opposite the cathedral. The showroom is full of fabulous things. Golden angels and beautiful, little, circular plaques with floral designs dangle from chains in the window, the sun catching their colours and scattering them like rainbows. Intricate, inlaid mirrors hang on the walls alongside pictures and panels made purely of stained glass. There's even jewellery, gorgeous rings, earrings, bracelets and necklaces tempting me with their colours and artistry. The lady shows us the selection of glass for the lantern, and we opt to stay with the original blue, green and yellow panels but decide to replace the broken red one with a deep mauve. I'm busy trying on rings now, but she's closing for lunch, so I have to abandon this venture, and we go off in search of lunch ourselves.

When we were in Autun last year for my birthday, we passed a particularly enticing pizzeria. We're here now, sitting in the shady garden opposite the restaurant, nibbling on grissini sticks and sipping glasses of chilled rosé while trying to decide between freshly baked pizza and freshly made pasta. We both opt for pasta, as the pizzas look enormous. Mr V orders a creamy carbonara, and I choose linguine with pine nuts, pesto, garlic and buffalo mozzarella. All is cooked to perfection. The linguine is al dente; the pesto, nutty and slightly rough textured. The mozzarella is deliciously tangy and melt-in-the-mouth creamy without being watery. The dessert menu is equally difficult to choose from, but in the end Mr V decides on a tiramisu made in a large wine glass, and I have an Italian twist on a rum baba—a limoncello baba—followed by a frothy cappuccino. I'm loving this. I really like Autun. I know it's only one day, but I really do feel as if I'm on holiday.

On leaving the town in search of the Roman amphitheatre, we see a sign for a waterfall, so we decide to make a little detour and go in search of that. The road twists and turns as it climbs through the forested area behind the town. It reminds me of driving in the Pyrenees, though not nearly so high. Halfway up we lose sight of the signs for the waterfall but pick up signs for *la Croix de la Libération* (the Liberation Cross), so follow these instead. I do love a mystery tour. The road becomes narrower and the trees denser, their upmost branches forming a vaulted ceiling shading the sun. Starbursts of dazzling sunbeams pierce the canopy, hitting the ground in pools of light that shimmer with the reflections of leaves agitated by the breeze. We mount a steep hill that descends even more steeply on the other side, making my stomach lurch as it does on a fairground ride. We climb another not so sheer and find ourselves on a vast plateau guarded on three sides by tall conifers, the fourth dropping away like an infinity pool, giving rise to spectacular views over the town and surrounding countryside. In the centre, stark against the deep-blue backdrop of sky, is the grey form of *la Croix de la Libération*.

It's so peaceful and calm; there's no one here except us. I'm in my element, photographing the light piercing the trees and the cross silhouetted against the sky. I'm now sitting on a simple stone bench, writing on a paper napkin from the pizzeria while Mr V strolls around taking photographs also.

We've given up trying to find the waterfall. From this vantage point, we can see a small lake that is close to the amphitheatre on the map, so we head down there.

* * *

Last year it was too hot to see the Roman amphitheatre as there's no shade there, but today is, as I said, ideal. The theatre curves around in a large semi-circle. The floor of the arena has been laid with grass, as have the spaces in between the terraces where the stone seats are missing. Just as at the monument of *la Croix de la Libération*, there are no other tourists but us, which I think strange, but I'm thankful we have the place to ourselves. I find it hard to imagine this elegant sweep of architecture to have maybe once been the scene for slaughter. It has none of the brutal atmosphere of the Colosseum in Rome, so I imagine instead plays and musical recitals and dances being performed here.

Even though it's much cooler than the last time we visited the town, it is still hot with the heat of the sun trapped in the hollowed-out centre without shade. So I take some more photos, and we leave.

We're now strolling around the equally almost tourist-free lake. Some people are milling about on the far side where there's a boathouse with kayaks and little yachts moored at a small harbour. But we're disturbed by nothing more than the rustling of the tall reeds at the water's edge. The sun is hotting up, so we fetch a picnic blanket from the car and spread it out beneath a willow tree. Here we are, shaded by the tendrils of branches that reach to the ground. I feel as if I'm in a fairy bower, with green-tinted sunlight filtering through. Mr V stretches out and promptly falls asleep, so I stretch out too with my head resting on his thigh and read my book.

I must have nodded off. My fairy bower is a lot more dismal than it was, the ethereal green light having turned to grey. The willow branches are swaying in what is an unexpected, fresh breeze, revealing a dark, charcoal sky through the parting leaves.

'Wake up,' I say urgently. 'I think there's going to be a storm.'

Mr V hastily gets to his feet. We gather up the picnic blanket and head back to the car. Huge raindrops begin to fall, landing on the ground in spots the size of saucers. A rumble of thunder stirs in the distance, and the spots come thick and fast. We're soaked and shivering by the time we cross the 50 metres of grass to where the car is parked; the temperature has plummeted. There's a loud thudding on the car roof. I can't believe my eyes. Giant hailstones the size of golf balls are raining down from a sky zigzagged with fork lightning. I thank goodness this didn't arrive while we were still on the top of the hill, surrounded by those tall trees.

We're now driving home with the windscreen wipers going nineteen to the dozen and the heating on. The holiday is over.

THERE IS A GREEN HILL

*I*t's the day after the deluge. The temperature usually cools down following a storm, but in this instance, it seems to have risen even higher. Solène promised some months ago to take me to a favourite place of hers, and she's chosen today of all days to fulfil that promise. She's just been to tell me that she'll come for me at 4 p.m., which is usually the hottest part of the day. I'm tempted to lie and say I'm busy, but this isn't my nature, so I smile and say thank you, that will be lovely…

Solène's car is like an oven, but she doesn't seem to notice. She's dressed in a strappy top, shorts and trainers. She's 74 years old, but her arms and legs are as toned as a teenager's. Her incredibly wrinkle-free skin is tanned to the shade of runny honey from working in the sun. She and her husband, Jean, tend to a small herd of cows that belong to her brother, plus they have a large garden and well-stocked *potager* to maintain; hence she is outdoors almost all day. We take the road out of the village then turn sharp left. I've never been in this direction before. If there's a view, I can't see it, as tall hedgerows mar it. Solène stops the car at a gate at the bottom of an extremely steep dirt track. *Surely we're not going to climb that in this heat?* But yes, we are. Off she strides. I feel dizzy at the thought. The sun is intense, and there's no shade. The track rises before me as I struggle to keep pace with this sprightly septuagenarian. I feign stopping to take photographs when in fact I feel on the point of collapse.

At last the summit is in sight, and the track enters a woodland area that's thankfully shaded by tall conifer trees. The branches provide a welcome coolness, but the roots set traps for my feet, as I'm only wearing sandals. This is *not* what I'd envisaged. Finally we come to a clearing. I can't see anything worth the effort I've just made, save that I *have* made it. The ground swells into a slight dome, so we continue to climb at a less arduous pace as we cross the clearing.

We're on the top of the rise, and I now see what was worth the effort. The ground gently slopes down to a circle of tall, straight-trunked pines in the centre of which is a wooden cross, the sight of which is even more moving than the splendour of *la Croix de la Libération*. Beyond the cross are views of the village and hamlet and the vast expanse of the Burgundy countryside. Solène moves away from me and surveys the scene, her frame silhouetted, as the cross was yesterday, against the backdrop. When she turns to face me, her eyes are filled with emotion.

'I love it here,' she says, 'but I envy you.'

I'm taken aback. This is *not* what I expected either. 'Why?' I ask.

'You have travelled the world,' she says, which is an exaggeration, as I've mainly confined myself to Europe.

Then she adds, 'I've never even been to Paris. All I know is here and cows.'

It shocks and saddens me that she's never seen the Eiffel Tower or Notre Dame, or visited the museums and art galleries, strolled by the Seine or eaten at a pavement café. If she was content with this, it would be fine, but her saying that to me indicates that she isn't entirely happy with her lot. I ask her why she's never been, as it's only an hour and a half by train from Dijon, and I make the trip regularly. She replies that she's never been anywhere on her own and marvels that I take airplanes alone, as she has evidently never been on a plane either. She says she had the opportunity to visit Paris once as she had a cousin who lived there, but her husband, Jean, wouldn't go. I hear a hint of resentment in her voice and tell her that she's welcome to come with me and stay at our apartment and I'll show her the city, but I know she won't...

We're back in the car and stop at a viewpoint. We get out and walk through a cornfield to take photographs of the cross in the circle of pines that's now immediately above us. Then the most wondrous thing happens. Disturbed by our movement, tiny, blue butterflies rise like a cloud of bluebell-coloured confetti in front of our faces. The contrast against the pale-yellow, sun-bleached corn is striking. There are hundreds of them, barely bigger than an ear of corn, fluttering around us, some landing on our shoulders and arms as we both stand motionless, hardly daring to breathe. It's a moment of sheer magic and beauty, provided for us by nature.

'You can't see this in Paris,' I say.

CALL THE MIDWIFE

I think we're at the end of what seems to be the longest cat pregnancy in history. Flaubertine is behaving in a peculiar way, following me everywhere and making a strange cry. I'm no expert, but her obvious agitation indicates to me that she's either in labour or soon will be. We've found a disused cat box that I've lined with a clean towel and put in the far corner of the garage behind the old bathroom window, propping it against the wall like the side of a tent. The box is a cube covered in fur fabric with a little arch for a cat to go inside and hide. I've put a three-sided box up against it, forming a courtyard with food and water so she can come out to eat and drink while still being enclosed, but she seems hell bent on getting into the house. This can't happen of course as Pussy Willow is in residence, and I fear she would attack any kittens born on her territory.

Flaubertine isn't the only vocal cat. The formerly silent Princess Tam-Tam has found her voice and regularly comes singing for her supper, or I should say whining, as she has the most unusually little singing voice that has now earned her the name Tammy Wynette, Tammy for short. So far from being the cat with no name, she's now become the cat with many.

* * *

There's no sign of Flaubertine this morning, so I'm presuming my instincts were right yesterday, and she's had her kittens during the night. The little shelter I made for her is empty, so she must have taken her chances amongst the other cats. I hope she's all right.

My instincts weren't right about Tammy, however. First I noticed that she had disproportionately large paws—'what big paws you have'—then that she had disproportionately large whiskers—'what big whiskers you have'. Then I caught 'her' spraying the bushes. So name number five, Tammy, is now Tommy—Little Tommy Tucker who sings for his supper.

* * *

It's late afternoon on the day after Flaubertine's 'lying in', and she's appeared in the garden wanting food. She eats hungrily then comes and sits beneath the table while I type. She's here now. I've asked her shouldn't she be with her babies, to which she replies, 'Yow,' gets up and trots off. Time will tell if this litter has survived.

What I've learnt today: I'm extremely bad at discerning the sex of a cat.

* * *

My friend Jayne has just arrived. She's like a small, shiny berry bursting with life, but life hasn't always been kind to her. This beautiful soul has been touched by much sadness. She's known the unbearable pain of losing a child and found herself suddenly widowed at the age of 52. I told her that whenever she was ready, she must come to Les Libellules to help heal her grief. I was delighted when she contacted me a few weeks ago to say that she was ready to come. Then fate played another cruel twist. Just before she was about to leave for France, her beloved mum, Elsie, died suddenly and the funeral was set for the day she was due to fly. But by sheer coincidence, she has a cousin who lives 45 minutes' drive from here, and she and her husband were going to the UK for Elsie's funeral, so I tentatively put it to Jayne that if she was up to it, to come back with them. So here she is, pottering about my garden, dead-heading roses, picking green beans and cutting back the dry leaves from the courgettes, totally in her element. She's singing along to one of my Yannick Noah CDs and doing a little dance as she flits from plant to plant like a busy, little bee.

Jayne has brought some haloumi from the UK, as I find it virtually impossible to come by here. The courgettes have been as prolific as the tomatoes, so here is a second recipe using them.

PUY LENTIL AND HALOUMI SALAD

Serves 2 as a main course or 6 as a starter

Ingredients

200 g (8 oz) Puy lentils
1 large courgette, finely sliced
1 tbsp olive oil
1 tbsp lime juice
2 just-ripe avocados, finely sliced
A good handful of pine nuts, lightly toasted
A handful of fresh mint, finely chopped
225 g (8 oz) block of haloumi cheese, finely sliced
Maple syrup or balsamic vinegar to drizzle over

Method

Cook the lentils in slightly salted water for around 40 minutes until soft, but not mushy, drain and leave to cool.

Chargrill the courgette slices and set aside to cool.

Mix together the olive oil and lime juice and toss in the avocado, cooled courgette slices and lentils, then gently mix in the pine nuts and mint.

Grill the haloumi on both sides.

Arrange the lentil salad on a serving plate and top with slices of haloumi.

Drizzle with maple syrup or balsamic vinegar if preferred.

Serve immediately.

HEIDI IN THE HAY LOFT

*T*he sun is setting on Jayne's first day at Les Libellules, and dusk is beginning to envelop us. We plan to go walking in the hills later to see the Milky Way, but first, as she's a trained masseuse, she is giving Mr V a much-needed back and neck massage. I've put on some chilled vibes, and scented candles are flickering on the table and the stone walls of the terrace. Mr V is stripped to the waist and reclining face down over a deep cushion on the very same table, while Jayne begins coaxing his knotted muscles and sinews to relax with the help of warm lavender oil. The smell is intoxicating and making my muscles and sinews relax by proxy. The solar lights dotted around the garden come on one by one, the last being the fairy lights around a branch of the feather tree. Or are they? Unbeknown to me, Mr V has planted a solar spotlight to illuminate the now not spindly rose bush in the centre of the garden; thankfully he's chosen a soft, warm tone, so the effect is muted and subtle.

Jayne continues to smooth and soothe until Mr V is lulled into a false sense of security. She now begins to knead with her knuckles as if she's making dough. Ignoring his little moans of protestation, she starts pounding his back with a series of quick karate chops. His moans are now groans; I'm enjoying this. Finally she resumes the circular action of her thumbs, probing deep into his previously tender spots whereon he gives a huge sigh of relief as all the tightness and tension flow away.

Ordeal over, Jayne wipes off the excess oil from Mr V's back. She tells him to put on a T-shirt and drink a large glass of water to flush out the toxins she's released. He takes himself to bed, not before issuing me with a *gilet jaune* and Jayne with a headlamp torch so we can be seen in the dark by any cars on the usually deserted country lanes. Then off we go, looking like a pair of navvies, to see the stars.

It's not quite dark as we walk up the lane. Ahead of us is a row of cows grazing on the hillside, their silhouettes black against a backdrop of vibrant tangerine. By the time we turn onto the lane behind the hamlet, they've disappeared into the darkness, and all there is to see is Jayne's torchlight. The stars appear as if by magic, and I tell Jayne to switch the light off so that we can appreciate them. She gasps as she, like me, has never seen them so tightly packed. We spin around, heads thrown back until our necks ache, then we lie in the road like snow angels, gazing at the sky.

Jayne is a free spirit, and as soon as she saw the little hay loft in which Mr V has insulated the sloping ceiling and boarded the floor, she was adamant that was where she was going to sleep.

'*Pourquoi pas?*' (Why not?) said Mr V when I told him. So I set about finding a duvet that she could double up and use as a mattress, and a pillow, sheet and blanket should it get chilly during the night. Mr V rigged up an electricity supply and installed a small table lamp and a CD player with some relaxing classical music. There's a new, double-glazed window and stable door, but the only way up is via a wooden ladder, so I've given her a bucket also should she need to visit the ladies during the night so she's not climbing up and down in the dark.

When we return from our star-spangled walk in the hills, we sit talking by candlelight with a glass of wine, then I escort Jayne to her humble lodgings for the night, see her safely up the ladder and leave her with a torch, a bottle of water, a flask of herbal tea and a book. She looks perfectly happy, but I've given her the key to get back into the house if she has a change of heart.

⁕ ⁕ ⁕

I've woken just before 7 a.m. All is quiet downstairs, meaning Jayne must have lasted the night. I get dressed and go out across the cobbles to the hay loft. And here she is, lying on her front looking down at me from the open stable door. Her face is glowing in the morning sun, and her eyes are shining as bright and blue as forget-me-nots. Her unruly, blonde curls have escaped from her little, blue beanie and are framing her face, making her look a good twenty years younger than she is. She's full of excitement. Apparently she woke in the night and opened the small window that looks out over the countryside behind the house. She tells me that the stars were like a magic carpet spread across the sky, and what was more magical was that she could hear owls calling to each other across the empty darkness. Life, it seems, has finally bestowed on her the illustrious key to open the door to happiness.

Mr V is busy watering the tomatoes and peppers, so we decide to go for an early morning walk while a flaxen cobweb of mist is still clinging to the dew on the fields. Jayne's excitement knows no boundaries; she's stumbled upon elderberries growing in abundance next to the field where the buttermilk cows are grazing. She tells me that she used to collect them with her father when she was young, and her mother would make elderberry jelly. On returning to the house, I set the table outside for breakfast, and Jayne disappears up the lane with a basket to collect the berries. Breakfast over, she's at the table, singing and dancing and painstakingly separating the berries from their stalks. She's carried on a wave of nostalgia as she shows me how her father taught her to remove them using a fork, carefully discarding the green ones until Mr V tells her that she must keep some as they provide more pectin than the purple and help the jelly to set. He really is a mine of information.

315

I'm overwhelmed by the joy it brings to see my beautiful friend emerge from her shell of sadness. Once again, Les Libellules has worked her magic.

Jayne is now stirring the berries in a large copper pan with an equal measure of sugar, pressing them with a ladle to extract the maximum juice to sieve off and make jelly once it's ready to set, humming to herself as she works. Her efforts make a meagre three jam jars full, but this was never about the jelly—it was always about the memories...

What I've learnt today: You must add underripe elderberries and blackberries when making jelly and jam, as this helps them to set. And never underestimate the healing power of nature.

ALL DRESSED UP AND NOWHERE TO GO

*J*ayne and I are all dressed up in chic, little shift dresses with eyebrows pencilled in and lipstick painted on, standing in the bus shelter waiting for the 7:25 a.m. bus to Beaune. I've never taken this bus before, so this is a bit of an adventure. It will be interesting to pass through the small villages en route to see more of the countryside. We're going to visit the Hospices de Beaune and the ramparts surrounding the town, then meet with Jayne's cousin, Annie, for lunch. We're both really looking forward to it.

The bus approaches, and the driver's face lights up with a look of sheer delight when he sees us. He's probably not used to having people waiting at the bus stop, let alone two small blondes dressed up to the nines at this hour of the morning. I mount the bus and ask for two tickets to Beaune, which are the princely sum of €2. A look of hesitation replaces that of delight as he plays out some internal battle, then his expression settles into one of disappointment.

'This is the bus to Montbard, *madame*,' he says.

'What time is the bus to Beaune?'

'It left at 7, *madame*.'

'But I usually see it pass at this time, and on the timetable it says 7:25.'

'Ah, but it's *les vacances scolaires*,' he replies with a fatalistic shrug.

The school holidays! All bus and train times change during this period. Why didn't I think to check the timetable yesterday? I step off the bus; he closes the door and drives off. So here we are, all dressed up and nowhere to go.

After a quick call to Annie to let her know what had happened, Jayne suggests that we go for a walk seeing as it's such a lovely morning and still cool and fresh as the sun hasn't properly risen. So off we go towards the village like a couple of townies in our posh frocks. Jayne would like to see the frescoes inside the church, but as usual it's not open; it must have been sheer fluke that Christelle and I wandered in last year, as every time I've been since, it's been locked. We look around the graveyard, and I show her the Napoleonic soldier's grave. It's impressive, but not as much as the frescoes.

We're on our way back down the hill leading out of the village, and right on cue, Jacqueline is at her door. She beckons to us to come inside and asks where we are going in our finery. I explain about the bus to Beaune and that we'd been to the cemetery.

'I'd really like to have shown Jayne the 11th-century frescoes,' I say, 'but the church is locked as usual.'

Jacqueline's little button eyes light up. She goes to a small wooden cupboard on the wall next to the door and takes from it an enormous key on a ring large enough to pass your hand through. It's the key to the church; she had it all along. She gives us instructions on how to pull the door towards us, put the key in the lock, push the door back then turn the key until the lock clicks twice and asks us to be sure that it's shut tight when we leave.

*　＊　*

Opening the door is proving more difficult than anticipated. Goodness knows how Jacqueline manages it. Jayne is tugging at the handle, and I'm trying to turn the key, only it won't budge. Then it dawns on me—half the keys at Les Libellules turn in the opposite direction to open the doors than you would expect. I try turning it clockwise, and, hey presto, it turns and clicks then turns and clicks again, and the huge, studded wooden door shudders open. After the bright sunshine outside, our eyes take time to adjust to the gloom of the interior. Then magically the light from the tiny, stained-glass windows seeps in, illuminating the frescoes and filling the church with a celestial amber glow. And the storm breaks...

Jayne has held in her grief for her mother ever since she arrived, and it all comes flooding out. She sits in one of the pews, shaking and sobbing, a huge well of emotion rising from the depths of her despair at not only losing her mother, but I suspect her husband also. I don't intrude and try to comfort or stop her. These are good tears; they are long overdue. After the storm, the calm. She sits in silent prayer, then finally looks up and smiles at me and says, 'Thanks, Lindy.'

This may not have been the day that we'd planned, but it is one far more spiritually healing.

⚘　⚘　⚘

Jacques has just arrived unannounced, asking if Jayne and I would like to come on a little excursion with him. The afternoon temperature has topped 38, so I'd prefer to stay indoors, but he's bristling with excitement, and Jayne doesn't like to disappoint him, so I agree.

Jacques has several cars in his barn, many bordering on classic, some bordering on vintage. Today's choice isn't one of them; it's a well-worn Volkswagen Polo with only two doors and what feels like horsehair blankets covering the seats. The gearstick is a metal rod with something resembling a golf ball on the end which has a tendency to come off in Jacques' hand when he changes gear. The air con is non-existent, with not even a plastic fan on the dashboard to cool us down. Jacques doesn't seem to notice the heat; he's puffed up like a peacock at the prospect of being out alone with two *nanas*. I laugh when he calls us this and say it's the first time I've been called a *nana*. Jayne is slightly insulted, thinking that Jacques has likened us to two grandmothers. I explain to her that a *nana* in French (pronounced 'nah nah') is a familial word for a girlfriend, used most frequently by young French men of African origin, and translates roughly as 'honey' or 'chick'. Pacified, Jayne quite likes the moniker.

We pass through the village, taking the same route I'd followed with Solène, then turn sharply to the right, climbing all the time. Below us a mosaic of muted-yellow fields appears like a mirage, blurred by the haze. It's baking hot in the car and opening the windows does little to help. We continue to climb until we reach an expanse of deeply rutted, rust-coloured earth that stretches as far as the eye can see. The horizon is broken only by a solitary tree, standing stark against the punishingly blue sky. We still have no idea where we're going, only that Jacques told us to wear good shoes. A fishing rod minus a line is balanced on the parcel shelf behind Jayne, and where the line would be is a plastic beaker bobbing like a mobile between Jacques and me.

He stops the car in the meagre shade of the solitary tree, and for all intents and purposes, it appears to me that we're in the middle of nowhere; it could be Death Valley as the terrain is so barren and the heat so intense. There's not a soul to be seen: no cars on the road, no tractors in the distance, not even the usual crop of crows picking their way through the recently ploughed soil. I'm glad I got changed out of my finery, applied liberal amounts of suntan lotion and brought a hat. Jacques marches ahead in pioneer fashion, using the fishing rod as a walking pole, his sturdy legs the colour of polished copper from being exposed to the sun on his twice-daily bike rides to the *boulangerie* for baguettes. Jayne and I struggle to keep up; our feet are sinking into the parched, powdery earth; it's like walking across uncooked pie crumble.

Jacques stops and points in the direction of a small copse of trees about 100 metres away that wasn't visible before due to it lying in a dip in the land. He slows down a little to explain that this is our destination. He's like a pony when it senses it's near to home and cannot contain his eagerness to forge ahead.

'I come here around this date every year,' he calls over his shoulder, as we're now lagging behind again.

Jayne mouths, 'Why?' to me, and I shrug in response.

Jacques uses the rod to point to the bare fields to our right.

'This is where my father and I harvested the hay every summer,' he says.

'Gosh, that must have been hot work,' says Jayne.

'So did you shelter in those trees to escape the midday sun?' I ask, now understanding why we are up here—we're on an annual pilgrimage.

'Ahh,' says Jacques, his eyes gleaming in his customary manner, 'there *is* more.'

At last we've reached the trees and their welcome shade. My hair is plastered to my head beneath my hat, and my cotton blouse is stuck to my back. Jayne is visibly melting, but Jacques looks as cool as a cucumber. The land not only dips but drops away in a sharply sloping hillside. The earth here is dry and shingly; we slip and slide as we descend, grabbing hold of brambles and bushes to anchor ourselves as we pass.

We've come to a halt at a small clearing which has ferns and branches strewn across it. Jacques begins carefully removing them, and sheltered beneath is a freshwater spring. It's about two metres in diameter and half a metre deep. The sides are lined with stones that are emerald green with moss. The water escapes in a feeble but steady stream from the rocks on the far reaches and trickles into the crystal-clear basin below.

'I come every year to drink from this spring,' says Jacques. 'This is where my father and I used to refresh ourselves and fill our water flasks when we were working in the fields. It is what keeps me so fit and virile.' He laughs.

He attaches the plastic cup back onto the end of the fishing rod with a wire loop and stretches out over the water to catch the drops of precious elixir, and drops they are. Jacques tells us that in the past, and indeed up until the year before last, the flow was much stronger, but the drought conditions of the previous two years have drastically reduced it.

'I was half afraid that there would be no water at all this year,' he says.

I think how sad it would be if it were to dry up after probably being here for hundreds of years.

We wait patiently as Jacques collects enough water for us all to taste. I wander a little further down the hillside and come to the edge of the trees. There in front of me, in a medieval vista, is Mont-Saint-Jean where we go blackberry picking. Seen from this viewpoint, it really does look as if I've passed through time and am looking on the scene as it was hundreds of years ago, the tall, grey stone fortress walls encircling the little village within.

Jacques calls to me to see if I'd like to be the first to drink the water. I would.

It is cold and crisp with an ever so slight mineral taste and has the same silky texture as Chablis. I've barely sipped more than a mouthful, but my thirst is completely quenched. My mouth feels alive, as if I've drunk a magic potion; maybe Jacques is right, and the water does have special qualities.

Next, Jayne stretches out over the spring to fill the cup and says the same as I, that she is instantly refreshed. I wish I'd brought an empty bottle, but at this rate of flow, it would be dark before I'd filled it. Jacques, however, fills a small hip flask and once again hides his secret spring beneath a bed of ferns and foliage.

On the way back to the car, we don't seem to notice the sun. Jayne and I begin to sing a little ditty in rounds that we both learnt as Girl Guides, 'Hei-di Hei-di Hei-did de li di, Hei-di Hei-di Hei-doh.'

Jayne certainly is embracing her inner country girl.

*　⚹　⚹

Back at Les Libellules, the peppers and tomatoes have finally ripened; the mint is in abundance, and after every evening when I pick a cucumber, I seem to find two replacements the following morning. This calls for one thing only—tabbouleh.

LINDY'S TABBOULEH

Serves 4 as a main course or 6 as a side dish

Ingredients

200 g (8 oz) bulgur wheat
½ a medium cucumber, cut into 1 cm (½ in) cubes
1 small red and 1 small green pepper, cut into small cubes
8 firm cherry tomatoes, cut into quarters
2 spring onions, finely sliced
1 level tsp fennel seeds
1 level tsp ground cinnamon
1 tbsp of good olive oil (I use Oliviers & Co Olive Oil with Mint)
1 tbsp lemon juice
1 tbsp balsamic vinegar (I use Greek balsamic with thyme and honey)
8 large fresh mint leaves, finely chopped
Freshly ground sea salt and black pepper to season

Method

Boil the bulgur wheat in 200 ml (7 fl oz) slightly salted water for 10 minutes then fluff with a fork, cover with cling film and leave to cool.

Mix the bulgur wheat with the cucumber, peppers, tomatoes and spring onions in a large serving bowl.

Add the fennel seeds and cinnamon.

Add the oil and stir well, then add the lemon juice and balsamic vinegar, also stirring well.

Cover with cling film and leave overnight in the fridge to absorb all the flavours.

Gently stir in the mint leaves and season as required before serving.

This will keep in the fridge for a couple of days and is a great dish to make in advance for a summer garden party picnic or barbeque.

It can be eaten as a main course with crumbled feta cheese, or as a side dish.

It goes perfectly with grilled fish and minted lamb chops.

SATURDAY NIGHT FEVER

*J*ayne and I have got our glad rags on again. We're going to Saulieu with Jayne's cousin, Annie, and her husband, John, to watch their friends performing in a band called The Flowerpots—three Brits and an Aussie playing '60s and '70s covers, so it should be good. Jayne and I are like opposites on a chess board: I'm wearing a black, crêpe-de-Chine dress, and she a white one; we're both wearing red lipstick so ready to party.

Expats have taken over the Café Parisien. I've never seen so many Brits in this part of France and have never seen any here in Saulieu and wonder where on earth they've all come from. The party seems quiet and sedate. The majority are seated inside, albeit with the windows folded right back, eating dinner and generally catching up. Most of the people I see are not locals but holidaying friends and family of the handful of Brits living in the Morvan region. They're all friendly and welcoming but obviously have a lot to talk about, and we don't want them to feel obliged to make polite conversation, so we take our drinks and sit outside on the terrace.

The evening is warm rather than hot, and most of the French customers are outside also. The Flowerpots have just begun playing, and they're really rather good. The first couple of numbers are laid-back '60s vibes. 'San Francisco (Be Sure to Wear Flowers in Your Hair)' is carried on the chords of a guitar onto the terrace, taking me back to a time before my time. 'Mr. Tambourine Man' follows, then the guys swing into the '70s, and Steely Dan's 'Rikki Don't Lose That Number' oozes out through the open windows.

I'm abruptly dragged out of the mellow mood that I've drifted into by the screech of brakes and a small, white van coming to a halt directly in front of Jayne and me. The door opens, and out comes Marcel, grinning from ear to ear. I forgot to mention Mr V isn't with us this evening because he's expecting Marcel at Les Libellules, but it now looks as if he will have a long wait. Marcel has installed himself in an impossibly small café chair that I fear won't take his weight; he's big and solid and not built for Parisian-style bistro furniture. I flash a warning look at Jayne, but too late, the words, 'Would you like a beer?' are already out of her mouth.

'Hotel California' is struggling to be heard over Marcel's booming voice.

'What the hell is this?' or words to that effect, he asks, cocking his head towards the café.

'It's a band,' I reply.

'They're rubbish,' or words to that effect, is his response. As he thinks the band is rubbish and I've reminded him that Mr V is expecting him, I'm hoping he'll drink his beer and go. But no, he's up at the bar getting another round in. I try to catch Annie's eye with a 'help me' expression, but she's deep in conversation. Bang goes my relaxed evening.

It's now dark. Coloured bulbs are lighting up the outside of the café, and the tempo has changed inside. Tables and chairs have been pushed back, and the band is belting out some rock and roll. Annie and John are doing an impressive, energetic jive routine; they're such a lovely couple, so in tune with each other. I envy Annie having a man who can dance. Mr V has two left feet.

Jayne in all innocence turns to Marcel and says, 'Let's dance.'

He downs his beer in one and is off faster than a greyhound after a rabbit.

'Was it something I said?' asks Jayne.

The French regulars standing at the bar are looking bewildered as the British invaders take over what is now a dance floor. Jayne and I push our way into the centre of the crowd and start singing along to '(I Can't Get No) Satisfaction', strutting our stuff like Mick Jagger. One regular, however, is busting to join us. A small guy of North African origin is gyrating away and even attempting to sing. He keeps looking at Jayne and me, and again before I can stop her, she's waved him over. This is a mistake; I feel it. He's going to be harder to shake off than Marcel, plus I think he's taken Jayne's 'come over' as a come-on.

Jayne's dance partner is really in the groove, and he's now attempting conversation. Jayne, who speaks neither French nor Italian, is answering him in a bizarre mix of both, with the odd, 'I can't understand you, love,' thrown in.

I'm edged out of the picture as he begins twirling and foot gliding, arms flaying around as if he's swatting flies, to 'Saturday Night Fever'. John Travolta would shudder at the sight.

A couple of French girls begin dancing with me and ask who our friend is. I tell them I've absolutely no idea, and they laugh. Jayne is mouthing 'help' at me, so the three of us surround her and dance her away to safety.

We decide it's time to leave and sneak outside, waiting in the shadows opposite for Annie and John to bid their farewells to their friends. Mr Night Fever has come to the entrance of the café, looking up and down the street for signs of Jayne. We shrink back into a shop doorway, holding our breath until he finally gives up and goes back inside, shoulders slumped as his Cinderella has disappeared into the night without so much as leaving a glass slipper. The evening has been wonderful, and contrary to what Marcel said (who says the same about all things non-French), the band wasn't rubbish; it was terrific.

Jayne has now left with Annie and John to spend some time with them before returning to the UK. So Heidi is no longer in the hayloft if anyone fancies taking her place…

What Jayne has learnt today: Don't offer random French men a beer or a dance, or you could live to regret it.

THE SOUND OF SILENCE

I once again find myself sitting in the garden at the end of a twelve-month cycle at Les Libellules. Midnight approaches —the witching hour when I must put down my pen. All is unusually silent except for the occasional hoot from a solitary owl somewhere high in the poplars. No melody of night-singing birds or chorus of crickets keeps me company as the final chapter draws to an end. Then the air is pierced by the eerily rasping mating call of foxes, carried on the silence across the fields opposite. It's a brutal, primeval sound, something that I'd never heard before moving here, but despite its harshness, it still thrills me to be so close to nature in all its forms.

In the minutes before the last evening of July becomes the first morning of August, I push back my chair and reflect on all the sounds that enthral me:

- Waves breaking upon a shingle shore.
- Gravel crunching beneath my feet.
- Water lapping against the side of a wooden boat.
- Logs crackling in a fire.
- The tinkling of cow bells.
- The click of a camera lens.

329

- The popping of a cork from a bottle of wine.
- The calls of frogs and crickets on a balmy evening like this.
- Birdsong.

The hour has passed, so I'll leave you with the thoughts of birdsong, crickets, frogs and foxes to reflect on your favourite sounds and say, '*A bientôt.*' See you soon.

GLOSSARY—CONVERSION FROM METRIC TO US CUPS

Flour: 125 g = 1 cup
Sugar: 200 g = 1 cup
Butter: 225 g =1cup (1 stick = 138 g)
Liquid: 250 ml = 1 cup

MESSAGE FROM THE AUTHOR

If you enjoyed reading this book as much as I enjoyed writing it, I would love to read your review on Amazon.

To see photos of my life at Les Libellules, you can follow me on Instagram at:
www.instagram.com/la.belle.vie.in.burgundy

Or come and join me and other memoir authors and readers in the We Love Memoirs Facebook group, the friendliest group on Facebook. www.facebook.com/groups/welovememoirs

BOOK CLUB QUESTIONS

1. Would you consider swapping a life in the city for one in the country? Has the book inspired you to do so, or put you off the idea?
2. The book follows the seasons in the French countryside. Which is your favourite season, and which did you enjoy reading about the most?
3. The six sections in the book are introduced by short poetry quotes. How well do you think they reflect each section?
4. 'What I've learnt today' snippets appear throughout the book. Did you learn anything from these?
5. The book contains original recipes. Do you plan to make any of the dishes?
6. Have you visited France? Would this book make you want to visit Burgundy?
7. Did you search for further information on any of the subjects or places mentioned in the book?
8. Could you relate to any of the author's experiences?

ACKNOWLEDGEMENTS

I would like to thank Ant Press and their brilliant editorial team, notably Jacky Donovan, for gently nudging me in the right direction with humour and professionalism, and diligently checking my recipes, and Victoria Twead for her expertise in formatting and attention to detail.

Also the extremely talented Mel Beswick for taking my original photos and transforming them into beautiful, rustic illustrations.

So many friends and neighbours have contributed to this book, some by sharing their knowledge of Les Libellules and the local area, others by sharing treasured experiences, giving me such a rich variety of material to write about. And of course, Mr V, whose get-off-the-hook line with every DIY disaster is 'another chapter'.

I am also indebted to the wonderful readers and writers that share the online community at the We Love Memoirs Facebook group. Truly the most supportive group there is.

Last but not least, I would like to thank you, the reader, particularly those of you who have taken the time to leave a review on Amazon and/or Goodreads for my last book, which I found very encouraging. These reviews are very important to a writer, so if you have enjoyed reading this book as much as I enjoyed writing it, please take a minute to leave one.

Printed in Great Britain
by Amazon